Think Like a Bird

BY THE SAME AUTHOR

The Unbridgeable Divide

Think Like a Bird

Alex Kimbell

First published in hardback in the UK
in 2000 by Airlife Publishing Ltd

Matador
12 Manor Walk, Coventry Road
Market Harborough
Leics LE16 9BP. UK
Tel: (+44) 1858 468828
Email: books@troubador.co.uk
Web: www.troubador.co.uk/matador

ISBN 1 904744 05 2

Cover. The author taking off from Dhala, a painting by David Shepherd OBE, FRSA, FRGS.
reproduced with his kind permission and with that of the Army Air Corps

Typeset in 11.5pt StempelGaramond by Troubador Publishing Ltd, Market Harborough, UK

Matador is an imprint of Troubador Publishing

Foreword

There have been many books and stories about flying, most of which have been written about the aircraft of the day and encompass the technological and electronic wizardry of the time. But time ever marches on, and many aeroplanes were 'king of the skies' in their own day – and in nearly all cases, their day did not last for very long. At the turn of the twentieth century there were box kites that could carry one man, and by the end of the same century stealth fighters and airliners capable of carrying many hundreds of passengers had evolved. Within this span of time lie the carcasses of many good aeroplanes, all now obsolete.

But as the mouse survived the dinosaur, one type of aeroplane has managed to survive throughout, and that is the humble light aircraft. For the light aircraft of today is essentially the same machine that it was in the 1930s. It may have shed a wing or two, or maybe is now embroidered with wheel-spats and a fancy paint-job, but the configuration, speeds, operating procedures – and in many cases, even the engine is still the same.

Every person who aspires to become a pilot will meet this aeroplane in one guise or another, for this is the machine in which they will learn to fly. And just as every pilot remembers his or her first solo, so they will remember the light aeroplane with affection.

This book is based upon such aircraft – namely the last of the era of fixed wing aircraft flown by the Army Air Corps, before the helicopter superseded their military role.

Although originally conceived and developed for the military, it is interesting to note that in many instances the aircraft have already outlived the helicopters that replaced them – for they are still essentially light aircraft, and as such are still flying, albeit in civilian colours.

The flying sequences related in this book are timeless and will be recognized by any pilot of any aircraft. One can write about pumping the flaps up and down only so many times, and by the time the reader has read half the book, they will have a good idea of how to fly an aeroplane. This is exactly what is intended, for entwined within every chapter is a flying lesson – together with the author's understanding of the 'poetry of flight.'

Hopefully this book will find its way to all those who have secretly nurtured an ambition to fly... or maybe make the seasoned pilot smile and shake his head.

Alexander Kimbell
Newton Ferrers
Devon

Acknowledgements

Many people have helped in the writing of this book. I would particularly like to thank Lieutenant-Colonel (Retired) John Watkins MC Royal Marines, who proof-read the original manuscript with the critical eye of one who served alongside me in the same campaign. Richard Checkley, for his enthusiastic involvement in this and our many other projects. Roger Neaves, a man who has spent a whole lifetime aloft, and under whose wings mine will forever be in shadow. Geoffrey Tantum CMG OBE, old soldier and lifelong friend and advisor. Ian Rawlings, whose knowledge and worldliness came into its own when the going became turbulent. My cousin Roger Kimbell, who dreamed the dream for so long before making it come true and thereby discovered the poetry of flight. Colnel (Retired) Ross Mallock, HQ Director Army Aviation, who proof-read the script on behalf of the Army Air Corps. Martin and Louise Eyre, without whose help the book would never have got off the ground. And finally Mr Summers... who has always been there when it mattered most.

To you all thank you.

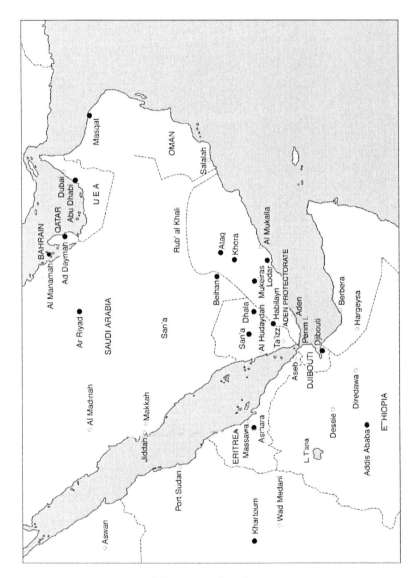

The operational area

Chapter 1

If it wasn't for the fact that you landed uphill, this strip would be too damn short, I reminded myself for the hundredth time, as in a cloud of dust I swung the aircraft round at the end of the landing run at the base of the mountain.

Blair's Field: I don't know who Blair was, but his choice of landing strip leaves much to be desired. Originally it was probably an outcrop of rock running out from the foot of the mountain. Over the centuries, generations of Arabs had cleared the wadi for cultivation and piled the stones into a heap. Then Blair came along, knocked it into an embankment, levelled it, and called it a landing strip. But what Blair didn't realise was that low level winds always follow the line of a valley – and his strip, set at ninety degrees to the wadi, meant there was always a vicious crosswind over it.

Moreover, Blair knew or cared little about airmanship, let alone safety. For the only way in is to land into the face of the mountain. Which, thank God, is uphill for the strip is so short that you have to put down on the extreme edge and use every available metre in order to stop. There is no margin for error, let alone an overshoot should you get it wrong.

For takeoff you do the reverse – except the mountain is now behind and the slope thankfully downhill. But it is still far too short for comfort – and with an altitude of 6000 feet, the air too thin to support conventional lift. Line the aircraft up; apply full power whilst standing on the brakes – and ignore the rattle of stones picked up and thrown back by the slipstream onto the fuselage and tail planes. Then, brakes off and lift the tail as soon as possible to reduce drag and howl down the strip in fine pitch, until you fall off the end and somehow mush into the air at minimum flying speed.

Anyway, we were down in one piece – and if I was honest I was only looking for an excuse for the awful landing I had made. It wasn't a landing but more of an arrival; I'd misjudged the strength of the crosswind, applied a fistful of power at the last second – which had done nothing to help, except lengthen the touchdown point – and only severe braking had stopped us in time.

It had been one of those days. The morning had started badly with a last minute switch of aircraft, and as my detail was only the 'school run', I had been left with XP777.

To look at, she was identical – or if anything, slightly less battered than the other Beavers in the Flight. Painted brown with khaki camouflage stripes, the only touch of colour being the yellow spinner on the propeller boss; she had slightly fewer chinks in her propeller from stone damage, and her tyres were marginally less cut about from landing on unmade runways.

The reason for this was simple: she was hardly ever used.

At sometime in her past, XP777 had been crashed in Germany. Workshops had rebuilt her, and her Flight Commander at the time had been only too pleased to palm her off to the Middle East when demand for more aircraft in this theatre had so dictated. And since aircraft are only machines, Workshops assured us, they are only made up of components; and each component has its own life, together with a plus and minus tolerance factor. So mechanically, the machine as a whole could not be faulted and was thus fully serviceable. QED.

But pilots learn to love aircraft and know better. And 'All the Sevens' was a Janus.

The radios were temperamental; the batteries boiled; the engine blew oil and never quite gave full power; she was impossible to trim and flew like a crab; the hydraulics failed and fuel wouldn't transfer. The list was endless with neither pattern nor logic. Every time she went up for an air-test, the pilots snagged her again to keep her grounded. She had been ripped apart and re-built more than any other aircraft in Army service – which was why her hours never ran out and she was still with us.

And now she had escaped from the hanger and was mine for the day, and together we were flying the ADS.

The Air Dispatch Service is a daily event, and being a 'bus stop run' not very popular with the Flight, which is why we work it on a roster basis. Takeoff at first light from our strip at Falaise for the fifteen-minute flight to Khormaksar, the combined military and civil airport at Aden. Load with mail, dispatches, spares and passengers – roughly in that order but on a first-come basis, and thence up country to Habilayn, which is the Headquarters for the Radfan operation. Dictated now by the needs of the Brigade, the rest of the day is spent fetching and carrying to and from the five satellite airstrips that surround the battle area, which are normally occupied and manned at Company strength. The terrain is mountainous and involves a high altitude strip landing every fifteen or twenty minutes; which is exacting flying, especially with the added pressure of keeping to a timetable throughout the heat of the day.

This morning in the half-light of dawn, XP777 started the day with a magneto drop during the pre-flight engine run up. I considered taxiing back and snagging her 'unfit for flight' there and then – to justify the point. But there were no other aircraft available, and we were already late, which would throw the ADS timetable out for the rest of the day. A mag-drop is not the end of the world and in this case, I reasoned, was most likely caused by an accumulation of oil in the bottom three cylinders, since the aircraft had been standing in Workshops for such a long time. The nine cylinders are set as radii of a circle – like spokes of a cartwheel – and unless the engine is turned over at regular intervals, oil drains down to the lower cylinders and settles there.

It is not in the manual, but if oil has accumulated one can sometimes clear it by burning it off by juggling the levers. First set RPM to fast tick-over, and increase the boost to maximum. Then by degrees pull back the third lever, which leans the fuel mixture. One shouldn't do this at ground level for it causes the engine to run hot – which is exactly what we are trying to achieve to burn off the oil. The steady blatting tick-over noise of the Pratt and Whitney becomes irregular as the engine starves. I watch the cylinder head temperature gauge rise into the red sector and hold it there. The engine backfires and I push the lever back to fully RICH, then quickly set the correct Revs and try the magneto switches again. Something has worked for they are now both within limits – *just*... and so long as I don't look too hard. At least I know the cause was oil and nothing more complicated, and as such will cure itself after an hour's running. So, and before they can change their minds, complete the remainder of the pre-flight checks whilst on the move, line up on the runway and takeoff.

We are light, and in the cool morning air together with the airstrip being at sea level, use only half the available runway before lifting off. Immediately airborne, I reduce the RPM and the ear piercing banshee howl caused by the propeller tips at near supersonic speed subsides to a gentler 'thrubbing' engine note. At one hundred feet I bank the aircraft forty-five degrees to port onto track for Khormaksar before raising the flaps. This not only cuts a corner and saves precious minutes, but also avoids overflying the camp. A Beaver at takeoff power makes an awful racket and there is no point in waking everybody up.

Up to now I have not spoken to anybody, for our control tower is rarely manned at this hour. With the aircraft trimmed to climb on track I turn to the radio selector box in the roof and select 'Com.1'. We carry four different radios, two VHF sets – a main and back-up for Air Traffic purposes; an HF set, which involves winding out a trailing aerial and is only used when we are in the middle of nowhere and outside VHF range; and finally an Army set which enables us to communicate directly to troops on the ground, and perform our main operational role.

I have been waiting for this moment with some interest, for XP777 has a new face smiling from the radio bank. It is one of the new UHF sets, which are coming into service to replace the No.1 VHF. Living in Workshops all the time has its compensations, and she is the first Beaver in the Flight to be upgraded.

'Khormaksar Approach, this is Army Five-Zero-One, Good Morning!'

Nothing... and I can't even hear my own voice in the headset, which is disconcerting. Or perhaps UHF sets behave like this? It's switched on; correct frequency – try again.

'Khormaksar Approach, this is Army Five-Zero-One. Do you read?'

Still nothing. Damn you, aeroplane! We are now entering their airspace and it is vital that I talk to them, for I am too low to overfly the field, having already positioned my approach for a long final to the active runway.

Deselect Com.1 and press Com.2, which is the backup VHF. It is a very old set with limited range and usually hisses for the first twenty minutes until it warms up.

'Khormaksar Approach, this is Army Five-Zero-One. Do you read?'

'Five-Zero-One, this is Khormaksar – you are barely readable with static, and why didn't you call earlier? We've had you on radar for five minutes!'

Oh you arrogant man, it would have to be you! I recognise his voice and all the pilots know him to be the most unhelpful RAF Controller on the Station. The word that as a young officer he failed to obtain his wings, and has carried a grudge against all pilots ever since. I first became aware of this some months ago, when I passed an airborne flight plan on the radio. He called me back some minutes later and told me to resubmit it as one of the legs computed to a ground speed of only thirty knots. What he didn't know, nor did I want the rest of the world to know, was that my task involved flying up and down reconnoitring an alternative route for a convoy. Operational sorties were absolutely none of his business – and I can do without his interference today.

5

'Zero-One, QSY Tower' I reply, and without waiting for an answer change frequency to Khormaksar Tower, who control all takeoff and landings, as well as all aircraft movements in the immediate area of the airfield.

The voice of the controller on the tower frequency I also recognise and indeed can put a face to, for I once flew him to Habilayn to inspect the air-traffic installation. He sits upstairs behind the tinted glass windows and sees and knows all that is going on. His voice is full of humour and warmth, unlike his bitter colleague who sits downstairs and shares a windowless room with the radar controller. He gives me the runway in use, the atmospheric pressure for my altimeter, outside air temperature and wind strength and direction.

'Khormaksar Tower, Zero-One, Copy.' I acknowledge, jotting the information onto my kneepad, for I can use this information as a basis to interpret the upcountry strip conditions throughout the remainder of the day.

'Ah, we are the morning ADS, running a bit late as usual, would it be possible to put down on the dirt emergency strip in front of our dispersal?'

'Affirmative Zero-One, there is no other traffic – and a staff car with a one-star plate arrived just about a minute ago, so you've timed it just about right!'

I swing to starboard away from the main runway, and line up on the emergency strip, which is parallel to it and ends conveniently in front of the fenced high-security area which is also the army terminus and ADS pickup point. This will save about half a mile of taxiing. A one-star staff car means a brigadier and is probably the Brigade Commander returning after a night away. We are almost on top of the strip and still at 400 feet – which although the right height for the main runway, now calls for an immediate steep descent if we are to get in. I chop the power, pull the nose up and select full flap.

'Tower, Zero-One – thanks for that. I'll land off this approach.'

Airspeed back now to fifty knots, I apply enough power to hold the speed steady just above the stall. She sinks like a stone. Remainder of the landing checks complete; speed nicely settled at fifty knots, we fly down an imaginary line to a point selected on the runway, with only the airflow from the propeller creating lift to the wings. This is the classic Army short landing technique and fine so long as the engine doesn't stop, for we are on the very back edge of the power to lift curve. Should the engine fail now, it would mean there would be no forced airflow over the wings and this together with insufficient forward airspeed would result in our falling out of the sky. A final burst of power to cushion the landing, and we are down, nicely on all three points with minimum landing run. Who needs a helicopter?

I swing off the runway, shut the engine down and roll the final few yards to the waiting mail truck and staff car, with the ADS schedule now back on time.

As well as the Brigadier there is the Brigade Major, a REME sergeant, and the Political Officer whom I last saw in Mukerius five months ago. There are also five sacks of mail and a small generator. It is a squeeze, but finally all is stowed with the Brigadier in front, occupying the co-pilot's seat.

Master switch – On; Circuit breakers – all On; Electrics – On; Mixture – Rich; Propeller – Coarse; Throttle – Set; Friction nuts – Tight; Carb-air – Hot; Instruments – Check and Set; Brakes – On and Locked; Fuel select – Front; Pump – On; Warning lights – On; Radios – Select; Magnetos – On.

We are ready to fire up.

To the uninitiated, starting a Pratt and Whitney can be likened to playing a church organ – and gives an equally satisfying noise at the end of it. Open the pilot's door a crack so your left hand can find the T shaped fuel pump handle, which needs three or four pumps. At the same time your right hand wobbles the yellow wobble pump under the bank of engine instruments to build up initial fuel pressure. Then transfer the left hand to the three switches under a safety guard. Forefinger to the left switch and press UP to activate the inertia reel, which is an electrically driven flywheel. Wait until it reaches peak revs, then with the middle finger press the next switch to operate the pre-start heater, and hold for about five seconds. Finally press the third 'engage' switch, which clutches the engine into the spinning flywheel and turns it over. After three of four agonising turns one cylinder fires with a bang and emits an alarming flame together with a cloud of exhaust from the short stack protruding from the starboard side. Thus encouraged, other cylinders take up the theme and fire spasmodically and in no orderly sequence, each outdoing the other with flame and noise. The propeller turns – click, click, click, click – whilst you *will* the engine into life, still wobbling with your right hand and holding the 'inertia' and 'engage' switches up with your left. Release them too soon and the animal you are trying to awaken will die; get it right and you are rewarded with that special harmony and crescendo of sound that only a radial Pratt and Whitney can orchestrate.

As she is warm, she will only need one pump of fuel with the left hand. Wobble with the right, pressure into the green sector on the gauge – and activate the inertia switch.

Nothing happens.

The fuel warning lights are on, so the main electrics are through to the panel, but the inertia motor remains lifeless. What now? Start by hand? There is a handle stowed for just this purpose but it needs a second person to crank the flywheel from the outside. But she started with no trouble this morning – and nothing has caused the fuses to blow.

FUSES!

Check the contact breakers again – which was the beginning of the Start Up sequence. They all look fully up – except for one in the middle, which is marginally lower than the rest. Possibly the Brigadier knocked it with his knee when he was clambering in with his grip. I reach across and press it up and it clicks into place. Wobble-pump pressure still up, reactivate the inertia switch and the motor starts its hum.

Sorry, XP 777, not your fault – but entirely mine for rushing. I have yet to learn to trust this aeroplane.

8

But you still don't fly straight, I add as an afterthought some ten minutes later, as with boost and revs set in a fast cruise configuration, I find the rudder trim incapable of holding the aircraft properly on course, and we progressively edge off to starboard. This first showed on the Direction Indicator and was soon confirmed by our track over the ground. But never mind, the morning is too good to spend niggling over details, and I'd rather be here than anywhere else. The air is sparkling and the visibility excellent – so much so that I can actually see the mountains eighty miles to the north and they are over half way to our destination. But as the sun climbs, so the visibility will decrease by the hour, until by midday when the temperature is at its highest, forward vision will be reduced to barely a mile.

It is good to fly at this time of the day.

From here to the mountains the desert rises 4000 feet, and then on entering the mountains will rise another 1000 feet as we follow the main wadi north for a further thirty-five miles to Habilayn. This morning instead of climbing to altitude before levelling-off on course, which is normal procedure, I opt to remain at 500 feet above ground level and climb with the slope. Four thousand feet spread over eighty miles will mean a touch under normal cruising speed all the way, with negligible extra time and fuel. Also, should there be any early morning cloud hanging over the mountains further up the wadi, which is possible at this time of the year, we will be at the right altitude to sneak under it and try for a low level straight-in approach to the airfield.

I add 'rudder trim' to 'UHF radio' already noted on the snag list I have decided to compile for Workshops. It is difficult to relax flying this aircraft.

We are four minutes ahead of schedule when we reach the mountains and the opening of the wadi beckons us in. Then, just when we really need it, the visibility decreases, and I can no longer see clearly ahead.

A moment ago every crag and gully was outlined with absolute clarity yet now the mountains that edge the path of the wadi are becoming hard to see, as though a mist

9

surrounds them. And more alarming, this mist is also beginning to conceal the path ahead, through the mountains.

All of which doesn't add up.

A glance through my side window confirms my doubts. The mountains on my left are still as clear as ever – so the trouble is from within. XP 777 has pulled another trick out of the bag and the windscreen is covered in a film of oil, obscuring forward visibility. By their very nature radial engines are prone to throwing a certain amount of oil at the best of times, but this sudden influx is most likely to be from the constant-speed propeller, the pitch of which is controlled by oil pressure acting against centrifugal force.

Add 'leaking CS seal' to the growing list and carry on. Fortunately I know the route, but with the amount of dust thrown up at every takeoff, the windscreen will need cleaning at every stop.

At Habilayn the resident mechanic confirms the leaking seal but assures me that it should not get any worse and clears the aircraft to fly for the remainder of the day. Whilst it is being unloaded I stroll across to the Air Traffic tent to make my number and to see who is on duty. Two senior RAF warrant officers, who by now must be nearing the end of their two-month stint of duty, man the radios. They are an essential link to us, for not only are they fully up-to-date with the tactical situation, but also conversant with the local weather and flying conditions to be expected in the mountains for this time of the year. When I first met them I discovered that they were both keen fishermen, and between monitoring aircraft movements, spent most of the day discussing where they would stand and how they would cast, were they on the banks of the idyllic English river shown in the centre page spread of an old fishing magazine.

The picture is still spread out in front of them, which pleases me. Even after two months they have not exhausted this topic, and it also tells me that nothing is seriously amiss. I interrupt and tell them about my difficulties with the aeroplane; that it is shedding oil from the propeller and also that I am restricted to the old No.2 VHF radio, which has manual instead of digital tuning, as well as lacking the range and clarity of the newer sets. They listen politely before turning back to their picture. This pleases me even more, for it displays exactly the right amount of indifference to be expected between those who fly, and those who are at the other end of the radio and control the airspace. But we are all wed to the same business, and although it doesn't often happen, and indeed is sometimes actively discouraged, I always find it's good to know the face behind the voice.

The next stop is Dhala with more mail and the Padre on his rounds. Dhala holds mixed memories for me, for it was here about a year ago I had a sudden attack of diarrhoea and sickness, which left me weak and retching. I remember lying under the wing and wondering whether I was capable of flying the aircraft back. This unlocked that other old enemy *fear*. Fear can be likened to a mental cancer and if allowed, will breed upon itself. Should fear present itself when you are on the ground, it will persist until the minute you are airborne, whence it will recede back into its hole, consumed by the business of flying. But should it present itself when you are aloft, it can be a totally different matter. As a service pilot we get paid additional flying pay – for which we are expected to cope with all weathers and conditions, every day of the year. In the two and a half years I have been flying in this theatre I have clocked just over two thousand hours flying time – together with three thousand landings. Statistics show that on average an incident will happen once a year – or every thousand flying hours – and it is then that you earn every penny of flying pay and usually in about five minutes flat. This is the time that fear will choose to emerge from its hole, and it must be recognised as such and then mastered and put away; else it will effect judgement. Adrenaline usually gets you through at the time, but you pay for it later – either the minute you land, or when sleep does not come that night and you lie awake in the darkness and re-enact what *could* have happened.

Flaps down, and back into Habilayn to refuel and a quick breakfast and on with the day. The airstrips are all old friends – some easy and some demanding. XP 777 is behaving herself apart from covering herself with oil and dust. Old faces, new faces, ammunition, spares and sacks of mail. The flying becomes harder as the day heats up and the temperature reaches the upper nineties. With the heat, new thermals appear together with vicious downdrafts near the mountains – but none of this matters nor indeed is taken into account by those waiting at the next outpost, all of whom have their own timetable and urgent reasons to reach their next destination in the quickest possible time.

And so to Blair's Field, the last satellite strip – and my worst landing of the day. It is four o'clock and we are still on schedule. I leave the engine running and lean out of my side window to fan my face in the propeller wash and wait for the passengers. I can't be bothered to clean the windscreen yet again and resolve to do it a final time before leaving for Aden. It will be a hard climb out of Blair's to cross over the mountain ridge, followed by an immediate descent back into Habilayn – so allow thirty-five minutes. What about the fuel? The wing-tip tanks are empty and the three belly tanks show the rear to be quarter full, centre half full and front just over half full. With careful management we have enough to get home, so there will be no need to top up at Habilayn, which will mean a quick turn-round – say ten minutes to load, or better allow fifteen as there is usually a full load of passengers going back to Aden. Allow an hour flight time to Khormaksar, say another ten minutes on the ground and then the final twenty minute hop back to Falaise – which will make it about quarter past six, and nicely in time for a long shower and a drink before dinner.

The camp at the side of the strip at Blair's looks very smart. The Coldstream Guards have recently taken over and already have erected two flagstaffs, one with the Union flag and the other flying their red and blue Regimental Colours. My passengers are also being seen off with due ceremony for it is the Colonel together with his Adjutant and the RSM, who have been visiting the company. Also there is the familiar face of the Gunner Forward Observation Officer who is always thumbing a lift, and finally a hopeful-looking cook together with rifle and all his gear, obviously on his first leg home for UK leave. As the rear passenger seats are all taken up, I indicate to the cook to clamber up into the right hand seat next to me.

Trims – Elevator three quarters Forward for this weight; Rudder slightly Left to counter the extra torque created by a short takeoff; Friction nuts – One, two, three Tight; Propeller – Fully Fine; Mixture – Rich; Carb-air – Cold; Fuel – Select Front tank; Contents – Check and Okay; Fuel pump – On; Flaps – Set to Takeoff; Instruments – Check and Okay, and reset the Direction Indicator to the Compass; Engine instruments – Okay and all in their green sectors; Pitôt heat – On; Hatches – All Shut and check passenger harnesses all Tight and Locked.

Ahead the strip wriggles in the heat waves and appears to be even shorter than it already is. Buzzards wheel against the garish yellow sky, over the area used as a refuse tip by the camp, and fortunately to one side of our line. To hit one on takeoff can be a messy business.

Standing on the brakes I increase boost and let the power build up. This is the worst strip of all for loose stones and I can hear them banging and rattling against the sides. After ten seconds of hoof pawing and before the cloud of dust creeps forward to envelop the aircraft, I release the brakes and check the swing with rudder and the aircraft slowly gathers momentum. In the AOP IX we used to lift the tail, which reduces the drag from the tail wheel and levelled the aircraft into its flying attitude, but the technique is different in a Beaver. The Beaver already sits in its flying attitude, and has a large steerable tail wheel, which is necessary to counter the torque produced from its 450 horsepower engine. So we don't push forward on the column, but keep it in a neutral position, and the aircraft will fly itself off. More stones rattling on the fuselage – that's strange, it usually only happens when stationary; the surface must be very loose. The halfway point is marked by a rusty can at the side of the strip, which is a useful marker, and normally at this point you can feel the beginning of lift. But not today. XP 777 is not developing as much power as she should. The rusty can goes past and we are now committed, for there is no longer enough room to stop. One of the passengers from behind is shouting above the din and someone bangs my shoulder, but I ignore it for I need all my concentration to *will* this aircraft to fly.

The end of the strip is approaching with alarming rapidity and we are still firmly on the ground. And then it disappears in an explosion of rocks and smoke.

We snick through the smoke and debris and immediately fall off the end of the embankment. Ease the column forward and we are flying – but only just, with the wheels inches above the wadi bed. Use the ground effect and let the speed build up and resist the temptation to climb. Now, swing left using rudder only, so as not to expose a wing and follow the line of the wadi using the high ground behind as cover. Obviously it wasn't stones rattling during the takeoff but hits from small arms fire, and we were the perfect target. We are still flying and, by keeping the nose down, the airspeed gradually picks up. Everything still seems to be working except that we are overheating and have been in fine pitch for far too long. I reduce the propeller revs back to 2000, and then one pump at a time, gently lift the flaps to clean the aircraft up. She obviously throws more hydraulic oil in fine pitch, for the windshield is running with the stuff. Should have cleaned it at Blair's when I had the chance. We are heading away from our destination but I decide to remain on the deck for at least another three minutes before even contemplating a climb, and then will climb still heading east, before turning back to over-fly the strip at a safe height. We used to do this in training; takeoff and hedge hop for five miles before climbing, and the same in reverse for landing; only then it was intended to conceal the location of the field from the enemy. And it was Europe where the air is cold and the fields never much above 300 feet above sea level, which made the aircraft handle like sports cars. And it was all good fun. Takeoff from Blair's, at a touch over 6000 feet above sea level with a full load and the temperature at 100 degrees, was not funny. I wonder why she wasn't developing full power? My right leg is trembling from the constant pressure of the rudder pedal. Even with the rudder trim wound hard over it still needs all my strength to keep the aircraft flying straight. Possibly the trim balance tab on the rudder got hit, for it is far worse now than it was before. Should I ask the cook sitting beside me to lend his weight on the dual set of rudder pedals? He is sitting with his rifle between his knees staring intently ahead, and seemingly unaware of anything out of the ordinary. I glance behind into the cabin and the colonel passes me a note, which he has scribbled on his pad. At least all looks well behind and obviously the cabin received no hits.

'Blair's under attack, can we turn back to assess the situation?'

Three minutes is up and it is time to climb. Increase revs to 2200 and ease the control column back and trim the elevators. Instruments – Check. Temperatures have dropped slightly and pressures okay. Fuel...

FUEL! From reading just over half a tank, the front tank now shows empty. I flick the selector to the rear tank, which still shows quarter full as it did on the ground before takeoff. Say fifteen minutes flying at climb power. Either the front tank has ruptured or there is a leak in the line – which logically must be somewhere between the selector switch and the engine. *Please let it be the former.*

A thousand feet and I start a gentle climbing turn to port. This is the way the aircraft wants to go and it eases some of the pressure from my leg. One-eighty degree turn at Rate One, and we are heading back on the reciprocal bearing, still climbing at eighty knots. Another four and a half minutes and Blair's reappears under the nose – with the altimeter passing through 8000, which gives us 2000-foot clearance above ground and out of immediate danger from small arms fire. I maintain the heading and rate of climb, for we have another 2000 feet to go before we can clear the ridge. Blair's is pockmarked with mortar smoke and obviously still under attack – which rules that out for an emergency landing, which leaves Habilayn as the only alternative. The Coldstream passengers are all peering intently out of the windows, with the Colonel using binoculars. He starts to scribble another note on his pad and I indicate the passenger headset stowed in its side pocket.

'Can we go a bit lower and see what's..?'

'Colonel, we are loosing fuel and I can't hang around.'

'But my Company...'

'I'll patch you into their frequency and you can talk to them direct.'

I reach to the selector box and press the button which connects the army radio, and tune the Brigade frequency to his headset; leaving my own communications still on Habilayn Air Traffic. At the same time the red Fuel Warning Light snaps on, which leaves me ten seconds to change to another tank. I change back to the front tank, which lasts for twenty seconds before the light comes on again, and then turn to the centre tank, which is all we have left. Obviously it is the fuel line, and our lifeblood is pouring away. The electric fuel booster pump is still on – which is normally used only as a precaution for takeoff. Should I turn it off, or will this starve the engine altogether? I can't think straight. Whilst the engine is still running, I think I'll leave it as it is. Six hundred feet still to climb. Say another minute and a half before I can reduce power and conserve fuel. We are heading due west and straight into the setting sun and the oil on the windshield makes it impossible to gauge the height of the ridge ahead. Once over the ridge we should be in VHF contact with Habilayn and then it is downhill all the way. In fact we may be able to get through now – and I think this situation warrants a PAN call, which is not a full-blown emergency, but will alert them that all is not well.

'PAN, PAN, PAN. Habilayn this is Army Five Zero One, do you read?'

'Five Zero One, this Habilayn, reading you strength four, pass your PAN message.'

I imagine them carefully folding up the picture of the river and immediately feel better. They can't actually do anything to help fly the aeroplane, but at least they are there and they will understand. A trouble shared is a trouble halved.

'Ah, Zero-One, we got peppered by small arms fire taking off from Blair's and are now loosing fuel. I'm not sure if we'll have enough to get back, so could you clear the field and stand by on this frequency? My position at the moment is inbound on a direct line from Blair's to you, approximately twelve miles out but I am still climbing to clear the high ridge abeam Capbadge.'

I can just make out the outline of the prominent jebel thus named, which we had a hard bloody fight to capture a month ago. It has been fully occupied since – giving our troops strategic coverage over the whole of the northeast sector of the battle area.

'Roger, Zero-One, we'll get things organised this end, and we'll clear this frequency for you. Habilayn Out.'

That was good of them. Between fishing casts they had remembered about the manual tuning on my old No.2 VHF set, and by clearing this frequency means I won't have the additional worry of loosing contact all together. I hear them contacting a RAF Belvedere helicopter that is on the helipad about to leave for Aden, asking them to hold their lift off – but am out of range to hear the Belvedere reply, which would have been worth listening to.

We scrape over the ridge and I immediately adjust the three central levers; throttle back to reduce boost, RPM back to 1650 to coarsen pitch and drastically lean the mixture, the combination of which will immediately halve our consumption from forty to twenty gallons per hour. The centre fuel gauge is flickering just above the zero and after a further second's hesitation I flick the electric fuel pump boost off and then push the control column forward. The airspeed builds up to 120 knots, with the engine turning so slowly that I am conscious of the propeller tips flicking round, out of the corner of my eye.

The Colonel is still talking on the radio and I check again that all the passengers are strapped in with their lap belts. The cook in the co-pilots seat has a full shoulder harness like mine on an inertia reel and I flick the lever forward to lock it. I scan the instruments, always returning to the fuel gauge which has stopped its flicking and is now firmly on zero; I wonder how accurate the gauge is and whether a hidden reserve has been built in? If I can hold this altitude for another ten minutes – no nearer twelve, with luck we should be able...

There is no hidden reserve and the Warning Light snaps on again. Fuel Booster pump back ON and woggle the manual pump to help it.

Ten seconds is a long time – and there is still no pressure on the woggle-pump – and the fuel warning light remains ON.

On the count of ten the engine gives a gentle cough and then is silent.

Instinctive reaction: convert speed to height and haul back on the column. Should have done this before, instead of sitting mesmerised by the light. We gain eighty feet and as the speed drops back through seventy-five knots I wind back on the elevator trim to hold the glide at that speed. Also with no torque effect from the engine, the rudder pressure seems to have eased a little and she is easier to keep straight.

Now, concentrate on the next sequence of the engine failure drill – which is to select a field in which to land and plan a circuit and approach.

Dear Lord, this is for real.

And there are no fields, just barren mountaintops into which we are descending at six hundred feet a minute.

Oh God, please help me now? No, that's not fair, I've done without You up to now, and I have no right to...*Oh God, is this really is happening? Come on get a grip; keep calm and fly this aeroplane. The wheel of fate has come round again and it's time to earn some of that accumulated flying pay.*

Fear; get back into your hole!

We are in amongst the mountains now, directly into sun with a filthy windscreen and I cannot see ahead. Better get a Mayday off before the mountains blank the radio. Casually now...

'Mayday, Mayday, Mayday. Habilayn, this is Five-Zero-One, Five-Zero-One, Five-Zero-One. We are out of fuel now and my engine has just quit. My position is – Ah, abeam Capbadge just coming up to the – Ah, got it! We're just coming up to the Wadi Rabwa. My heading is due west and I'll try and put down in the wadi bed. We have six souls on board. Mayday, Mayday, Mayday.'

There, that's done and I feel in command of myself again. *And thank you God* – for the only course of action presented itself even as I was transmitting, when I suddenly realised my exact location – and that the mountains instead of being unknown and hostile were familiar – albeit still far from friendly. And at the foot of them, like a white snake, winds the Wadi Rabwa. I had discovered this valley by chance just before the Cap Badge battle, when I directed Hunter ground-attack aircraft onto a target not far from this spot – and at the time the wadi was the only place to keep out of their way. I remember thinking at the time that it was no place to have an engine failure, for the dried up riverbed is narrow and twists in all directions as well as being strewn with boulders the size of parked cars. And now Fate has destined this to be XP777's final landing ground – and the wadi is waiting down there at the end of our glide, if I can find enough airspace to reach it, threading through the mountains with a dead engine. There's no time to find the location on my map to give them an accurate grid reference, so I hope they can find it.

'Mayday, Mayday, Mayday. Army Five-Zero-One, Five-Zero-One, Five-Zero-One; this is Habilayn. Your Mayday message received and we are alerting Rescue. Be warned, enemy activity in your vicinity and we have alerted two fighting patrols that are in the area. Good luck, Zero-One. Habilayn. Over.'

I click the 'send' button twice to acknowledge and then de-select the colonel's headset from the army set and flick the switch to 'intercom'.

'Colonel, I'm afraid we are out of fuel and I'll have to find a spot to put the aircraft down. Please check that you and the other passengers are strapped in as tight as possible, and lean forward to protect your head with your arms before impact.'

I turn round and his eyes widen and hold mine for a long second before he nods. In his position I don't suppose I could think of anything to say either.

The slope of the nearest mountain is catching us up and I apply a fraction more back pressure to stretch the glide. It falls away again and I catch a first glimpse of the Wadi Rabwa, like a twisting white snake at the foot of the mountains. It reminds me of skiing down a slope in the Alps and seeing the village and resort beckoning from far below. If we had an engine this would be fun – but as it is, and measured against the nearness of the rocks, it is frightening to see how quickly we are descending. From what I can see, the valley seems to open up a bit further on, and as such offers the only possible place to land. But can we stretch the glide that far?

Also there seems to be a further complication in the shape of a large black hillock of rock, which is directly in line with our path, and which we will have to clear first.

Ease back a touch more and the speed drops to sixty-five and I re-trim the aircraft again to hold it. She is wallowing now and not far off the stall. The hot air currents reflected from the rocks do not help and call for large movements of aileron and rudder to keep the aircraft straight. *Come on 777, I know you have been abused in the past, but fly now, like the thoroughbred you are.*

We are too slow, and she is impossible to control at this speed. I wish I could see more to gain better perspective. Inch the column forward again and build the speed back up to seventy. This immediately sacrifices some height and the slope starts to catch us up again, but at least the controls are firmer and she is flying again. It is tempting to try ten degrees of flap, but this will just slow us – and theoretically she will achieve maximum glide distance with a clean wing.

'Haven't we got any parachutes?' This from the adjutant, pointing to the parachute wings stitched onto his right sleeve. He is obviously unaware just how close to the mountain slope we are, for there's not nearly enough height for a parachute to deploy, even if we did carry them. Which we don't, for in our aircraft they would take up too much valuable room – and a long time ago somebody reasoned that at our slow landing speeds, it is a damn sight safer to stay strapped into the aircraft.

Nonetheless it makes me smile and brings back another early memory from training, when we used to wear parachutes – or rather sit on them as they were designed as part of the seat of our Chipmunk training aircraft. Because of this we were obliged to attend a skimpy course in the gymnasium on how to control a parachute whilst descending and how to land without breaking your legs; and the course concluded with a lecture from a visiting RAF warrant officer who glared at us from the rostrum and announced that *anybody* who voluntarily jumped out of a *serviceable* aeroplane needed their heads seeing to... To conclude, he gave us a résumé on how to land in the sea, which up to now we hadn't even considered, so intent had we been on preserving our limbs.

'...It is very difficult to determine height when descending over water, so the odds are that you will punch the quick release button whilst still several hundred feet up, and *plummet* to your deaths. The more *cautious* of you will hesitate – until inevitably you will leave it until too late, and you will splash into the water and sink. Furthermore, in your struggles to escape you will find you are hopelessly tangled up in the control lines of the canopy. *There is no cause whatsoever to panic.* Just swim to the surface and stick your nose under the canopy and you will find half an inch of God's *Fresh Air* to breathe. Next, using the knives – which I see you all have sheathed in your flying suites – cut yourself free and then all you do is to find a seam of the canopy. Follow the seam – remember a parachute is rather like a large orange – not forgetting to breath in the air gap above as you go, and after about ten minutes of struggling you will eventually arrive at the hole in the middle. *Turn around* and...'

But today only a black rock face awaits us, for the hillock, which I had seen in the distance, is still obstructing the only level ground, only now noticeably larger in the windshield and still very much in the way.

With all tanks sucked dry, at least she shouldn't burn when we hit.

The constant pressure on the right rudder pedal is becoming unbearable and my leg is trembling and becoming numb with the strain. It is too late to ask the cook for the use of his leg, for this slow speed calls for large movements of elevator and rudder and his feet would now be in the way. I try easing it up and immediately the aircraft skids to port which, at just above stalling speed, could flick the aircraft into a spin if not caught in time.

But maybe even this would be preferable to flying head on into a rock face, which is fast becoming the only alternative. I cannot stretch the glide any further and we have neither the height nor speed to avoid it.

'*If you misjudge your final approach in a Beaver when force landing into a field, and have neither the height nor speed to avoid flying through the hedge, there is one final trick you can try to avoid this embarrassment.*'

The voice of Mr. Summers materialises in my headphones.

'*Try dumping full flap, very quickly. It is only to be used as a last resort, but it may balloon you into the air to give you clearance for the hedge – but at the expense of the remainder of your flying speed and you will fall out of the sky, and without doubt will suffer the indignity of a heavy landing.*'

I drop the nose a fraction to build up an extra knot of speed, select the flap lever to down, and when impact seems inevitable pump the flaps hard down. The aircraft hits a wall of air and rears up like a startled horse.

The black rocks scrape by.

Then, as predicted, we fall out of the sky.

XP777's final landing may have been undignified but she looked after her passengers to the very end. In a nose high attitude and fully stalled the tail hit first, followed a split second later by the main wheels, puncturing both tyres on impact and a second later ripping off both undercarriage legs. The remaining forward speed was then dissipated by a boulder about the size of an office desk, which dismembered the propeller and finally wedged itself under the engine cowling. After the prolonged silence of the glide, the noise was horrific – and then silence, save the ticking of the cooling engine and the final winding down of the gyros.

We all clambered out.

Then had to dive for cover, as we came under attack from unseen rifles. The colonel took charge and organised all round defence with the assorted collection of side arms we carried. I gave my 9mm pistol to the Adjutant who seemed to be without one, and then crawled back to the aircraft to retrieve the SMG that I kept under my seat – but also as a last act of airmanship to check that everything had been turned off. I needn't have bothered because I found the aircraft completely shut down. At some time during the final moments of the descent, my fingers had automatically performed this final ritual.

I found the machine gun together with two charged magazines and then as an afterthought unclipped the Vary Signal pistol and a box of red cartridges. Things were hotting-up outside and I could hear the colonel shouting for me to get back. I gripped the control column for the last time and looked at the array of now dead instruments.

Thank you, old lady for getting us down safely – and I'm sorry to – and then, on an impulse found my knee pad and tore up the sheet with the list of faults I had been compiling for Workshops. Final check to the clusters of radio switches on the roof. All off. And then a glance outside and up through the two glass panels in the roof, which are there to see out when in a vertical bank. A patch of blue sky is visible far above, framed by the shadows of the surrounding mountains. That's where we should be now, winging our way home to dinner in the Mess in an hour and a half. Instead of this hole. God, I'm exhausted and have run out of energy to face this latest turn of events. How on earth did we manage to corkscrew down into this patch of ground?

Thank you, God, for... The rattle of small arms fire is continuous now, although no shots have hit the aircraft yet.

You are somewhere there in that patch of blue far above... This is becoming something straight out of the Wild West, and I can hear the ricochets whining off the rocks.

And You heard...

Chapter 2

I sit in the cockpit for a moment longer, adjusting to the ground, and then take off my helmet and place it on the co-pilot's seat – the final after-flight ritual. With my ears free from the headphones I immediately become aware of the noise of the small arms fire and with it the realisation of the predicament we are in. My mind is still aloft, re-living the final descent and crash landing. Poor old 777, at least she'll no longer be the target for every pilot to snag and keep grounded, for she will never fly again.

God, I feel drained and the feeling has still to come back into my right leg, from being locked onto the rudder for so long.

Come on... It is time to become a soldier again.

Machine gun, and two loaded magazines from under the seat; vary pistol from its clip and box of cartridges. That's all I can salvage for now, so let's go before they realise I'm here.

I make a run for the rocks and throw myself down behind the nearest outcrop, followed by spurts of dust in the sand, which I realise must be bullets aimed at ME! It's different when you're flying; these bullets are suddenly very real. The Colonel and RSM are both behind the rock with 9mm pistols drawn.

'Ah, that's more like it, Sir' the RSM says, relieving me of the SMG and magazines, and then 'God, look at the state of it!' as he examines the barrel.

It is not worth protesting and being an infantryman the SMG will doubtless be more effective in his hands rather than mine. But nonetheless I feel a bit miffed, for the only reason I fly with a machine pistol under the seat is that I'm a notoriously bad shot with a handgun. I've always liked the idea of being behind a spray of bullets rather than individually aimed shots.

'Colonel' I say rolling over to face him 'I seem to be left with only a Very pistol to fight this war...'

'Never mind, I don't think there are more than a dozen of them, and they're rotten shots, else they would have hit you. So tell me, what's the situation?'

'I got a Mayday off to Brigade, and they know where we are. They warned me that there was enemy activity in this area, and apparently there are two fighting patrols out. I think it is just a case of sitting it out and waiting for the cavalry to arrive.'

A fresh volley of fire splinters the rock over our heads. Then the Adjutant's voice calling out that the enemy were moving round to our right flank.

This is getting too close for comfort, and is exactly the reason I left the walking army and went flying...

✳ ✳ ✳

I first came into contact with the flying side of the Army whilst sitting on top of an armoured car in Germany.

Out of nowhere, a Skeeter helicopter landed, and out got my Colonel, who sauntered over and asked me for a lift back to Regimental HQ. The Skeeter then lifted off, did a graceful pirouette before dipping its nose, and at only a few feet above the ground disappeared behind some trees.

What a way to go! And that, I thought, is the job that I want to do.

I thought about it for the remainder of the exercise, the germ of an idea, and the more I thought about it the more I wanted to know about flying in the army. I asked a few people, but nobody seemed to know much about it, other than it was a small elite force and far too specialized for them, and anyway, if I wanted to fly, what was I doing in the army?

At the end of the exercise there was the usual post-mortem, followed by a dinner night in the Brigade HQ tent

– one of those bizarre customs peculiar to the British army, and contrived so that participants at all levels may have the opportunity to meet their opposite numbers, as well as any foreign delegates who had taken part. The tent was still in its tactical location, which meant it was in the middle of a wood, and as usual it was pouring with rain and entrance was gained over a bridge of squelching duck-boards, placed to span the worst of the mud. But this did not deter standards in any way; inside, the silver was on the table and the mess staff properly attired in their starched white jackets.

You never know with these semi-official parties and I had not been looking forward to it very much, but in the event it turned out that I knew a few of the people and it was good to catch up with some familiar faces and swap experiences until dinner was announced. By this time we'd all had a drink or two and when I eventually discovered my place I found myself sitting next to a Gunner captain whom I had not met before and who turned out to be the pilot of the Skeeter I had seen the other day. At last! Here was the very man who would know all about it.

'How do I get to wear a pair of those?' I asked him, nodding at the wings on his chest.

'If I was given a pound for every time I've been asked that,' he said in a tired voice, 'I'd be a very rich man. Do you *really* want to know? And which version would you like, the long or the short?' He sat back and looked at me, and I noticed he was drinking water. Perhaps he had thought my interest merely perfunctory and was thus disinclined to talk.

I told him I'd seen his Skeeter the other day and that I was genuinely interested, and then also mentioned that I'd done a bit of flying – strictly as a passenger and mostly with my father who had owned an Auster for many years.

'Hmm. More important, how long have you served with your Regiment?' he asked, looking at the two pips on my shoulder. He had a weary look about him and seemed rather old to be still a captain.

Perhaps that was it! Maybe he had been flying generals for the last two weeks and, having been the prima donna amongst their exalted company, now resented being placed near the bottom of the table, in strict accordance with the pecking order of his rank.

'Four – coming up to five years...'

He sat for a moment, and then seemed to make up his mind.

'Well, I merely mentioned it because you have to have at least five years' service before you can even apply for the flying course. And then a lot depends on your CO, and if he's willing to recommend you. A lot of senior officers don't like funny hats,' he said guardedly, glancing at his light-blue beret on the table behind us. 'And if he *does* recommend you, you've then got to ask yourself why he wants to get rid of you, having just spent five years training you? Or, is he *genuinely* interested in your career? A lot depends on that and it's very easy to fall between two stools and damage your long term prospects in the process.'

'How come? I'd have thought that being an army pilot would have enhanced your career?'

He sighed and looked at his watch, which was one of those fancy black-faced affairs with a sliding outer ring and three or four buttons for triggering multiple other functions. Amongst the dials he discerned that perhaps here was somebody who was genuinely interested and maybe even worthy of the long version; and with that, launched into what appeared to be a well-rehearsed résumé of army aviation.

The Army Air Corps in its own entity, he told me, was extremely small. So small that it only numbered about eighty officers and senior NCOs in the permanent cadre, and the highest rank that one could attain was brigadier. It was formed from the old Glider Pilot Regiment and the Royal Artillery AOP Squadrons, and even now, after five years, was little more than a training organisation. They did not even have enough of their own people to administer the Army Air Corps Centre at Middle Wallop, and this was staffed by the Royal Armoured Corps. And more to the point, apart from the permanent cadre, the majority of army pilots were regimental officers and senior NCOs from all arms, who were seconded to the Army Air Corps for a three-year flying tour.

'So, if it works, what's so wrong with that?' I interrupted. He stared at me for a moment and frowned.

'Work it out for yourself, you're a regular officer; you know as well as I do what you've got to do to plan your own career. What ambitions do you have, and how are you going to get there?'

I thought for a moment, and then decided to give the stock answer. 'Well... I suppose go to Staff College and – and hopefully to command my Regiment at some time...'

'Exactly!' He looked at his watch again and then clicked one of the buttons twice. 'Useful for timing the time of flight,' he said mysteriously, and then looked up again. 'And how do you intend to educate yourself, to qualify for entry into Staff College?'

I decided to carry on with the official line. 'Well, I suppose to gain as much practical experience... and in as many different branches as possible at a Headquarters, starting at Grade 3 level?'

'Right! You must be about due for captain? So tell me, how are you going to find the *time* to go off flying for three – maybe four years, in this career plan of yours?'

I could see the point he was making, for the path to the top is strewn with thorns. And you also need more than your fair share of luck. But the whole business was beginning to intrigue me. Surely things didn't happen this way?

'Don't let me put you off' he went on. 'I did it – but then I'm a Gunner, and a lot of senior Gunner officers are ex-AOP, which makes it a lot more acceptable. And if you like flying, undoubtedly it's the best job in the army! You *can* fit it in, lots of people manage it, but you'll find they're all at senior lieutenant or junior captain level – which is where you are now, for that's where the only career slot is.'

'But you said something earlier about *damaging* your future prospects?'

'Well, you've got to look at it from both sides. What about the Army Air Corps? They've invested a lot of time and money in you. Have you any idea how much it costs to put someone through the flying course? Once they've trained you, they need to get their full money's worth – so who do you suppose commands their Flights and Squadrons?'

'Their Permanent Cadre?'

'In many instances, yes, but the point is, how do they get their money's worth from all the other people they've trained to fly?' He paused for a moment, and then didn't wait for an answer. 'I'll tell you!' he said, 'a second flying tour. They invite you *back*, and this time, if you're any good – and believe me, you've got to be good to get through in the first place, they'll tempt you with a *command*. And *that's* where you can blow it! By the time your *second* tour expires, you'll have lost another three years and probably be over the top for promotion. Your regiment will have lost interest in you, because they've got to look after their young officers who are pushing up from below, and suddenly you could find your carefully planned career structure has gone to pot... I suppose you *could* try for the Army Air Corps permanent cadre, but they don't have many vacancies – and inevitably none will be at your seniority!'

I wondered whether he was on his second flying tour and had just come to terms with the fact that he had blighted the remainder of his career. Now *that* would account for a lot, and would certainly explain his age. To cover my thoughts, I gestured towards his glass with the wine bottle. He put his hand over his glass.

'Thanks, but I'll stick to water. I'm flying first thing in the morning...'

'So what incentive is there?' I eventually asked.

'That's just it, there isn't one!' He sat back and shook his head sadly. 'But people still do it. Once you get the flying bug... D'you know, I've come across no end of excellent and experienced pilots with *thousands* of hours of flying time, and they've all fallen between these two stools! They're now stuck at their present rank, doing odd stores jobs at the end of the railway line, with little or no prospect for the future, and begging to be called back for another flying tour. But there just aren't enough jobs for them at their level of seniority. You can't have senior majors filling all the flying positions – there are few enough vacancies for the young pilots as it is, and especially since many of the flight commanders are still captains! I suppose that's why the RAF is full of flight lieutenants who seem content to remain at that rank as aircrew. Not many seem to get through to squadron leader and go on to a command. They must have had the same problem that army aviation is only now just beginning to face. The trouble is, the Army Air Corps is just too *small* and too *specialised*...

'If you *really* want to fly, the best advice I can give you is to restrict it to one tour, and make sure you time it carefully. Enjoy it and then forget it and get on with your career as a soldier.' He looked at his watch again and then pushed his chair back and got up. 'I've got to get some sleep, I've been on the go all week. Nice to chat to you, and I'm sorry if I've painted a gloomy picture.' He collected his beret from the table and made to leave, then paused and leant over the back of my chair.

'Mind you... You could go for the whole hog at the *start*, and apply for the permanent cadre and change your badges. I understand on the grapevine they're taking a few subalterns now, and the more junior you are the more likely your chances of being accepted. But if you do that, just bear in mind that your career prospects could be limited, because there's only one Brigadier Army Air Corps. And you'd have to come clean and declare your hand with your Regiment from the start. You'll need your Colonel's recommendation, and what happens if you fail the course – why should he want to take you back? That's one you'd have to play *very* carefully and will need careful thinking about...' He gave a depreciating smile, and left me sitting with my wine.

I went to bed that night and tried to piece it all together. It didn't really make sense, and why was it so unsettling?

More to the point, was it worth jeopardising – or at the least disrupting – a settled career for the sake of a bit of extra flying pay and the glamour of wearing a pair of wings? I thought about my Regiment and how happy I was to belong, and drifted off with the thought that, on balance, it really wasn't worth it.

I woke up to the sound of a cartridge detonating, followed by the stuttering roar of an un-silenced engine. I peered out from my tent flap and saw the Skeeter enveloped in a cloud of blue exhaust smoke and the rotors slowly turning. Last night my dinner companion had told me it was an up-rated Gypsy Major engine – essentially the same engine block which, in one form or another had powered every British light aircraft since the Tiger Moth, only in this case was set crosswise behind the bubble cockpit. And instead of the main rotors being two-bladed and made of metal like every other light helicopter, the Skeeter had three blades made of wood and covered in fabric – again the same as a Tiger Moth's wing. Also since they were connected to a British engine, they rotated the other way to American machines, the same as the propeller turns the opposite way

Saunders Roe Skeeter – two seat light reconnaissance helicopter '...in spite of its age it could still fly out and knock spots of the American Bells and Hillers...' (*Courtesy Army Air Corps*)

on a fixed wing aircraft fitted with an American engine. All this made the Skeeter light and responsive to fly; and in spite of its age it could still out fly and knock spots off the American Bells and Hillers that were only now coming into service.

I saw him putting on his helmet and then fiddle with something on the roof. Then he gave a casual wave to the attendant soldier standing by, and the engine note changed as the rotors bit the air, and the nose dipped and he was gone...

And so I applied.

As so often happens, the first major hurdle turned out to be no hurdle at all. My colonel thought it was a great idea, and contrary to the cautious advice I'd received, thought the Army Air Corps, in one form or another, was bound to develop into the cavalry of the future – which was the very reason the Royal Armoured Corps had stepped in to administer the Army Air Corps Centre. He then went on to tell me about his previous appointment at the War Office where he had been involved with the re-establishment of army aviation, and the battle they had had to keep it away from the clutches of the Royal Air Force. And how, in order to clinch this, there were now moves to further de-centralise aircraft by forming Air Troops within regiments, thus rendering them untouchable and firmly out of bounds to everyone else.

'There's bound to be a bit of infighting at the start, but I shouldn't let it worry you. If I were your age I'd go for it... and try for the permanent cadre; it's a wonderful chance to get in on the ground floor. You'll see! Army aviation is here to stay, and the Army Air Corps will soon be large enough to stand on its own feet, and it certainly won't have to rely on seconded officers forever... Tell you what, best if we don't dine you out, for the odds are you won't pass the medical, let alone the flying course – so when you're sent back, we'll dine you back in instead! Oh, and for God's sake get a haircut; the rest of the army takes great score about these things...'

Nothing happened for three months, which made me wonder whether my application had gone astray, but then it all arrived one morning neatly packaged.

Far from going astray, somebody had been very busy on my behalf, and had co-ordinated the next two moves with the maximum of forethought. First I was to report to RAF Biggin Hill where I would undergo the medical and aptitude tests required for potential aircrew, but more important, the dates for this three day event had been chosen to coincide with the next sitting of the AAC Board which convened but once a year at the MOD for the sole purpose of selecting applicants for their permanent cadre.

I caught the night ferry from Ostend and made my way up from Dover to Biggin Hill, where I found the flying medical and aptitude tests were one and the same for all three services, administered on their joint behalf by the RAF. The majority of people were youngsters straight from school applying for flying commissions in the RAF or the Fleet Air Arm, which made the few soldiers like myself (and all with a minimum of five years service) feel somewhat elderly and rather out of place.

At the end of three rather intense days I was told that I was sound of mind and limb and suitable for aircrew training.

The interview with the Army Air Corps Board was scheduled for the following morning, so I stayed a further night at Biggin and caught an early commuter train from Croydon and walked from the station to the Ministry of Defence.

I don't know what my Colonel had said in his recommendation, but the interview with the Board went smoothly enough. I was extremely conscious that once again I needed a haircut, and in the rush of the last few days had not had time. Let alone for an interview of this magnitude. Fortunately I was able to fall back on my scant knowledge of flying, which had started when I was eight years old when my father used to fly down to Exeter to pick me up from school. In retrospect, I don't think this had much bearing on the outcome of the interview, but at least it broke the ice and allowed my enthusiasm to show through.

After about forty minutes they compared notes and then had a huddled conversation.

Finally the Chairman looked up. 'Well, army flying is a bit more *exacting* than that required at your father's flying club, so we'd best see how you get on with the flying course and then, subject to your pass level and gaining your wings at the end, we'll let you know when you can change your badges.'

And that was that.

My Joining Instructions followed shortly after and informed me that the next Pilot Training Course would assemble at the Army Air Corps Centre, Middle Wallop on Monday 4 June, and since accommodation was scarce it was advisable for single officers wishing to 'live in' to report to the Mess Sergeant on the previous day.

There were a number of Wallops on the map, and true to its name, Middle Wallop was in the middle of them all and I had no trouble finding the airfield as it bordered the main A343 Andover to Salisbury road, about half a mile up from the village. The airfield and main camp were on one side of the main road whilst the Officers Mess and married quarters were on the opposite side. It was a typical RAF Station layout with the mess set back and standing in its own grounds, with a large sweeping drive and a place where you could park. RAF Messes tend to be much the same and are all built to accommodate large numbers of people in transit, which makes them somewhat impersonal, but they are comfortable enough for all that and couldn't function any other way.

'Ah yes, here we are sir!' The Mess Sergeant said, ticking my name on his list. 'Your quarters are round the back of the building. "H" block in the spiders, you can't miss it and you can park your car there. We like to keep the *front* of the Mess clear of vehicles, sir, if you would remember that in future? We've put you in room six, and you'll be sharing it with Mr Wilson, a gunner officer, sir. Accommodation is always a bit tight at the start of a course, but you'll probably find you'll have a room to yourself after a few weeks. That's what *usually* happens anyway. Oh, and dinner starts at *eight* on a Sunday, sir, dress informal. Thank you, sir.'

I drove around to the back and 'H' block was one of a number of wooden huts joined together to form a cross, or 'spider'. Most likely they had originally been erected as temporary accommodation to solve an overflow situation; but as so often happens, once the arrangement proves to be satisfactory and convenient, the 'temporary' becomes 'permanent', and is then passed on as an easy option by the succession of people whose job it is to be in charge of accommodation; especially if they don't have to experience the 'temporary hardship' themselves. Perhaps the next twelve months would not be quite as comfortable as I had first thought.

I found Room Six at the end of one of the spider's legs, and also Roger Wilson who had arrived some twenty minutes before me.

'Hi!' I said as I entered. Instead of responding in like form the occupant stood up and solemnly offered me his hand, which, after a moments hesitation, I equally solemnly shook and announced my name. He was obviously a stickler for correct procedure. Having formerly introduced ourselves we took stock of each other, both conscious that first impressions were important, especially if we were to share a room for the next twelve months. And as sometimes happens, we took an instant liking to each other. We were of similar age and build and the first thing I noticed about him were his eyes, which had depth and a permanent twinkle. But then I reeled back with surprise when he greeted me with a blustering and over-hearty manner, which sudden-ness came almost as an assault and seemed strangely at odds with his otherwise gentle demeanour. But I was soon to learn that this was his way to cloak the shy and sensitive person he really was and once he was sure of a person, his heartiness faded away.

We unpacked and sorted the room out and then walked

across to the main building for dinner. Although we had only just met, an unspoken bond was already beginning to develop – as so often happens with two new boys who are drawn together on their first day at school – whereby should they join forces at the very start, it can create a unit-strength which can then be drawn upon to face all the unknowns, as well as a rock foundation from which whatever hardships in store can be endured.

After dinner we walked across the road to have a look at the airfield.

Middle Wallop was once a Royal Air Force fighter station and was built in the days when fighter aircraft had piston engines and could operate from grass runways. The airfield became redundant with the advent of the jet fighter, which not only needed metal runways but also a lot more space than Wallop could offer. This was when the army took it over, for a grass field was entirely suitable for their light aircraft and helicopters, and there was more than enough space. And Wallop proved to be ideal in every other respect, with plenty of hangars, various workshops, a large administrative centre, numerous offices, barracks, mess halls, married quarters, et al. And all conveniently situated on the edge of Salisbury Plain, the army's favourite training area.

Roger and I took it all in and then climbed the steps to the control tower where there was one person on weekend duty. We stood on the outside balcony and looked over the field saying nothing, but both wondering what the morning would bring. It was one of those still, velvet evenings that only occur in high summer and just seem to linger on. We could smell the grass, which was freshly cut. *Was this to be the battlefield? Or would it be...?* I looked up at the sky. Roger had obviously been thinking along the same lines, for without turning broke the silence. 'United we stand...?'

And so our pact was sealed.

* * *

'This is the De Havilland Chipmunk' our new Flight Commander announced, as the twenty-two of us regarded the bright red and silver aeroplane parked nearest to the door of the hangar. The hangar was crammed full of identical aircraft, all slotting together like an enormous jigsaw puzzle. Some near the back had their cowlings off and were being worked on by mechanics. 'And this is the aeroplane in which you will be taught to fly...' he went on, with only the merest hint of doubt creeping into his voice. 'They are painted red and silver to distinguish them as aircraft belonging to Elementary Flight, as well as being the colours the RAF adopt for all their basic trainers, although, as you see, we have put ARMY on the sides...'

The Flight Commander had introduced himself as Major Chris Walsh and wore the distinctive light-beige service dress uniform of the Army Air Corps, which made him one of the chosen few. He was young to be a major and we wondered what his background was, but his only interest was the job in hand and he continued to tell us about the Chipmunk, walking round and pointing to the various parts as he came to them.

'From conception, the aeroplane was designed as a basic trainer, and as such is very forgiving should you get into trouble, but like most training aircraft it needs firm mastery in order to fly well.' He undid the cowling and showed us the Gypsy engine and then jumped up onto the low wing and slid back the cockpit canopy, revealing the two seats in tandem, each with its own instrument panel and controls. 'These aeroplanes' he said from his vantage point, 'are constructed of metal, which makes them extremely strong – which is just as well as they take unbounded punishment from course after course of trainee pilots, but they are also built to withstand negative-G forces, which makes them an ideal aerobatic aeroplane.'

He then jumped down and showed us the tail wheel and how, when in a flying attitude, its diminutive area offered far less drag than a nose-wheel; but when on the ground, obviously made the aircraft sit back. 'This makes the aeroplane difficult to taxi, for you cannot see where you are going because the engine's sticking up in the way. Therefore in order to see ahead, you have to swing the aircraft from side to side as you go along.' Finally, he told us, Chipmunks were the only aircraft used by the army in which the pilot carried a parachute. Not that we were expected to jump out of the aeroplane with them, but they were there to be strapped to our bottoms before clambering in, and then used to sit upon, because the seats were hollowed out for this purpose and an ordinary seat cushion would not fit.

Back in the crew room Major Walsh outlined the flying program for the duration of our stay with Elementary Flight. The program was designed to take sixty flying hours. First we would learn to fly the aircraft from scratch, then having gone solo, there would be a halfway test at thirty hours followed by a final handling test at sixty hours. During the whole of this period our abilities would be continually assessed to see whether we would be suitable to progress to the next stage of the course, which would be either on to helicopters or advanced fixed wing.

'But first you have to go solo,' Major Walsh said, looking at each of us in turn. 'And this is measured by a very simple yardstick. You've got to go solo within ten hours.

'Your instructors are all civilians – although you'll find that most of them are ex-Royal Air Force or Navy. As civilians, they're under contract to the army to teach you to fly. And as with every other contract, they have a strict budget to adhere to – which you will find, will rule out any form of leeway or favouritism. Their budget allows sixty hours per pupil. Not sixty-one, or sixty hours and ten minutes; but *sixty* hours exactly. And within this time frame you first have to go solo, *then* learn how to navigate so you can find your way home, *then* how to cope with emergencies, *then* how to perform aerobatics, *then* how to fly on instruments, *then* to fly at night, and so on. And believe me, every minute is needed and accounted for. Each part of the flying program has been allocated a set number of hours, and you cannot rob Peter to pay Paul. The rules are fixed.

'Given enough time, you can teach a *monkey* to fly, and the whole point of the army flying course is to achieve a series of progressive standards, each within a set period of time. There are no ifs, buts or maybes, and if you can't keep up, you will be OUT.'

He then went on to tell us that throughout the course, should any standard – or indeed satisfactory progression towards that standard – not be achieved within the time allocated, we would be put 'on review'. We would then be given one chance to redeem ourselves and if successful would be reinstated; if not, we would be failed and returned to our unit – or RTU'd.

'Right, that's the flying side of the program, but as your Flight Commander I also have the additional burden of matching this with your progress through ground school' Major Walsh went on. 'Depending on the weather we try to divide your days equally into flying and ground school. Ground school is where you will learn about the principles of flight, basic navigation, engines and airframes, rules of the air, meteorology, aerodrome procedures, and a lot of other things to do with the business of flying.

'And, as with the flying program, your progress will be monitored on a day-by-day basis, so you cannot afford to slack. There will be an examination at the end of each week, which you will have to pass in order to progress to the syllabus for the following week. And again, if you do not pass, I'm afraid you'll be out – for there will *never* be enough time to go back and retake any of the exams.'

In practice, he told us, this procedure had been found to be fair, both to the student and the course as a whole; for should a student fail a test, be it on the ground or in the air, it was unlikely they would fare any better in the more demanding tests to follow. It also ensured that the course as a whole would progress and not be held back by a single or a number of individuals.

I looked across at Roger and he gave a grimace, which left me wondering how long we would continue to be the joint occupants of Room Six?

We'd had a busy morning. We'd been to the Medical Centre where our heads had been measured for a 'bone-dome', as flying helmets seemed to be called. We'd been to the quartermasters and drawn light-blue RAF flying over-alls, together with an evil looking dagger which we were told to keep sheathed in the special pocket found on the left leg, and which purpose, heaven forbid, was to cut your way free from a crash... We'd collected flying boots, a pair of expensive-looking kid-leather gloves, some interesting navi-gational instruments and a blue RAF logbook – the perma-nent significance of which we were yet to perceive; all of which had buoyed us up with an air of expectancy of great things to come...

But now our spirits were totally deflated. How could we survive a whole year of this – to be under a microscope for every minute spent in the air as well as having to pass a weekly ground school exam?

At first sight Wallop was proving to be unlike any other training establishment any of us had encountered. No regard was given to our past experience, regiment, age or rank, and from the very first day our status was made perfectly clear: we were *students*. Wallop spawned its own hierarchy together with its own demanding standards; and if you did not sport a pair of wings on your chest, you were a *nobody*.

'We were going to take you up for your air-experience flights this morning,' Major Walsh concluded. 'But time is getting on and I see it has started to rain. Air experience is best demonstrated in fine weather, so hopefully the front will have passed through by tomorrow morning. Ah yes. There is one final thing. About your flying suits...'

Our flying gear, we were told, was to be kept in our lock-ers, and flying overalls were to be worn *only* for flying and not at other times about the camp. Certainly they should *never* be worn in the Mess. And whilst we were students of Elementary Flight, such was the temporary nature of our status and possible duration, our flying suits should remain unadorned ...

Permanent staff and the squadron pilots who were based at Wallop obviously had different rules, for their flying suits were adorned with wings, badges of rank, squadron badges and other personal paraphernalia. They were also worn for most of the day, wherever the wearer happened to be, and had that comfortable 'lived in' look about them. The ultimate apparel was worn by Skeeter pilots who were issued with leather fur-lined flying jackets – though why a Skeeter was deemed to be a colder aircraft to fly than any other was one of those aviation mysteries, and remained as such until they went out of service.

The following day the warm front was still with us, with low cloud and blowing rain. We changed into our blue flying suits and made our way to the crew room to see what fate awaited us.

A very large man with a ruddy complexion was standing by the door bellowing my name. 'God, you all look the same, which one of you is...? Ah, so there you are! My name is Mister *Avery*, and I *hope* it is going to be my *pleasure* to teach you to fly...'

So this was to be my instructor upon who so much depended.

The others were going through similar introductions and I saw Roger claimed by a small wizened man of uncertain age, who's face was a mass of deep lines, and who spoke with a strong Polish accent. It struck me then, and I have often pondered upon it since, that so often people can be type-cast by the job they do, or at least by some professional likeness – be they farmers, bankers, soldiers, accountants or publicans; but there is no stereotype for a flyer, and irrespective of age or nationality, they seem to come in all shapes and guises.

Mr Avery looked and behaved like a sportsman, and it therefore came as no surprise when I later learnt that he used to play a useful second-row for the Inter-Services rugby, as well as flying a Shackleton for RAF Coastal Command. And looking at the size of him, I couldn't help thinking that a four-engined Shackleton was a far more suitable aircraft for a person of his stature than the diminutive Chipmunk. But like many large men he could be deceptively agile, and even when encumbered with the seat-pack parachute strapped to his bottom, managed to ease himself into the confined cockpit space with a minimum of effort, albeit born from much practice.

The first thing he told me was that when in an aircraft, all instructors would be addressed as Sir, and when on the ground, the use of Christian names was frowned upon, and he would be addressed as *Mr Avery*. Apparently this was a tradition that stemmed from the Royal Air Force and was insisted upon by the Station CFI (Chief Flying Instructor) who was a serving RAF wing commander. I couldn't help thinking that the formality of this salutation was a little unnecessary, especially since I was used to the other extreme; for in my regiment it was customary to address everyone up to the rank of major by their Christian name, and thereafter by their rank, be it colonel or general; this never seemed to cause any offence, let alone any breakdown of discipline, or indeed respect. But perhaps this was all part of our new status; and when in Rome... especially if it was to be a question of survival.

'And what's more, I hate this sort of weather,' Mr Avery boomed, looking out of the window at the rain which had by now set in, reducing visibility to a few hundred yards. 'Come on, we might as well go flying.'

The rest of the course had settled down with their instructors, who had all decided not to squander precious flying hours in the rain. There were charts and models that could be used to familiarize students with the rules of basic airmanship or how the flying controls of an aeroplane worked, and were kept in the crew room for just this occasion.

'You'll learn far more with the real thing' Mr Avery growled, as we waddled out with our parachutes strapped to our bottoms, and clambered into a waiting aircraft. 'You sit in the front, the instructor always sits in the rear seat, and don't *touch* anything.'

De Havilland Chipmunk – two seat basic trainer. 'You sit in the front, the instructor always sits in the rear seat, and don't TOUCH anything.' (*Courtesy Army Air Corps*)

We took off and remained under the cloud base, which was about 300 feet, while he contacted Boscombe Down on the radio. We were then cleared for a radar climb and bored our way up through the cloud. At 6000 feet we broke out into the sunlight – my first time into that special world, and into which only a pilot can open the door. Here, he demonstrated what the others were learning in the crew room far below. How an aeroplane is rigged to fly straight and level at its designed cruising speed, and when trimmed correctly you can actually take your hands and feet off the controls. Put the nose down, and the aircraft will go faster and, surprise surprise, will also turn – because it has been rigged to fly straight and level at its cruising speed. To keep the aircraft balanced you must apply rudder, and the correct pressure to use can be seen from the Turn and Slip instrument on the panel in front of you, but try to feel it through the seat of your pants. In a climb the opposite occurs, and as the airspeed falls back, so you have to apply the opposite rudder to keep straight.

'Right, you have a go now, and use that cloud as a reference – you have control.'

'I have control . . . Sir!'

And so it began.

To start with, the training flights were restricted to thirty or forty minutes a day, after which time it was considered that your level of concentration would become saturated, and you could absorb no more. We learnt how to fly straight and level, and then progressed to climbing and descending, followed by turns, and finally onto the circuit, where all this was put together.

The circuit consists of taking off into wind, climbing straight ahead, whilst bringing in the flaps as the speed increases, to climb 'clean' at seventy knots. It is meant to be a 'square' circuit, so all turns are ninety degrees, and unless specified otherwise, to the left. So at 400 feet, turn ninety degrees to the left, whilst continuing to climb to 800 feet, which is the circuit height. Level off and increase the speed to ninety-five knots, then turn left again – and you are now running down wind, and hopefully the runway is just over your port wing tip. Complete the down wind vital actions for landing, and remember to call 'Down Wind' on the radio, then throttle back to 1200 RPM and turn left onto the base leg and you start your descent. Speed back to seventy knots and select half flap and trim. Almost in line with the runway and at approximately 400 feet, a final turn to complete the pattern and bring you back into wind; select full flap and the runway should swing in just under your nose. Call 'Finals' to the tower and reduce speed to sixty-five knots. Fly down an imaginary line to the threshold of the runway – at exactly sixty-five knots, and adjusting the rate of descent by the use of more or less power. Over the fence, power off, and hold the aircraft level just above the ground. As the speed drops off, gradually ease the stick back so the aircraft will stall, neatly on to its three points on the ground. Complete the landing run with discriminate use of brakes to keep the aircraft straight. And that is all there is to it.

It sounds easy, and the circuit pattern and method has not changed since flying began.

But there are degrees of acceptability. Anybody can fly a sloppy circuit and land at the end of it. Not so if you wanted to become a service pilot, and from the start our heights, turns, and speeds had to be exact, with no plus or minus tolerance admissible. This was to stand us in good stead for later when we progressed to the techniques for short-strip landings – where the approach speed is the vital factor.

But this was yet to come.

By the time I was ready for the circuit, I had used up five and three-quarter hours from the allotted ten. Mr Avery told me not to worry, and that I was about average; but secretly I doubted whether I could master the circuit in the time remaining, and subconsciously began ticking off each minute spent in the air, which only added to the pressure.

With one exception, the rest of the course were suffering in much the same way, and seemed to have split into two groups – those who were mastering it, and those who were not. Mess life began to dwindle, and Roger and I spent most evenings in our room, helping each other to revise for the weekly ground school exam, or sometimes rigging up a makeshift throttle and joystick to one of the beds and flying imaginary circuits.

The one exception was Jeremy Colquahoun. Jeremy was a Guards officer and the reason that he alone remained above all this, was simple.

He could already fly.

Not only did he possess a Private Pilots Licence, but also he also actually owned his own aeroplane! Naturally enough he asked permission to keep his aircraft at Middle Wallop, which request posed considerable deliberation from the administration, eventually ascending to the highest level before the answer came back – in the negative. Wallop, he was told, was a military airfield and as such no provision could be made to hangar civilian aeroplanes. Unabashed, Jeremy made arrangements to hangar his aircraft at Thruxton which was the nearest civilian aerodrome, and only some eight miles away.

So he alone remained apart, and was the envy of us all (which we passed off as indifference) especially when he used to fly home at weekends, where he had his own private landing strip.

But soon our envy was to turn to grudging admiration.

Without doubt, the most baffling subject at ground school was meteorology. To divine the weather is more of an art than a science and the subject, together with its long-suffering teacher was thus treated with the greatest obeisance and respect. It was included early in the program for two very good reasons. Firstly it was useful for every pilot to have a working knowledge of this as early as possible in his flying training, and secondly it was acknowledged that it could take a lifetime to understand properly... especially when trying to forecast the weather for the British Isles.

It therefore came as no surprise when a series of summer fronts appeared out of nowhere and descended upon Wallop with the usual low cloud and blowing mist and rain, to the extent that one Monday morning it was declared as 'beyond limits' and unsuitable to continue with our 'circuit-bashing', which was the stage we had now all reached. Instead, the instructors would give a series of impromptu lectures in the crew room.

Half way through the first lecture a breathless Jeremy burst in, muttered his apologies for being late, having been 'held up', and took his place in class. Later during the break we learned that he had indeed flown home for the weekend, and as usual, timed his takeoff for the return trip at first light in order to arrive in time for work. The weather was appalling with low cloud, rain and little visibility; but he pressed on and eventually found Thruxton, where he hangared the aeroplane, jumped into his car and drove like mad for Wallop – only to arrive and be told that the weather was too bad to fly!

The following week he turned up with a young Labrador bitch at his heels, and thereafter the two were inseparable. Jeremy explained that the gun dog was at a crucial stage of her training and unless she received his constant attention, could be ruined for life. This explanation was accepted, but the line was drawn at the dog riding in army aeroplanes, although she was quite used to flying home with him in his own aircraft.

By now the frontal systems had passed through, and June was again at its sunny best – which made the temperature inside the wooden hut that was used for meteorology lectures, akin to an oven. Soon after Jeremy's dog had become a member of the course, the temperature was insufferable and mid-lecture we were given a break, and all tumbled outside for a breath of fresh air.

For the second half of the lesson the door was left open, but this made little difference to the sweltering heat. The dog was lying beside Jeremy in her usual place; tongue out and panting like a steam engine. Finally the meteorologist snapped: 'For Pete's sake Jeremy, I can't hear myself talk! What with helicopters revving up and hovering outside and that damned dog of yours panting... if you've *got* to bring that animal into my class, at least you could *train* it to shut the door...'

Jeremy deigned not to look up from his desk, and after a moment casually drawled 'Just shut the door, Judy ol' girl'. Without hesitation the dog heaved herself up, glared at the instructor and then sauntered over to the door and slammed it shut with a single swipe from her front paw. You could have heard a pin drop. The dog looked round in surprise, then dismissed us all and ambled back and flopped down to resume her panting.

We forgave Jeremy for being able to fly.

The weather remained fine, which was important for it offered continuity, and we flew every day during the last two weeks of June and first two weeks of July, and as our familiarity increased, so the duration of our flights were extended to an hour or just over, which we found we now could take in our stride.

'God, it's twelve-thirty!' Mr Avery said, sliding back the canopy. 'My wife's going to kill me – I'm meant to be at a lunch party in five minutes, so just pull over there will you?' He clambered out from the rear seat and stepped onto the wing. 'You've still got half an hour before lunch in the mess, so just go off and do one more circuit on your own, and then take the aircraft back to dispersal. Oh, you'll find she'll perform a lot better without my weight...'

I was taxiing out to the end of the runway before the full significance hit me. *This is it! But I am not nearly ready yet; what if... what if?*

'Wallop, Charlie Five Seven, ready for takeoff.'

'Five Seven, this is Wallop, is this your first Solo?'

'Wallop, Five Seven, yes. – Er, yes.'

'Five Seven, Wallop, switch your landing lights on – just as an indication to the rest of the traffic, and you are cleared for takeoff.'

I opened up the throttle and the unladen Chipmunk leapt into the air.

Am I really on my own, flying this thing? Flaps up, check temperatures and pressures in the climb, and stay on the correct heading. Four hundred feet already – that was quick. Rate one turn to the left and watch the DI turn through ninety degrees. Eight hundred feet, level off. APT – Attitude, Power, Trim. We are not far enough out yet; she climbs much more quickly with less weight. Leave it for another minute. There! That's about right, now turn downwind, and I've lost ninety feet. Good job Mr Avery isn't sitting behind. Vital Actions for Landing. Brakes – Set; Mixture – Rich; Carb-heat – On; Fuel pump – On; Contents – Sufficient for overshoot; Flaps – we'll do in a minute; Instruments – Check. Damn! Now I'm twenty degrees off course. Sorry, Mr Avery. Where were we? Ah yes, Pitôt heat – On; Hatches – All shut and Harness is Tight. Time to turn onto base leg – – and I've forgotten to call the Tower.

'Wallop, Charlie Five-Seven is downwind for landing.'

'Five-Seven, this is Wallop, the wind is down the runway at fifteen knots and you are Number One for landing. Call again on short finals.'

'Five-Seven.'

Swing round onto base leg and reduce the power to 1200 RPM – and hold the nose level and wait for the speed to drop. Eighty knots and flaps down to half. Trim. She is not sinking nearly fast enough. Take off a touch more power. That's better. We are a long way from the field – just angle in a bit and try to cut the corner. The wind must have picked up. Five hundred feet and we are coming up to inline with the runway. Round onto finals, and drop full flap. Speed back to sixty-five knots and just a trickle of power. At last, she is sinking nicely. Last check round the cockpit, instruments all okay, now concentrate on the field ahead.

'Wallop, Charlie Five-Seven on finals.'

'Five-Seven, you are cleared to land.'

Watch out for the buffeting and be ready for the extra sink when you pass over the trees just before the threshold. There! Arrest it with a touch of power, and we are through, and still online. Over the threshold, still a bit high, and we are going to overshoot the first marker of the runway, where I had intended to touch down. Never mind, there's plenty of field ahead, and it will be less far to taxi. Now, hold her back, power right off, come on, we are nearly there, back, back with the stick, and –There! We are down, and a real greaser!

I relax, grinning from ear to ear. And immediately the aircraft takes charge.

The braking system on the Chipmunk is an antiquated throwback to the time when light aircraft were first fitted with brakes. It consists of a handbrake which, when fully applied will lock both wheels. For turning on the ground, there is a differential linkage to the rudder pedals, and by pulling the hand brake half on, and then pressing the appropriate rudder will activate the brake on that wheel only.

I had relaxed too soon, and straight after that textbook landing the aircraft started to swing to the left. I sat frozen, willing it to stop, then jabbed down on the right rudder. But it was far too late, and by now the aircraft's momentum had taken over. The starboard wing dipped towards the grass, and in a series of juddering lurches the Chipmunk swung right round, tearing up the grass, finally coming to rest facing the way we had come. In aviation terms, we – that is Chipmunk and I, had discovered the ground loop.

And with it, Mr Avery, who hadn't gone to lunch at all, but had been in the Control Tower watching all along. He slid the canopy back from the outside and shouted over the slipstream.

'Go on then, turn it round and do another circuit! You've still got over an hour's credit left out of your ten, and I bet you can't pull off another touch down as smooth as the last one. Oh, and *try* not to wander all over the sky on the downwind leg, this time...'

Like birds leaving the nest, we all went solo within the space of two days. All, that is, excepting five who did not make it. The first casualty was claimed by ground school, which at this stage of the course was deemed to be unusual, and the other four ran out of hours before they were ready to go solo, and so were RTU'd.

Having mastered the circuit, the next twenty hours were spent in developing and polishing our newly learned techniques, together with some cross-country navigation and an introduction to 'upper air work' – mostly advanced turns and spins as a prelude to aerobatics which were to follow. We also learned what to do in case of an engine failure, both on takeoff and also whilst en-route.

Without warning Mr Avery would close the throttle from the rear seat, and inform me in a casual voice that our engine had ceased to function. The first few times I sat mesmerised by the sudden silence, with hands and feet frozen on the controls, imagining the enormity of the situation. But then I got the hang of it, and with the first faltering of the engine my eyes would dart to the throttle and see it moving slowly back on its own. Next, check the lever that controls the carburettor heat to stop it from icing. *Ah, yes, he's remembered to do that*, so, hard back on the stick to gain as much altitude as possible, and as the speed falls back catch it and trim the aircraft to glide at seventy knots.

'Engine failure..! And stop beating the gun! See if you can get yourself out of this one...'

'Engine failure. Roger,' I acknowledge, and then start a verbal commentary to let him know what I am doing and thinking. 'Convert speed to height, and trim to glide at seventy knots. Check round the cockpit, and see if there is anything obvious which has made the engine stop. Fuel is okay, and I can't see anything else. Right, pick a suitable field, which we can land in. There! Ahead and to the left, a grass field with a clump of trees in the middle. That should do, can't see any cattle or livestock, only watch out for those power lines that are running along the southern border. Now, which way is the wind? We took off on runway 21, so the wind is from the southwest, which means it's coming from the direction of that ploughed field there. We're running roughly downwind at the moment and our height is passing through 1500 feet with the altimeter set on the area QNH, which is roughly sea level. The ground is approximately 300 feet above sea level here, so our actual height above ground is 1200 feet, and from now on I'll deduct 300 feet from the altimeter. As a safety precaution, I'm just going to rev. the engine to make sure the carburettor hasn't iced up.'

I open the throttle and give the engine a five-second burst, and manage to gain fifty feet whilst doing it. There is a snort from behind.

'Time to get the Mayday call out – "Mayday, Mayday, Mayday, this Charlie Five-Seven, Charlie Five-Seven, Five-Seven. We are a Chipmunk training aircraft and have a total engine failure. Our position is abeam... ah, about seven miles due west of Winchester and just east of the village of Kings Somborne, and our intention is to force-land in a grass field. Mayday, Mayday, Mayday". There, that is that. Now, how are we doing? I'll do a left-hand circuit and turn crosswind now, half way across the field. No! Second thoughts, we're never going to have enough height to go all the way round, so if I drop flap now and kill some height, I should be able to go straight in from here. Half flap, speed sixty-five knots, passing through 900 feet – less 300 which means we are about 600 feet above the field. Good, I should be able to make it in from here. Round into wind, and drop full flap. Speed steady at sixty-five, we are drifting sideways a bit, and the wind seems to be coming from that corner, so adjust our line. The surface doesn't look too bad and I'll land just before the clump in the middle, and run towards the corner...'

'I have control...' from Mr Avery '...I think even you could have got in there all right.' And the engine bursts into life again.

Back in the crew room we go over it in detail, and then on following trips it would happen again, only each time the 'convenient' field became harder to find and further away. And the recovery with engine was left later and later, until the day came when we actually landed in the field, and the game became sudden reality.

The next hurdle was the thirty-hour check, which was conducted by Major Walsh and with whom I had not flown before. Roger had had his check the day before, and told me he had got through by pretending it was his normal Polish instructor sitting behind, and just flew as he had been taught. So I adopted the same philosophy, and all went well, and was also cleared to continue to sixty hours.

But the morning queue for the showers in H Block was now noticeably smaller, and the thirty-hour check claimed another casualty, which further reduced the course to sixteen. Several of the double rooms were now only occupied by one person (as the Mess Sergeant had prophesied) and it was also sad to see how attitudes were changing, whereby people were becoming increasingly wary of allowing friendships to become too close, in case it was to be their turn next. Roger noticed this first, and by now we knew each other well enough to be able to voice these thoughts. We discussed it one evening, and both recognised and acknowledged the value of our partnership, which strengthened our resolve to win through. Room Six, we told each other, was lucky, and neither would have dreamt of moving out.

By now it was early September and still perfect flying weather. The fields below turned from green to gold, making the ancient hill forts that abound around Salisbury stand out in stark contrast to their surroundings. Or perhaps it was that now I had time to observe these things, as the minutes in our logbooks slowly built into hours, and another page turned over. For the first time I began to feel confident in handling the aircraft, and instead of being an ordeal, flying began to become a pleasure. But this was soon to be shattered when we started aerobatics, and the Chipmunk I thought I knew, suddenly took on another dimension, and with it my newfound confidence.

We used to practice over a disused airfield nearby.

First we were taught to loop, which is fairly simple. Mr Avery talked me through. 'Pick a nice line feature, like that straight road there, and we'll do a loop and try to end up on the same line and at the same height. Ready? Right, first dive to increase speed to 120 knots. Remember left pedal to keep her balanced. Then back with the stick. Right pedal as the speed falls back. Ease-off the backpressure when inverted to make the loop nice and round. Now screw your eyes up and hold your breath, because you'll find that as soon as we are

Chipmunks in formation. '...the Chipmunk I thought I knew suddenly took on a new dimension, and with it my newfound confidence...' (*Courtesy Army Air Corps*)

inverted, various bits of debris will float up from the floor and land in your face. No matter how often the ground crews vacuum the cockpit, this always happens – it's like somebody throwing a waste paper basket into your face! Now, sit back and wait for the earth to reappear.' The horizon swims back into view and suddenly we are pointing straight down. 'Remember, left rudder again as the speed passes through 100 knots and keep the backpressure on the stick. Now, rescue the engine from its stuttering, because it doesn't like being inverted, and here we are, straight and level again, at our original height, and there is our road still pointing straight ahead. Right, you have a go...'

From loops, to rolls, barrel rolls, spins, sustained spins, stall turns, and Immelman turns, Mr Avery's booming voice in the headset was always there, talking me through the manoeuvre. Then came the time when we were told to practice them solo, and on the first occasion I climbed to 9000 feet before plucking up courage to start the sequence. And whether he was there or not, Mr Avery's voice always talked me through – and so it would remain for the rest of my flying career.

Away from the circuit we were also introduced to instrument flying. The Chipmunk was equipped with a full blind-flying instrument panel, which meant it could be flown 'blind' through cloud or at night.

Providing it was in the right hands.

Those who were to continue with advanced fixed wing flying would ultimately be expected to fly in all weathers; and in order to do this would first have to obtain an 'instrument rating', which allows a pilot to fly in IMC conditions (Instrument Met Conditions), and is in itself a separate course on its own. At this stage it was included to give a working knowledge of what was required, and enough to enable us to get home, should we ever be caught out or become lost above cloud.

On cloudy days, Mr Avery would take me into the overcast and then hand over, where at first we practised all the simple flying manoeuvres from straight and level to turns, and then turning whilst climbing or descending. If the weather was cloudless, a hood was fixed over my half of the cockpit, which made it impossible to see out. After four carefully logged hours in the Instrument Flying column of my log book, I was ready for more advanced manoeuvres and these gradually became more difficult, culminating with Mr Avery's full aerobatic sequence, when he would hand the aircraft over half way through a loop or a barrel roll. But most aerobatics are positive manoeuvres and as such are always instigated by the pilot in command. Which is all very good for training and learning to handle the aircraft, but not likely to materialise in actual instrument flying conditions.

Except for the spin.

And this is fully realistic, for a spin can develop after an aircraft stalls.

An aircraft flies by virtue of a balance of four forces. These forces act about the centre of gravity of an aircraft in the form of a cross. There is an arrow pointing up which is the lift; countered by an arrow pointing down, which is weight; then an arrow to the left, which is thrust or speed; and finally this is countered by an arrow pointing to the right, which is drag. And so the cross is complete, and with forces correctly related, the aircraft will fly. Thus a stall can be brought about by the pilot who deliberately places the aircraft in an attitude whereby these forces no longer balance – as would happen if he reduced the power and pulled the nose up, which would result in a reduction of speed, which in turn would cause less flow of air over the wings and so less lift, and (by virtue of its attitude) more drag; thus weight would take over and the aircraft will stall and fall out of the sky. Alternatively it could happen as a result of a combination of external circumstances over which the pilot has little control. Supposing an unseen hand suddenly burdened the aircraft little by little with additional weight? There would come a time when there would no longer be enough power available to create enough thrust for sufficient air to flow over the wings to lift this additional weight. Then, suppose the same unseen hand simultaneously altered the critical aerofoil section of the wing itself, to become so distorted that it could no longer create lift?

The unseen hand is out there, for both these conditions can occur with an accumulation of ice. And the combination of moisture and temperature that make for icing conditions is usually prevalent in cloud. Any cloud, so long as the outside air temperature registers between twenty and thirty degrees. It may be there. Or it may not... this time.

So Mr Avery would stall the aircraft and let a spin develop, and then wait for a few turns before handing over. And from the instruments you first had to determine which way the aircraft was spinning, before applying the correct procedures to recover.

Which I found most terrifying.

Nearly seven hundred flying hours would pass before I would again hear Mr Avery's voice booming in my headphones, talking me through the recovery procedures as my aircraft spun out of control in cloud. Then, even though distracted by all else that was happening, I would know their incalculable worth.

With practice I began to recognise the scope and characteristics of each individual instrument. Some would react instantaneously whilst others lagged; but if you made allowance for this, together they became complimentary with each instrument contributing to give a constant picture of the aircraft's in-flight conditions. For it is only by using and understanding the instruments that you can learn to put your trust and complete faith in them and then finally learn to ignore your own senses. Because the instruments will always be right.

Then followed the intricacies of radar assistance, holding patterns and letdown procedures, all of which brought a new dimension to flying. At last semi-confident in this newfound world, and able to climb up through the weather to the world above, Mr Avery decided to throw his final spanner.

'Right, we have a partial electrical failure, and the Artificial Horizon, Vertical Speed Indicator and the

Direction Indicator are all u/s. Here, stick these sticky blanks over the face of those three instruments.'

Only the Airspeed, Turn and Slip, Compass and Altimeter were left.

'If you are straight and level at cruising RPM, your *speed* will remain constant. Think about it, *speed* can tell you so much. If you are diving it will increase, and if you are climbing it will fall off, so why do you need a Vertical Speed Indicator to tell you if you are going up or down? Likewise, the Direction Indicator is a *luxury* because it only echoes what the compass already tells you. So why not *just* use the compass? You have a Turn and Slip Indicator which tells you *just that*, so you don't *need* an Artificial Horizon – anyway they're always the first to topple when you need them most, so it's best not to rely on them too much. Now, settle down and do everything *gently* and *use* the instruments intelligently. We're on 240, so remain on this heading and take us down through this clag and see how you get on. You have control.'

It was like asking a recently blinded man to throw away his stick. But using a 'limited panel' began to teach me more about flying than all that had preceded it.

For the monkey was being taught to think.

Yet as pride will always precede a fall; so at Wallop, lightning will always strike on a Monday. It happened without any warning, as is the way with lightning, and its devastating bolt hit but one target: 100m six, H Block of the spiders – which still had its two original occupants.

Roger had been falling behind with his instrument flying, and now had used up all his allocated hours; which meant the system automatically put him on 'review'. He had one chance to redeem himself: a check flight with the Flight Commander, whose decision would then be final.

And I had fallen behind at ground school, and had fluffed the Principles of Flight paper in last Friday's examination.

The Flight Commander asked to see me. 'You've done quite well up to now' he said, leafing through a thick sheaf of reports, all bearing my name. 'In fact, I see you went solo in eight and a half hours, and have maintained that lead ever since... which is to your credit, and your flying would appear to be slightly above average. But your ground school results are not so good, and looking at these, it would seem that each week you have only just managed to scrape through.

'Now, you know the rules, and...' He looked up from the reports.

I waited for the axe to fall.

'But then, thinking back I remember it took *me* an age to grasp some of the theory... I think, and in view of your flying results, I'm prepared to give you another chance... so I'm going to place you on review. You will take that paper again; or rather it'll be a similar paper used on another course. And you've *got* to get a grip of it, and I shall expect at least an eighty-percent pass mark. You can use this office, and I'll arrange for someone to sit in and invigilate – say eight o'clock next Wednesday evening? This will be your one and only chance, and if you don't pass, you'll be RTU'd. If you pass, you'll come off review, but I shall keep a close eye on your weekly results and I will expect to see a marked improvement in your ground studies...'

That evening Roger and I sat in our room and commiserated over a bottle of scotch. Our partnership had worked well up to now and we had confided and helped each other with most things; his strengths often being my weaknesses, for his ground school results had always been above average, but he had sometimes found the flying hard work.

'Tell me about it?' I ventured at last.

'I don't know... I'm okay when I can see out, and I can *see* the aeroplane responding to my controls. But on instruments... I don't get claustrophobic or anything. And I get on well with my instructor. It's just something inside me... Sometimes, when in cloud, I just can't *believe* the instruments. I feel – in fact I know we are in turning, or in a dive – every sense in my body screams this at me. Yet the instruments still show that we're flying straight and level. And in the end I usually follow my own instincts, because the instruments – well they *could* be wrong. You can't even *see* how they work, and you can only trust their face value; how can you *totally* commit yourself – and have *blind faith* in something that is man-made, when every sense in your body tells you otherwise?'

He topped our glasses up and went over to his desk and found his Principles of Flight file.

'Come on, there's no point in our both going down. At least I can get you through this exam. Let's start from scratch, and just stop me when you are not sure of something.'

The following two evenings were spent pouring through his notes, which he patiently and methodically expounded upon, until suddenly it all began to come together and finally the subject made sense.

He had a theory, he told me, which had worked for him when he was at school, and which he was now applying to ground school. 'Everybody has got a brain, and it's got to fit into your head. Think of your head as a bucket; you can only fill it until it's full, and then it spills over. Now, take a look at the plethora of different subjects we are learning at ground school. Every week, more and more – and all of it bits and pieces, with no two subjects relating; so much, that you can no longer apply reasonable logic to the situation, and so build a subject up that way. Frankly, my bucket can only take so much! So, to make room, I deliberately empty the pail, and forget what I learned last week! Easy!'

Although bizarre, this made a certain amount of sense – and if it worked for Roger, at least I could try it! So I deliberately forgot all the other subjects and concentrated solely upon Principals of Flight.

Late on Tuesday night Roger gave me a final test, and announced with a grin that out of twenty, I had only got one question slightly wrong.

We had a final scotch, and by now the level was just below the label.

I held the bottle up. 'Do you believe this, Roger?'

'What..?'

'Well, you can see the level of the whisky in the bottle. And if you think about it, that's all an Artificial Horizon tells you. Only with this bottle, you can actually see the liquid and there's no hidden mechanism relaying the information to a clock face. So there is nothing to doubt. Could you put your complete faith in this bottle? Enough to quell those instincts of yours? If so, why not take it with you when you do your check tomorrow?'

The following afternoon Roger secreted the bottle of whisky in his flying suit and went off for his review check. He could have made a good tale from it; how the level wasn't quite right and just needed to be a sip or two to make it lower, but this was not his way. He told me afterwards that in fact he didn't actually have to resort to looking at the bottle at all, and the mere knowledge that it was there, was enough to give him confidence. And his instrument test went without a hitch. Likewise that evening I retook my exam, and with my newfound knowledge of the subject, managed to get all the questions right.

Before turning in on Wednesday night, we drank to our partnership and our release from review, and finished the remainder of his Artificial Horizon.

Having learnt to fly in cloud, it was relatively easy to put this knowledge to further practice by flying at night, which we found was not nearly so difficult.

Most airports have electric lights that are permanently focussed onto the metal runways and light up the scene as though it were day. Middle Wallop, being a grass field, had no built-in lights and it was done the old-fashioned way by lighting flares and placing them on either side of the runway in use. Initially we were quite nervous, but soon found that to fly a circuit in the dark proved to be no more difficult than it was during the day – and needed about as much adjustment as it does to drive a car at night. Anyway, we soon got the hang of it and managed to go off solo and complete three of four circuits, before the end of the session.

September drew to a close, and with it our sixty-hour marriage to the Chipmunk. The final week at ground school terminated with a mammoth exam, and I found myself having to scrape the bottom of my bucket. But all went well and once over, I emptied the bucket and concentrated solely on the forthcoming Final Handling check, which was to be taken by none other than the CFI himself.

He was very brusque and businesslike, and fired questions about the aircraft as we walked out. 'What's the wingspan? And the tyre pressures? And what range would you expect with one-up in still air?' Fortunately I had been warned of this, and had all the answers off pat. 'Hmm. Well let's see if you can fly it.'

The check lasted a little over an hour, and we did everything in the book. The weather was hot and humid with the odd thundercloud and I was soon running with sweat under my flying suit. I made a bodge of the first loop, going round in a series of jerks, and not ending up in line with the ground feature I had picked. There was a deathly silence from behind. This, I had been told was his pet subject, for if you could not perform aerobatics with precision, meant you could not really fly the aeroplane properly. I thought of the ignominy of returning to my Regiment at this late stage, and without thinking, forgot about Rome and reverted to my regimental way of thought.

'I can do better than that, Wing Commander, let's give it another go...' And this time we went round as though Mr Avery was doing it. Then, without being asked, followed on with the sequence of aerobatics that Mr Avery favoured, one flowing gracefully into the other. May as well be hung for a sheep as a lamb. Halfway round the final barrel roll the engine faltered and died.

'Engine failure...' the voice said from the back.

'Yup, okay,' I said, caught completely by surprise. Then, with my newfound confidence: 'I'll talk you through it...' whilst trying to recover what speed we had left, trimming to glide at seventy knots, and looking out for a field.

We ended the test by doing a flapless landing, followed by an overshoot and then another landing with the engine off, and finally taxied back to dispersal. Just in time I remembered not to taxi too fast and to weave the aircraft from side to side, which was another thing the CFI was a stickler for, and one that was so often disregarded or considered nonessential by this stage.

The debriefing was held in the Flight Commander's office.

'I don't care which Regiment you belong to, but when flying you address me as *"Sir"*, and not *"Wing Commander"*. And also, when I instruct you to do something in the air, let alone on your Final Handling Test, you do not reply *"Yup"*. Flying is a serious business, and your attitude needs to *sharpen up*. I shall note this in my report. But..' and here he gave a grudging smile. 'You *are* safe to fly a Chipmunk. Well done, you have passed.'

But the axe fell on another three who were not so lucky, and even more surprising, one of these was Jeremy, who failed his sixty-hour check. This, considering the head start he had had over the rest of us, left us stunned with disbelief. Maybe he had acquired too many bad flying habits prior to the course, we never did find out. But along with Judy, he packed his bags and drove out of the gate.

Which left thirteen – and all determined not to make the number unlucky.

On our last morning in Elementary Flight crew room we were told that we were now qualified for a civilian Private Pilot's License, which came as an unexpected bonus, and with it the satisfaction of knowing that even should we fail the remainder of the course, at least we would have something to show for it all.

We collected our flying gear and I took a last look at the Chipmunks lined up in the hangar. On an impulse I dumped my gear on the floor and climbed up onto a wing and slid the canopy back. I smelt the familiar Chipmunk smell and it brought back all that we had been through together. Then I carefully closed the canopy so that it locked and jumped down. They were pretty aeroplanes but... there was something unsettling about them... and I turned and walked away.

Chapter 3

They were pumping bullets into the Beaver now, and no doubt will claim that they had shot it down. I wonder what'll happen to it? It's certainly worth salvaging – just for the engine and systems alone, so long as they don't blast it all to bits first. Somehow it's an undignified end for a fine aeroplane – for although XP 777 was a Janus, it wasn't altogether her fault, and she more than made up for it in the end. They all have their own little ways, but generally speaking the Beaver has always been the perfect pilot's aeroplane.

Thinking back, I never learned to have the affection for the Chipmunk as I later did for the AOP IX and the Beaver. I remember looking at them on that last day. All lined up in the hanger in their silver and red paint – almost like a line of whores waiting for their next customers. Perhaps that was it, although blame should be levied at the workman rather than his tools. But there was no taking away the fact that throughout the whole of the Chipmunk period we were constantly under threat of failure. That learning curve set against the time factor was by necessity a fixed entity, but it allowed for no deviance. And woe betide anyone who fell below that curve, for it was almost impossible to climb back. I was lucky in being given another chance with the ground school exam, and also extremely lucky to have had Mr Avery as an instructor, for he saw me through thick and thin. But others were not so lucky, and a lot of good people went down. So the Chipmunk itself still remains an enigma, for to grow to love an aeroplane you must be able to relax and enjoy it, and somehow we never had the time for this luxury.

And I haven't the luxury to daydream now, as more and more shots pump into the Beaver. At least it won't burn...

'I think I'll move over to those rocks over there to get a line on them' the RSM announced. 'No good having three of us bunching behind this rock, and it's hardly large enough anyway. Here, Sir, you'd better take this – I'll hang on to your SMG', thrusting his 9mm. pistol and a box of ammunition into my hand. 'It's got to be more use than a flare-gun – only don't drop my pistol in the sand!' And crouching low, made for the outcrop of rock on our right flank.

The colonel and I looked at each other, both wishing that we had thought of this. 'You cover the left flank, up to the Beaver, and I'll cover straight ahead' he said, then called out to the Adjutant. 'Tim, where are you?'

'Over here, sir, behind and about fifteen yards to your right. I'm with the cook who has a rifle and about thirty rounds of ammunition remaining. We're wedged in nicely and have got a good field of fire to our front. I've just seen Mr Fowler and he's making his way further around to the right. The Political Officer is unarmed, but he's with the Gunner officer who has a pistol, and they are both in the outcrop behind, and a bit further up.'

A fresh volley of rifle fire came from our right, followed by the distinctive chatter of the SMG.

'Right, sir, I've got a bead on them, and they are moving back towards the aircraft', the RSM called.

'I've counted fourteen of them, sir' the Gunner FOO called from behind 'I can see where most of them are from up here, pity I haven't got a rifle – they are well out of range of my pistol. I'll stay up here for the moment whilst I can see what's going on, and I can also cover our rear. I can soon come down to help if anyone's in trouble.'

'Right, that's the best we can do for now' the colonel called out, 'Mark your shots, and let me know if you are running low on ammunition. We'll just have to keep them off until help arrives. Mr Fowler?'

'Sir!'

'Can you give me covering fire? I'm going to move my position towards you a bit.'

The SMG resumed its chattering, and the colonel slid back, then sprinted to his new position.

Which left me on my own. I loaded a red flare into the Very pistol, then rolled on my back and fired into the air. If a patrol were on its way, at least that would give them an indication of our position, and they'd know we were still alive. Or even better it could be seen by a helicopter, and I strained my ears for the first sounds of the familiar 'womp, womp, womp', made by an approaching rotor, or better still the distinctive buzz of a Scout. Now, in spite of all the old rivalry at Wallop, a helicopter would really come into its own...

* * *

We sat in the lecture room and watched through the window as the new intake assembled outside. They seemed to be a large course, but then I counted and made it twenty-three, which was only one more than we had been. Well, good luck to them all...

This was the morning we were to be divided – some to learn to fly helicopters and the remainder to continue with advanced fixed wing. No choice had been given to those who had been sponsored by regiments to fly the Sioux helicopter – which was to be the standard aircraft for the Air Troops, and already now in the process of forming to become integrated into some Cavalry and Gunner Regiments. And in the event, the future Air Troop pilots took up the majority of the places available on the rotary course.

I had opted to continue with fixed wing, with the knowledge that if all went well and I was accepted into the Army Air Corps, there would be ample opportunity to convert to helicopters at a later date. Besides, I had only just scratched the surface of fixed wing flying, and it still had so much more to offer. Helicopters were essentially short-range tactical machines, and ideally suited for this purpose. But they were not designed to fly on instruments and their air space was firmly restricted to under the weather. Nor were they economical to use over longer distances, for the simple reason that they could only carry a limited weight of fuel. Mr Avery had given me a taste of what pure flight was about, and it was this aspect I wished to pursue.

'Helicopters?' he boomed in my headphones in his best undertone, when we discussed the subject one day at 9000 feet. 'You wouldn't get one up *here*, for a start. Of course they're good for what they do, but they don't *fly*.' He eased the Chipmunk into a gentle turn, then dipped the nose and flowed into a perfectly executed barrel roll, to demonstrate his point. 'No, they don't fly; they just *defy gravity* in every possible way. You sit in a glass bubble, hanging forward in your straps, jerking up and down and they stink of paraffin. It is not a *gentleman's* way of flying.'

So we went our different ways, with eight going to Rotary Wing to learn to fly the Hiller, which was the helicopter used for basic conversion from fixed to rotary wing, before going on to the Sioux or the more sophisticated Scout. Roger had decided that choppers were to be the thing for him ('...and I don't want to see the inside of another cloud again...') and since the flying programs for fixed and rotary wing were kept firmly apart, meant we would no longer fly together. But the spirit of the course was still to remain intact, for the two halves were still to unite for ground school and every other function.

The remaining six including myself, were told to find new lockers for our flying gear in the hanger next door which was the home of Advanced Fixed Wing, and where we were introduced to the last of a long line of army Austers, the AOP Mark IX.

Initially I thought the AOP IX would be much the same as my father's Auster Autocrat, which was a re-engined civilian version of the AOP V, but I couldn't have been more wrong; for here was a completely different aeroplane. The general configuration – that of a high wing over a spacious cockpit with two seats side by side and another one behind, was the same. But there it ended, for she was much larger and squarer looking and altogether more purposeful. Instead of being covered overall in fabric, the wings were part metal and part fabric, whilst the tail plane and fin was all metal. She had big fat tyres and wheels that were set on single struts, which actually were large hydraulic shock absorbers – and from its inception the aircraft had obviously been designed to operate off the roughest terrain. The engine was a 180hp fuel-injected Blackburn Bombardier, made more purposeful in that it could only be started with a cartridge – as well as delivering twice the power of the 90hp Cirrus Minor fitted into my father's Autocrat. Primarily developed for directing artillery fire (hence the quaint army nomenclature of Air Observation Post), we were told that in the field the AOP IX was also used for supply dropping, leaflet drops, target marking, night illumination, reconnaissance, casualty evacuation, message pick-up and liaison work – all of which gave an indication of the content of the course to come.

Training, we were told, would to be split into three parts. First, we would have to learn to fly the aircraft in the conventional manner, which would be judged at a thirty-hour check. Then, to learn to fly the aircraft tactically – and in all weathers, which would be judged at a sixty-hour check. By this stage, having logged a minimum of 120 hours, students were deemed to be competent to fly the aircraft automatically and with a degree of safety and so were ready to progress to the final phase, which was to put into practice all the various roles expected from an army pilot. The final phase was scheduled to take a further eighty flying hours, during which time there would be a Final Handling Test, again flown with the CFI.

In the meantime ground school would keep pace with this program – much on the lines as before (including a weekly examination), and as well as continuing with certain major subjects in greater depth (notably principles of flight, meteorology and engines and airframes for our respective new aircraft), there would be additional subjects including: advanced navigation, airways procedures, flight planning, signals, air photography, a knowledge of aviation medicine for casualty evacuation, air recognition, gunnery and finally tactics. Tactics covered a multitude of subjects (with the syllabus taken straight from Staff College), and this we were told, was the major stumbling block of the whole course, both on the ground and in the air.

So we went back to work.

The instructors in Advanced Fixed Wing were civilians as well as serving army pilots, under the command of Major Ian Ball RA DFC. Major Ball was an army pilot of the old school and had flown gliders as well as every mark of Auster AOP, and still wore the old Gunner wings (with Royal Artillery bomb instead of the army crown and lion), on his chest. He had grown up with every development and aspect of army flying and was a fund of knowledge, all gained from practical experience. Moreover, we were to find that he was extremely approachable and by nature a patient and understanding man, which made him a first class teacher.

From the very first day we perceived that Advanced Fixed Wing was run on very different lines from Elementary Flight. Whether this was school policy or as a result of

Auster AOP IX. '...She had big fat tyres and wheels that were set on single struts, which were hydraulic shock absorbers – and from its inception the aircraft had obviously been designed to operate off the roughest terrain...' (Courtesy Army Air Corps)

Major Ball's personality was hard to say, but from the start an adult relationship between instructor and student was encouraged, which immediately induced a relaxed atmosphere and made us feel that we 'almost belonged'. Instructors were there to help rather than judge.

This was further enhanced when I met Mr Summers, who was to be my instructor for the first part of the course to thirty hours. In every way he was the extreme opposite to Mr Avery. He was of slight built with a shy, hesitant manner and a master of the understatement. Quietly spoken and exceptionally modest by nature, had he been an actor he would have been cast as a junior cleric, which belied his past as ex-airline pilot with many thousands of hours, as well as having flown Mosquitoes for the elite RAF Pathfinder Force. He was one of the most gifted pilots I ever had the privilege to fly with.

'This is the aeroplane' he said in a sad voice, as we regarded the AOP IX in the early morning October drizzle, prior to starting the pre-flight external check. 'But she really is quite *remarkable* in many aspects...' His voice trailed off, and I followed him round to inspect the ailerons. 'You'll find her light on the controls and very agile. Look; see these *droop* when you lower the flaps, to decrease the aspect ratio of the wing. That's quite neat, and you'll find you will be able to fly in and out of the most *impossible* places... Most aeroplanes are designed to fly in the air, but this one was designed to fly near the ground...' I helped him to open the starboard cowling of the engine, '...But she takes such a *time* to get anywhere.' He removed the oil dipstick and peered intently at the level, then shook his head and sighed. 'Yes, she must be one of the *slowest* aeroplanes ever invented.' He pulled down on the wing-strut and noted with satisfaction as the movement was taken up by the shock absorber contained in the undercarriage leg. This seemed to remind him of something else. 'Oh, and she also has a *bite*, which is interesting, but it can be rather annoying. It always happens without warning, and you can't *make* her do it, but I expect you'll find out during the next thirty hours... Now, let's see if we can make it *go*. No, no, *you* sit in the left seat, that's the *captain's* place, I'll just come along for the ride...'

Once airborne he became a different person. His melancholic air vanished, and every thing about him became acute and alive, for he was now where he belonged. At first, possibly fearing ridicule, he was hesitant to reveal his innermost thoughts, and no doubt would have continued to teach this monkey to fly the aeroplane by numbers. But once he perceived that he had a genuine disciple, he opened up and began to share his world – which almost amounted to a creed, and embraced everything to do with the business of flying.

Sitting side by side meant we could converse, as well as share the controls of the aircraft, which made communication easy as well as instantaneous. After my clumsy attempts he would take the controls, and the aircraft that I had been pushing around the sky, would suddenly come to life. It was as though it became a part of himself. He would set the altimeter according to the pressure given by the tower, then would never need to glance at the instrument again. He *knew* his altitude as a bird instinctively knows what height to fly. His turns, whether level or climbing or descending became a fluid extension of his brain, and in level flight the needle of the altimeter never wavered. Regardless of however steep we banked in a tight turn, the needle and ball in the Turn and Slip instrument remained balanced, for he *sensed* his aeroplane and needed no instruments to show whether he was skidding. And always his eyes were outside the cockpit, where they belonged, rather than driving the aircraft around the circuit chasing a set of numbers.

'You've come across the Wallop monkeys? Well you can teach one of those to fly an aeroplane by numbers' he told me. 'And if you eventually manage to teach a monkey to fly, there is nothing to stop him from pinning a pair of wings on his chest, and calling himself a *pilot*. But there is a vast difference between being a pilot and becoming an *aviator*. A pilot is someone who... Well look, I've known experienced airline pilots with thousands of hours, and yet they will

'.. you'll find you will be able to fly in and out of the most impossible places...' (*Courtesy Army Air Corps*)

always remain as pilots, because they merely *drive* their aeroplanes according to the book, which anyone can do by reading the Pilot's Notes. To become an aviator you must start to *think* like a *bird,* and that way you will always be ahead of any situation'.

'Think like a bird' he said as we ran downwind on our first circuit. 'See the shadows of the clouds as they track across the airfield? They tell you the direction of the wind aloft. Now look at the windsock, and you'll see it points at a slightly different angle. *That* is the direction of the wind at ground level. Now *use* this knowledge and you can bisect the angle and adjust your approach leg accordingly and compensate for the difference, then there'll be no *need* to use lots of power to get the runway back into line when you turn onto finals. See the trees at the boundary? In sunny weather, trees produce shade; so there'll *always* be descending air over trees, and when you know this in advance, you *won't* be caught out by the downdraft and have to resort to a fist-full of power at the last critical moment. And see how the leaves flicker and are flattened by the wind? They react a lot quicker than the windsock will ever do, and you will soon be able to judge the wind speed from them.'

One night some weeks later, I became lost during a long cross-country navigation exercise ('An *aviator* never becomes lost, at worst, he becomes *temporally uncertain* of his position...') and it was then he taught me about the wind. 'Once you understand the wind, it will become your *friend*; if you do not understand it, it will always be your enemy...'

I went solo in the AOP IX in three hours, and by following and imitating Mr Summers, strove to become an *aviator* from the start, rather than remain just a pilot; and during this process I grew to understand and love the aircraft as well.

Should one ever admit to *loving* an aeroplane?

I put this to Mr Summers one afternoon, when he was showing me how to edge my way through an assembly of cumuli, without resorting to the radio and outside help.

'It's funny how some things stay with you for the whole of your life' he replied. 'I suppose I must have been about four years old and I was at Sunday School, looking out of the window, daydreaming, when suddenly the parson thundered *"Thou shalt not worship false idols"*. And, do you know, to this day I have always regarded people who keep *gnomes* in their garden with the *deepest* suspicion, and I always feel uneasy when I'm wandering through a garden centre and am suddenly confronted with rows of stone images – they can play *havoc* with the imagination...' He looked at me and smiled, 'But isn't an aeroplane just such a false idol?'

I had to agree. We passed around the final buttress of cloud and the sky ahead was clear.

'In which case, I suppose we'll just have to go along with breaking the Fourth Commandment, for I cannot think of another word that embraces all the feelings you can develop for – what *must* be more than just a machine?'

The AOP IX was a delight to fly. As Mr Summers had foretold she was light and responsive, and was free from most of the in-built foibles found in a training aircraft such as the Chipmunk. Instead of the handbrake steering arrangement, there were toe brakes set on top of the rudder pedals, which were far more responsive and easier to use when taxiing. But you had to be wary on the ground, for the light airframe was sensitive to cross winds, which meant keeping the joystick pointing into wind, as well as holding it hard back, for with the relatively powerful engine it was very easy to lift the tail if you used too much throttle. Once lined up, the aircraft was extremely eager to fly and the take-off run was just a skip and a jump. No longer did you need a boot-full of rudder during the climb, and fuel injection made the engine respond instantly to the slightest throttle movement as well as having no carburettor to ice up. She was roomy and comfortable to fly (which was just as well, for the duration of the sorties were soon to stretch to between one and two hours) and the high wing and large cockpit windows made for excellent visibility, all of which, as her pedigree bore out, made the perfect army aeroplane.

The most notable characteristic was the aircraft's ability to fly slowly, whilst still remaining under full control. The flaps were hydraulically operated, with a roof-mounted lever that you pumped to whatever degree was necessary, which was invaluable for flying slowly. To raise the flaps, all you had to do was to flick the selector lever up and the flaps retracted automatically, driven up by the flow of air against them, which made for a smooth transaction and your hands could be busy elsewhere. The slow flying ability was further improved by the aileron drooping mechanism which was activated when the flaps were lowered, and allowed both ailerons to droop to a maximum of ten degrees, thereby changing the profile of the wing to increase the lift/drag ratio.

To work out of short fields requires the absolute mini-mum takeoff and landing run, and in order achieve this, the preceding approach and round-out must be flown as slowly as possible. Which, in real terms means just above the stall. Each AOP IX had its individual stalling speed, as well as an additional factor that varied according to the weight of fuel and passengers carried; and the only sure way to find out was to actually stall the aircraft and make a note on your kneepad of the exact speed when this occurred. Thus it became routine to check this every time we flew. At some-time during the sortie we would simulate the approach conditions, with flaps down and power set to 1200 RPM (which also gave extra lift to the wings from the propeller slipstream), and then note the exact stalling speed of the particular aircraft we were flying. Then, should a strip landing be called for, the approach speed could be quickly calculated by adding five knots onto the stalling speed noted and the landing made at this speed. With five knots in hand, the rate of descent could be adjusted by the use of power, and you could stretch or shorten the approach to land on a particular spot. Once down, the power was chopped, which killed the 'false lift' created by the propeller, and the aircraft would stop in only a few lengths.

November, and it rained nearly every day with the cloud base rarely exceeding 300 feet, but still we flew. We practised short takeoffs and landings at five knots above the stall at every opportunity, and always at the beginning and end of every sortie. We had our own corner of the airfield where we could rejoin and fly a low level circuit, out of the way and under the other traffic, to land on a marked-out area that represented a short strip.

On every flight we also tried to include a simulated engine failure, and I soon discovered that like everything else, Mr Summers had firm ideas about this.

'*Whenever* you fly, and *whatever* the purpose of your flight, you should *always* be looking and assessing suitable places to land. It is no good going off to *practice* engine failures, because they just don't *happen* that way. And you don't *wait* for the engine to stop before you look for a field, you should *know* that you have just passed over one. That way you will be *ahead* of the game, and you might stand a chance. And there's no point in *cheating*, because the engine will always stop when you least expect it to happen, and the only way to *practice*, is by trying to surprise yourself. Like, now!' And he chopped the throttle.

We were flying at 500 feet just under the overcast, over the centre of Andover. Which was bad airmanship in the first place, for at that altitude I shouldn't have been there and should have given the town a wider berth. I stole a sideways glance at Mr Summers, and saw that he knew that I knew. And furthermore, from the twinkle in his eye that that was precisely the reason he had chosen this moment to chop the power.

'Ah. Sorry about being here in the first place – an *aviator* wouldn't have stacked the odds against himself.' I converted speed to height and trimmed to glide. 'But, it so happens, in this instance, it was an *operational* necessity to fly over the town', as I fluttered my fingers over the panel to show him I was looking for a reason for the stoppage. 'So we'll just have to do the best we can. You might like to add that in your flight report when we get back?' He was smiling, and inclined his head. '*Mayday, Mayday, Mayday.*' I went through the procedure, and ended with '...my intention is to force-land on the school football pitch, just north west of the town centre.' And with that I lowered the nose and swung the aircraft through 180 degrees, whilst pumping down flap at the same time, and the football pitch swam into line, nicely set up for short finals.

'Okay, Lindbergh, well done. Perhaps you *are* beginning to learn – better not go too low and disrupt the children's lessons. Climb back up and resume your course.'

The following day I was flying solo returning from a low-level navigation exercise, and heedful to his advice, chopped the power on myself, without the usual precautionary look beforehand. I was flying at our customary 400 feet, from which height I could see only one suitable landing ground, which happened to be a field we had used before. Or rather than 'field', it was an advanced landing strip and used for this purpose, as it resembled many of the strips currently in use in Malaya. It was of particular challenge as it was little more than a clearing extending like a finger into a wood on the side of a hill, and the usable dimensions were only slightly larger than the marked strip we used on the airfield. You landed up the slope, regardless of wind direction, using the gradient to bring you to a halt – hopefully before entering the wood at the top. With careful use of power it was perfectly feasible.

But now, without power, it would have to be judged just right – for the layout of the field and its surrounds was such, that should you proceed with the approach to short finals, you were then committed to land. The hill ahead of you, together with the tall trees on its summit now made too great a gradient to out-climb with an overshoot, and the only way to extricate yourself from the situation was to land, turn around and then takeoff again downhill.

All this flashed through my mind in a matter of seconds, for I only had time to trim the aircraft to glide and then swing right seventy degrees and we were lined up to land. Everything looked fine, and having landed there before, I decided to carry out the drill to its conclusion as though it were the real thing, and so was committed. There was a slight downwind element which made our ground speed higher than normal, but the timing of the approach was right and soon after, the wheels rumbled on the grass – an acceptable, albeit somewhat hurried engine-off landing. I had to use a fair amount of power to taxi up the gradient to the final summit of the hill and I had to complete the pre-takeoff vital actions on the move, for it would have been difficult to get going again had we stopped. But there was enough momentum to swing round and then, facing down the slope, it was just a matter of opening the throttle and we were off.

I was pleased with my efforts and wished I could have shown Mr Summers. In his Machiavellian way he would have probably taken the wind from my sails, by chopping the power again now.

And so I did just that.

Oh my God! Don't even think about it. I'm at 200 feet, in a climbing attitude at 60 knots, facing the wrong way and no power. But it could have happened just like this... Nose hard down, and keep the speed up. With no power, how much height will she lose in a one-eighty? Try it and see. We were taught never to do this; if you have an engine failure on takeoff, always land straight ahead, because there'll never be enough height to do a one-eighty turn, as well as keeping the nose down to stay above stalling speed. But there is nowhere to land ahead, and I can always abandon the exercise and use power to get myself out of this if I have to. Round we go. God this aeroplane does fly! And with takeoff flap still down, the drooping ailerons are really coming into their own. There! We are round and there is still height to spare... and if anything we're nearer the strip and better placed than last time. Remember, we are landing down wind, which means we're a lot faster over the ground. In fact, if anything, we are now too high. That can soon be remedied. Drop full flaps... and we are now committed to land. Speed is too high, come on, nose up a bit – think like a bird. We are just hanging in space and not descending, some unseen eddy must be giving us additional lift. Come on, land! This is becoming serious; we're still far too high, and the trees are approaching. It's too late to climb out with power... we have GOT to land. But still she floats, almost in ground effect, and RISING with the slope! And we are going to hit the trees.

Time for drastic action. Haul back on the stick and stall her in. A lot of noise but we are down, and nothing the undercarriage can't cope with. I take my hat off to whoever designed it. Toe brakes full on, and the wheels lock... there is no stopping power and we must be skating forward on the wet grass. There is a post and wire boundary fence and a ditch beyond. Come on, what would Mr Summers do?

But in the end it wasn't Mr Summers who came to my rescue, but Mr Avery's face shouting through the windshield. In the nick of time I remembered the termination of my first solo with that ignominious ground loop, and how the Chipmunk had swung right round in little more than its own space.

Which, to avoid disaster, was the only thing to try.

Hard right rudder and brake, stick back, eyes shut... and round the AOP IX went, juddering and shaking just the same as last time, with the port wing dipping down and just missing the fence; and then all was quiet and we were facing back the other way, perfectly positioned for takeoff.

I had a lot to think about on the way home. With ten degrees of flap and aileron droop, the gliding qualities of the AOP IX were almost akin to a glider. We lost very little height in that one-eighty turn with the engine off; and then that last business, when we landed with a downwind component and how she floated on and on, just a few feet off the ground. I wondered whether to discuss it with Major Ball; foolhardy or not, explain the circumstances, and how the situation *could* have arisen. And in this instance, the only way to avert an expensive disaster had been to execute a ground loop; and the fact that had I not sat through one in the Chipmunk, I don't think it would have even entered my head. Perhaps there was a lesson here – and maybe it should be included in the training syllabus, so trainee pilots knew what to expect; or at the very least it could be included in one of the many discussion sessions we had?

I called Wallop, and joined the main pattern, slotting in between two Chipmunks that were doing enormous circuits and dragging in on finals using lots of power. I rounded-out as near as I could to the first marker, to allow plenty of room for the Chipmunk that was following. The wheels brushed the grass and the aircraft settled down onto her three points without a bump, and a very different performance from the last landing. We rolled on, and the Chipmunk swished by on my left, still fifty feet up.

It was then that the AOP IX decided to extract her revenge.

In slow motion, the starboard wing lifted up and decided to fly again, whilst the port wing remained firmly stalled. I applied full right rudder to stop her from turning, and held the stick hard back. We carried on, with only one main-wheel running on the ground and there was absolutely nothing I could do, except watch the port wing tip as it dipped lower and lower towards the grass. After about ten seconds, the starboard wing decided it had had enough flying after all, and just as gently lowered itself back down, until we were rolling along on all three wheels again, as if nothing had happened.

I couldn't believe it, and it was the final straw after a more than eventful trip. And what had I done to provoke it?

I taxied back to dispersal, called 'Clear, complete' to the tower, and switched off, to be met by Major Ball and Mr Summers who were both laughing all over their faces.

'I *told* you she would bite you at some time' Mr Summers said. 'That's the AOP IX's party trick, and her only vice. They *all* do it, and it usually happens after an exceptionally smooth landing. It is *always* the starboard wing that picks up, and all you can do is sit there and wait for it to drop down again. We've had the designers onto it, independent aeronautical experts, engineers – who tried moving the centre of gravity, and any *number* of experienced pilots, and *nobody* can come up with an explanation!'

That characteristic remained with the AOP IX for the length of its service, and when finally retired was the reason why the aircraft was never awarded a civilian Certificate of Airworthiness, and able to join its AOP III, V and VI predecessors, many of which were given a further lease of life and indeed are still flying on the civil register today.

'I'm glad you experienced that wing-drop,' Mr Summers said the following evening, as we walked back from the aircraft, which I noticed was being prepared by the ground crew for another flight. 'Because you'll know how to cope with it if it happens tonight.'

'Tonight?' I queried. 'There's no night flying on the program?'

'I know' he replied. 'But they are going to prepare a tactical flare path for the Beaver conversion course, and I thought if you're not busy we'd join them and do a spot of night flying. See you here at about eight o'clock?'

A tactical flare path was not a flare path at all, and merely consisted of two Land Rovers parked at an angle of forty-five degrees and set back on either side of the strip, with their headlights on so that the beams merged together to form a pool of light. Which was what you had to land in. To indicate the direction of the strip, a red hurricane lamp was placed on the centreline at the undershoot, and a white lamp placed at the other end. And that was that. To takeoff you started in the pool of light and aimed for the white lamp; and to land you flew down the approach, lined the red and white lamp up (although the red lamp was often difficult to find, and easily confused with the rear lights of the vehicles), and rounded-out in the pool of light, with the white lamp still ahead to keep you on line.

We slotted in amongst the Beavers, took off and then cleared the circuit to the northeast.

'I think we'll wander over to Greenham Common and see if they can take us for some GCA's.' Mr Summers announced. 'I've *heard* that the American controllers actually get *paid* for every GCA they undertake, which is why they are always so very friendly.'

It was typical of Mr Summers to initiate me to a GCA at night, and it was the one instrument approach I had not covered with Mr Avery in the Chipmunk. The Ground Controlled Approach is used for landing in restricted visibility, having been 'talked down' to the ground by the radar operator in the tower, who's sophisticated radar's can determine your height and glide path as well as your distance and position to a centreline. It is a good system and easy to use especially as it takes all responsibility away from the pilot, who merely has to fly exactly as instructed by the radar controller. As a letdown procedure it is a vast improvement to the old 'radio range' – which was a narrow radio beam the pilot had to intercept for direction, whilst using a series of ground beacons situated on the approach which activated a light in the cockpit, and so indicated the range to touch down. But already the GCA was fast being superseded by the ILS (Instrument Letdown System), which again uses ground beacons that transmit to a composite instrument in the aircraft showing distance, heading and glide scope all on one dial, enabling a pilot to initiate a descent at any time of day or night, without calling upon the services of specially trained radar operators waiting permanently on stand by. The AOP IX did not carry ILS, which is why we opted to use the GCA at the American Air Force base at Greenham Common. This was by no means the nearest facility, but had been found to be the most obliging, purely as a result of their pay structure.

I set course in the rough direction of Greenham Common, which was about thirty-five miles away. Again this was typical of Mr Summers, who from years of flying knew the exact course and distance to all the major airfields, and airily assumed that everyone else knew this as well. The weather was perfect, and although it was cold, for the first time that month there was not a cloud in the sky, and the stars were very bright. Navigation was made easy by the lights of the towns on route, and from our track I soon determined that there was little or no wind to bother about. 'I think all flights should be conducted at night.' Mr Summers said, echoing my thoughts whilst turning the instrument lights down to their minimum setting. 'The weather is always so much calmer, which makes for such *smooth* passages. Also, there are no *idiots* flying – or at least very few,' giving me a sideways look. 'And flying at night somehow gives you *time* for philosophy; almost a sense of *completeness* that you never have time for during the day; it's almost as if you are looking down and sharing the world with God.' He looked at me, and then away, as if he had said too much. 'Ah well, we're not up here to dream, so let's use the time for some *useful* instrument practice.'

We spent forty minutes going through the majority of the syllabus required for the Instrument Rating exam, which I was now nearly ready for, and then rounded this off by calling Greenham Common, where we completed three GCA's treating them as the real thing, with my head in the cockpit and he looking out as safety pilot. The first we broke off at 150 feet and did an overshoot, the second we took down to 50 feet, and we landed off the third, all on instruments. We then did an instrument takeoff and climbed to the east before clearing their zone.

'Just keep on taking her up' he said as we passed through 4000 feet. 'It's ages since I've been this high in this ditch-loving machine, and it is such a *glorious* night.'

We climbed up and up, and at 10,000 feet the whole of southern England was spread out under us. We could also see the lights of northern France lighting up the southern sky. The air was still, and it was as though the aircraft was in its own timeless orb, and completely stationary. Then he cut the power.

'Oh no!' I said.

'Engines still fail at night, you know.'

'But, well...' I did a rapid mental calculation as I trimmed the aircraft to glide. 'If this were an engine failure, my intentions would be to spiral down and land at Greenham Common again. Even one of your monkeys could do that – with or without the aid of that controller, it would be a doddle. So, instead, how about trying to glide all the way back to Wallop? We are at 10,000ft, still air, rate of descent will be about 350ft a minute, thirty-seven or eight miles to run, do you think we could make it?'

'Now there is an *aviator* talking' he said. 'Go on, why not? Give it a try, Lindbergh.'

There was no noise, save the whisper of the slipstream brushing over the aircraft and the subdued mutter of the engine at tick over. From 10,000 feet we slid down an imaginary line, both totally captivated by the situation. No longer were we instructor and pupil, but two flyers sharing something very special. Had it been day, there would have been other distractions, but night made it magic. I was very aware that he could have flown the aircraft with far more accuracy, and focused all my concentration on holding the glide speed steady, and the aircraft perfectly balanced. Had I been on my own, I probably wouldn't have done this so meticulously. The lights of Andover drew nearer and with them, as if on a string, the lights of Salisbury beyond. There was a black hole in between, which we both agreed must be where the airfield was.

Better give them a call.

'Wallop, this is Lima Two-Three, rejoining from the northeast. Range about twelve miles, and request permission to rejoin for a straight-in approach?'

'Two-Three, Wallop, we've been waiting for you. You are cleared to rejoin. Tactical flare path on runway 24, and the QFE is 997. Call again on finals, and we'll get the lads to switch the vehicle lights on for you.'

'Lima Two-Three.'

Like a ghost we flitted over Andover at 2800 feet, a shadow against the stars. By watching the lights of the cars, I managed to pick up the route of the A343, which runs past the field. It was going to be a near thing. Without reference points, there was no way of judging the distance. I completed the vital actions for landing, and then eased back on the stick a fraction, to stretch the glide.

'Leave it where it was' growled Mr Summers. 'You were flying quite nicely until then.'

'I don't think we're going to make it.'

'Neither do I, but Pilot's Notes say the best glide performance is achieved clean at seventy knots. Anyway, it was a good try... The best thing to do now would be to put the power back on, rejoin overhead and sort yourself out. Then you'll be able to establish where the flare path is amongst all the other lights, and...'

'Mmm-mmm.'

Yesterday's experience was still churning over in the back of my mind. And how, with half flap lowered and the ailerons in their droop position, the aircraft had kept on floating and floating and wouldn't land.

'You disagree?'

'We're not going to make it. So, if this *was* for real, and with nothing to lose, I'd try ten degrees of flap...'

'Well, you're the captain, so do what you think best...'

By now I could just pick out the lights of the Mess to the north of the road, and the camp complex to the south, and the blackness of the field beyond. The distance looked about three miles to run. And the altimeter was passing through 950 feet. Okay, let's try it. I flicked the flap selection lever down, and pumped until the indicator showed ten degrees, and then re-trimmed to glide at sixty-five. We hung there.

'Wallop, Lima Two-Three; it's difficult to pick out the flare path from this angle, could you get the Land Rovers to flick their lights on and off?'

'Two-Three, Wallop....'

We were now on the edge of the black hole and our height was down to 450 feet. Suddenly lights flicked on and off, near enough straight ahead, and roughly where I had hoped. With the position confirmed, the two hurricane lights suddenly materialised, and I turned left fifteen degrees to line them up.

'Wallop, Lima Two-Three on short finals to land.'

'Two-Three, you are clear to land, there is no wind and no other traffic.'

I left everything as it was and we whispered on down. It was as though the aircraft knew what to do, and there was no point in disturbing it. Blacker shadows of trees and fences became discernible as we neared the ground, then for a long space there was nothing, and then we were there, flicking through the pool of light. Mentally I eased the stick back a fraction, and the aircraft sighed and landed itself. I still left it alone as we rumbled on towards the distant hurricane light, and there was no wing drop. Eventually momentum ceased and we sat in the dark savouring the final moment, until we became aware again of the engine, still idling at tick over revs.

'I enjoyed that very much' Mr Summers said quietly. 'I timed it; it took twenty-eight and a half minutes from when I cut the power to the time of landing. That's the longest glide approach I have ever done. Lucky the field was where it was, for we couldn't have stretched it much further.'

We taxied back to dispersal and I called the tower and bade them good night, and then switched off.

'That's probably our last flight together' Mr Summers said as we sat for a moment in companionable silence. 'Which was why I asked you to fly tonight. You're scheduled for your thirty-hour check tomorrow with Major Ball, but if you fly like you did tonight, you should be all right. There's a new instructor called Sergeant Bateman who'll be with you most of the time to your sixty-hour check. You'll be his first pupil, so behave!'

We climbed out and he looked at his watch. 'I don't usually do this, but would you care for a little *cordial* in the Mess?'

The next day was the last day of the month, and the four of us sat in the crew room bringing our logbooks up to date. Totalling the monthly summary showed I had flown thirty-one hours and twenty-seven minutes during the month of November, which was nearly a third of my total time, which now stood at ninety-seven hours and fifteen minutes. The fact that it had rained virtually every day in November made for greater significance, for the Chipmunks had been grounded for most of this time. Looking at the others made me wonder whether there were any monkeys left amongst us?

In spite of being of like mind and sharing similar ambition, my four companions on the Advanced Fixed Wing course could not have been more different – which again compounded my earlier observations: there being no such thing as a stereotype flyer. We all shared the same experiences and had the same learning curve to adhere to, but here the similarity ended and our attitudes were refreshingly different.

John Foster was a Light Infantry lieutenant, and his every mannerism somehow echoed the furious quick-time adopted by his regiment. His speech was delivered in a high-toned staccato, often to the confusion of the Air Traffic Controllers who's ears were better tuned to the more hesitant transmissions proffered by student pilots. As well as his speech, he walked, ate and wrote all at the same desperate pace. At first I thought his movements were as a result of a general nervous disposition, but it soon became obvious that his mind was even further ahead, as though impatient for the rest of him to catch up. He flew in much the same manner, with quick precise movements, darting around the circuit and landing in a series of swoops. But however uncomfortable a passage, his mind was already there, which was what really mattered.

Guy Marshall was an Irish Guards captain, who walked everywhere with a stout hazel stick, which he only put to one side when he entered his bed or an aeroplane. He was always immaculately turned out and even his flying overalls looked as though they had been tailored for him. He spoke in a slow drawl, and never raised his voice nor affected surprise, no matter what the situation. Later in the course we were to be teamed together for many of the tactical exercises, and I could not have wished for a more agreeable or reliable partner. Nor could we know that within four years his wings would be clipped forever; but still we were destined to meet again and help each other in highly unusual circumstances.

Sergeant Barker was in the REME and already wore a light blue beret, for he was an aircraft engineer, and previously attached to the REME Workshops at Wallop, before deciding to try for his pilot wings. He was an excellent person to have as a fellow course member, and his knowledge of all things mechanical proved to be a boon to those of us who were not so blessed with a similar mind.

And finally there was Harry Harrisson. In any course or collection of people, there is always one who, for better or worse, stands out; and Harrisson was the self-appointed course humorist. Apparently he had always assumed this role; and whatever the outcome had revelled in the notoriety it brought, however short-lived. Within our first week at Wallop we had all heard how he had been thrown out of his public school for some prank that had seriously backfired, and how with parental influence, he had somehow got into Sandhurst, eventually to be commissioned into a county regiment. As a junior cadet at Sandhurst he had made his name at the puzzled expense of his company sergeant-major, who was one of those splendid individuals – which only the army can produce (and are so often caricatured, but splendid nonetheless), and who had trouble pronouncing his H's.

'My name is Company Sarn't-Major 'Oskins, and you young gentlemen will address me as Sir!' as he walked up the line. 'And 'oo might you be, Sir?' stopping in front of Harrisson.

'Arrisson, Sir.' He mimicked without batting an eyelid.

'Arrisson?'

'Arrisson, sir.'

'And 'ow do you spell that, sir?'

'With a *Haytch* an' a *Hay* an' a *Har* an' a *Har* an' a *Hi* an' a *Hess* an' a *Hess* an' a *Ho* and a *Hen*. Arrisson, Sir...'

By now a captain, Harrisson had buffooned his way through the army so far, and could see no reason why he should change his style merely because he was learning to fly an aeroplane. So what was so different? Besides, away from his regiment, rule-bound Wallop offered unbounded scope, as well as a whole new audience to entertain. And he certainly lightened the atmosphere in the crew room; with howls of laughter coupled with exaggerated hand movements as he recounted how he managed to fall out of a stall turn, or nearly landed on top of somebody else. But on a one-to-one basis he could be extremely plausible, which helped dispel any inner doubts, as well as winning over the goodwill of his instructors; and so he had managed to survive the hazards of Elementary Flight, and progress thus far in Advanced Fixed Wing. And this morning was thirty-hour check time on the AOP IX.

Major Ball took me first. We were flying XR 239, which pleased me for it was the same aircraft Mr Summers and I had used last night – as well as the one that had looked after me during the forced landing episode on the previous day; and if you could forgive the wing drop, was a sweet aircraft to fly.

'How are you coping with ground school, these days?' Major Ball enquired in his disarming way, as we bored up through the overcast under the surveillance of Boscombe Radar.

I kept my eyes on the instruments and cautiously replied that I felt more confident with most of the subjects to date. In truth, since my earlier fright, I had been working extremely hard, and religiously set aside at least three hours for homework every evening before and after dinner.

''Well, Chris Walsh asked me to keep an eye on your weekly results, and you seem to be keeping up okay. Some of the subjects *are* difficult to grasp, so if you *do* find any difficulty, for heaven's sake come and talk to me, and I'll try and help. That's what I'm here for, and it often helps to have someone else explain it. There's no middle course in the flying business; you've got to remain right on top of everything – so for your own sake you mustn't allow yourself to fall behind like you did last time. Now, whilst we are in this clag, let's do some instrument practice...'

We did about fifteen minutes of recovering from unusual attitudes, during which time I took the opportunity to note the stalling speed on my knee pad, and then followed with a QGH – which is a letdown procedure using the direction-seeking radio facility of the tower, and once overhead you fly a prescribed course whilst descending. We then returned low level to the strip, where I put my previously noted stalling speed to good use when he asked for two short landings.

'Okay, that's all. Mr Summers speaks well of your flying, and I'm the last person to query *his* judgement. I hear you had an interesting glide back to the airfield last night? Anyway, well done and I won't waste any more of our time. I'll keep the engine running, and send 'Arry 'Arrisson out, will you?'

The total time spent on my check had lasted forty-two minutes.

Unlike Harrisson's, which lasted for well over two hours, and he was still flying when we went off to ground school in the afternoon. The lessons were quiet without him – and so they were to remain, for we never saw him again. On hearing he had failed his thirty-hour check, he just packed his bags and left without saying goodbye to anyone.

I think if it happened to me, I would be tempted to go the same way.

* * *

The next morning I met Sergeant Bateman, who had just arrived from his instructor's course, and I was to be his first live pupil. He was a rotund jolly looking person of diminutive size, standing only a little over five feet in his flying boots. He had an open friendly face and talked with a strong Yorkshire accent. He stood grinning in front of me and his whole demeanour conveyed totally the opposite from that expected of an instructor, as well as the authority bestowed upon that species. I had half intended to ask about the protocol concerning who was going to call whom Sir, when on the ground or in the air, but in the event this never even became an issue and from the very first meeting we both knew that we were going to get on, he being there to teach and me to learn. He had a bundle of maps in his arms, and suggested we grabbed the corner table in the crew room, '...Because the first thing Ah'm going to teach ye, is how t' fold a map properly.'

Up to now we had used the standard aviation map, which covered the whole of Southern England and showed airfields, airways, radar installations and all other data of interest and relevance to the aviator. Sergeant Bateman's maps were standard Ordnance Survey 1:50,000 maps – to the scale and detail favoured by hikers for long distance walking.

Which was why he had so many of them.

'Ah've managed t'get the whole set, which covers the whole of our low flying area...' he confirmed, '...and ye're going to need them all. So first you fold them like this, then this, and then into a concertina like this, so you can open them page by page like a book when ye're flying, and then turn them over like this, so ye can use the bottom half, still nicely folded.'

Next, we put them in order and numbered them using a simple grid, and then superimposed this grid over the low-flying area already marked on our large Southern England maps for easy reference.

'Now when ye're low flying, things happen fast, and to be ahead of the game ye've got to be looking out all the time,

Approximate Low Flying Area around Middle Wallop

or happen ye'll kill yourself. But at the same time, it's absolutely *vital* to know exactly where you are at all times. And I mean *exactly*, In spite of the fact ye won't have time for more than a fleeting glance at the map, happen ye'll get the chance. And you certainly won't have the luxury of *height* to compare it to features on the ground. So your map reading must become instantaneous as well as accurate, and that's the only standard there is, and ye'll be examined on your map reading on your next flying test.'

He let this sink in for a moment, then went across to the stationary cupboard and came back with a sheet of card and a biro.

'So, how do we get you there? It's all to do with time and distance, so let's look at that. Put your right hand on the card.' I did as I was bid, and he drew round the outline.

'It's best to think in time rather than distance. Right, go to the scale at the bottom of that map, no, not the statute

91

miles, ye'll find nautical miles are easier. Now, place your forefinger on the scale. What is it, half a nautical mile? Good, your fingers are about the same size as mine. Right, try your fore and middle finger tight together on t'scale. Mile and a half? Good. Right, when ye're flying clean, the trick is to select the RPM to give you an airspeed of ninety knots, and at that speed ye'll cover a mile and a half in one minute. Right, now try the span across your hand. Three miles? That's two minutes if ye're clean, or, if you are on half-flap, throttle back a bit to give sixty knots, and ye're on a mile a minute. Easy! And it works, so when people ask you for your ETA, all ye have to do is to flick your hand across your map and bingo! The most useful one ye'll find, is to stretch your fingers apart, and measure the straight line between tip of thumb and tip of little finger. That's it, try it on t'scale and it should be six nautical miles – or four minutes flying if ye're clean.'

I tried it and it was so. I then measured the prominent dimensions of my hand and fingers and marked the card in minutes flying at sixty or ninety knots.

'Good, keep the card as a crib for now, but ye'll soon learn to do without it, and then your hand will become your personal time-ruler forever more. Now, what's the most important feature you need to know when ye're low flying?'

'Ah! Railway lines?'

'No, no, they're just a useful guide for direction – oh, and while I think about it, if you are using a line feature to follow when ye're low level, always keep it on your left hand side. *Especially* around here, because then you won't hit somebody coming t'other way. And believe me, ye're bound to meet somebody, especially if the cloud is on the deck. No, the most important features to know are wires. More people have been killed by flying into wires than owt else. So I want ye to mark in red all the high-tension wires on all your maps, so ye'll know they are coming.

'The low flying we are going to do is tactical. This means ye'll be at about fifty feet and just the right height to cop a wire. Remember, if you see a line of high-tension wires – or any other wire for that, always cross over as near to post, or pylon as possible. Then ye'll know the wires are underneath you, because midway between pylons the wires sag, and it's difficult to judge their height. The other thing is, if you *don't* see the posts in time – and this often happens, always go *under* the wires and not over. And always be wary of any clear space between trees or high hedges – especially near buildings or a farm. Happen the posts will be hidden in the trees, and there'll be a wire strung over what you thought was a clear gap. Again, if you *are* caught out, always go under – there's usually enough room. For if you pull up violently in front of a wire, the odds are ye'll go into a high-speed stall, and skid straight into them. By going under ye're always in full control, and you can see them the while.'

We started as he meant to go on, and for our first sortie, taxied over to the marked strip in the corner of the field.

'Right, take me to grid reference 473926, low level, which means not above fifty feet, using the ground as conceal-ment.'

I sorted through the maps and found the grid reference – which was the corner of a wood, two maps away.

'We're on t'ground, so use the opportunity to sketch your route in. All the maps are covered, so use a chinagraph pencil. Ye won't always get the chance, but you'll soon get the hang of it.'

Whilst Sergeant Bateman looked out of his window, I drew the route onto the two maps. From the field north to Grately, then nearly up to Tidworth where I would turn west, to avoid overflying the town, and then onto Salisbury Plain, and west nearly to Warminster, where the grid refer-ence showed my destination to be. I also noted the various line features and high-tension wires on route.

'Okay, you ready? Then line up and let's go'.

I called the tower, lined up and opened the throttle. The usual hop and a skip and we were airborne. I trimmed to climb at sixty-five knots and felt upward with my hand to flick the flap selector up to bleed off the flaps. He stopped my hand halfway, then reduced the power.

'Ah know it's against every pilot's instinct to take the power off on takeoff, but that's what we do. We're airborne, we've got the speed, and we're already at eighty feet – so we don't need takeoff power; we're on our way! Leave the flap at ten degrees; ye'll find it a lot easier to navigate if you keep the speed down to sixty, like I said. Now follow your route, get back down to under fifty feet and aim to use the ground to give as much cover as possible. That's it, down into the dips and keep below that tree line.'

And so flying revealed another dimension. The red wires marked on my maps took on a real significance, as well as how to fly an accurate course whilst constantly deviating to avoid ground features; or more to the point how to intercept the original track again by using time and distance calculations, which we found were necessary for even the shortest detour.

Because at fifty feet you cannot see.

The rules that govern normal aviation make it illegal to fly low other than for takeoff or landing. This is understandable and accepted by all professional pilots, for not only does it cause fright and upset to people (and animals) on the ground, it is also extremely dangerous. Most pilots revel in being let off the leash occasionally and will indulge in this, the most exhilarating of practices; but unless authorized can face the ultimate penalty – which is the loss of their license, as well as a hefty fine. The severity of this penalty is usually enough to deter most pilots – and certainly all professionals who earn their living aloft. But human nature being what it is, some low-time pilots are still tempted to risk their lives, and the lives of others, especially when they show off – which usually takes place near the ground.

For aeroplanes belong in the sky and not near the ground.

But for better or worse, we had to fly outside these rules. We had our own designated low flying area, which covered many square miles of southern England, and it was an operational necessity to learn how to fly at the minimum possible level. And it took many hours of practice, for until we

AOP IX in the Malaysian jungle. '...and aim to use the ground to give as much cover as possible...' (*Painting reproduced with kind permission of David Shepherd OBE, FRSA, FRGS and the Army Air Corps*)

were able to fly at fifty feet in all weathers, we could not accomplish the other tactical roles, all of which start from this base. At first we found it tremendously exciting: how to skid the aircraft round in a flat turn using a hollow in the ground, for an uplifted wing is the first thing to give your position away; or the various ways to sneak up to a position using hedges and trees as cover. But as our experience grew, so with it came caution and the realization of the dangers involved.

The level of concentration demanded by this sort of flying inevitably brings its own fatigue, and for this you must be your own judge. At what point do you refuse to fly a sortie? *Know thyself*; for as an operational pilot you are only useful for as long as you are alive to fly another day.

After a month of flying never much above treetop height, it came as a refreshing break to return to the upper air, the respite being the occasion of our instrument rating tests. By now we had accumulated the prescribed amount of flying hours, and as usual the examination was to be conducted in two parts, first a paper on the ground followed by the actual test in the air. The written paper was encompassed within the normal ground school program, and as such did not reach the proportions of becoming a 'special event', with the happy result that the four of us took it and passed almost without realizing it. Likewise, instead of a build up of apprehension prior to the flight test, I found myself looking forward to it, for with the recent concentration of low flying, I had missed this other extreme of the flying spectrum.

A Royal Air Force examiner, who was not very familiar with propellers, let alone the slow-flying Auster, took the test. After a few derogatory remarks about the simplicity of the machine, I found myself wishing that I could show him the full potential of the aircraft, performing as it was designed to do, a few feet above the ground. But instead we climbed up through the overcast to the world above, where he put me through my paces for an hour and forty minutes before we descended to the earth again. As in my thirty hour check, I managed to make a discreet note of the stalling speed during the procedures, and at the end of the test rejoined low level to the strip, where I had the satisfaction of watching him go rigid with his eyes glued incredulously at the airspeed as the AOP IX at last came into her own, and the perfect aircraft to demonstrate the army definition of a short landing.

We all passed, and met afterwards in the crew room feeling very pleased with ourselves. Mr Summers was there and made a point of coming over to tell us that this was one of the major milestones of a flying career, and was the first step to becoming *professional* airmen. Which pleased us even more. On comparing notes, we discovered that I had not been the only one to receive derogatory comments about propeller aeroplanes and the Auster in particular, and each had retaliated in his own way, so much that by the end of the day the poor man returned to the Air Force with very different ideas about propellers and how the army put the AOP IX to use.

* * *

'Now if you fly as Ah've taught you, and you conceal yourself properly, you should make a difficult target for enemy small arms fire, as well as ground t'air missiles.'

I sat up and gave Sergeant Bateman my full attention, for up to now I had thought that merely by sitting in an aeroplane would somehow make me invincible.

'So if ye're doing a good job – like actually hitting target when ye're artillery spotting, the enemy may think you to be of sufficient nuisance value to get rid off. Happen he might even get t' know you after a while, especially if ye're working the same sector. So rather than waste his ground to air missiles, another way would be to ring up his Air Force, and whistle up a couple of fighters to shoot you down.'

I had difficulty in following the full logic behind his argument, but nonetheless the subject was becoming more interesting by the minute.

'Anyway, it's included in t'course, and Major Ball has arranged for some RAF fighters to come and shoot you down this afternoon. They'll be using camera guns, and you'll be able t'see films afterwards.'

Major Ball came into the crew room and confirmed that he had made the final arrangements, and the attacking aircraft would be Hawker Hunters, but he didn't know how many. Start time would be 1400hrs and the stage to be set over Salisbury Plain. Guy Marshall and I were to fly two aircraft at 2000 feet and establish a flyline on an east-west axis between Tilshead and Netheravon, whilst John Foster and Sergeant Barker would fly another two aircraft on a north-south axis, crossing our flyline roughly in the middle. The Hunters would only have ten minutes fuel to spare on the sortie – which was a realistic time for battle conditions. The most effective evasive manoeuvre, he told us, was to execute a slow turn whilst descending, so that you were always dropping away under the fighter's gunsights, and forcing him into a steeper and steeper dive. In order to survive we would have to spot the attackers first. On a one to one basis, the odds were favourable; for once on the deck you should be able to out-manoeuvre the fighter for the required ten minutes. But, if they got their act together and used two fighters against one, the odds would be against you, and you would be lucky to survive.

We got together before we took off and agreed upon a common radio frequency, as well as a rough plan that Sergeant Barker would head off north, John Foster south, Guy Marshall east and myself to the west once we got jumped, and thus hopefully we would separate them. And the first one to spot them would call 'Break' on the radio, which would at least give us a sporting chance.

It was an unnerving business, and by 1400hrs Guy and I were on the second pass of our flyline, flying in loose formation. The all round visibility from the AOP IX is good, with the exception of a major blind spot over each wing, so every few seconds I lifted a wing in order to scan this area of hidden sky. It was amusing to see Guy doing the same. At the halfway mark we saw the other two flying south and cross our line slightly ahead of us. Then one of them did a 180-turn and headed back to the north, which struck me as a sensible idea as it would present four different single targets instead of two pairs, so I did the same and headed back for Tilshead again.

Tilshead coming up under the nose, so round again onto zero-nine-zero and click the stopwatch. Now, what's the distance of the flyline? Two stretched hands over the map, that's twelve miles or eight minutes. So watch out for the others in four minutes.

I watched the clock and sure enough as the hand swept up to four minutes, there were the other three converging and we all crossed each other near enough to wave.

Two minutes later, John Foster called 'Break'!

I was still flying east so immediately throttled back, put the nose down and started a one-eighty to the right, whilst looking out in every direction.

'A pair have just gone over me in close formation, heading south.' John Foster again.

DI swinging through two-one-zero, which means they should be somewhere straight ahead. There! Ahead and below. God, they are shifting. And difficult to see as they are painted in camouflage. Why do aeroplanes seen from the air always look like fish? Now they are separating, one turning right and the other left – which if he carries on round will bring him straight at me. With its sweptback wings and tail fin it looks like a shark, rather than any old fish. Carry on turning and hold the rate of descent. How many more of them, I wonder? The sun flashes on his cockpit and he's trailing black smoke. God, what a sight! It looks beautiful, but now he's coming straight for me! Carry on turning. No, hold it! If I carry on it'll present my tail to him. Two-four-zero. Hard over and swing back the other way, and increase the rate of descent. His wings flick up into a vertical bank as he tightens his turn. But I think he's left it too late – he wasn't expecting my change of direction, and I'm now inside his turning circle. Still in a vertical bank he flicks past my tail and the air around me is distorted in heat waves from his exhaust. Check the left turn, and bank back to the right again to continue onto two-seven-zero. There's the other one, heading north. Look behind, and the sky is still clear. I wish I knew where the rest of them were. There must be more than two? Passing through one hundred feet, temperatures and pressures all in the green, and steady on two-seven-zero.

The landscape is at last beginning to take its proper shape. There's an extensive wooded area ahead, with what looks like a firebreak running through. If I can get in there, I should be safe. Throttle back, and slowly feed in flap and we are back to our customary sixty knots. Skip over the fence and we're in amongst the trees, with just enough room on either side of the wings. It looks as though it opens out ahead, into a central clearing – yes, it's like the hub of a wheel and there are more firebreaks leading off like spokes. Bank hard right, and duck back into the next but one, which

Hunter. '...it looks like a shark, rather than any old fish...' (*Courtesy Phillip Jarrett*)

is heading roughly north. There are two people walking with a dog. Another Hunter roars overhead heading west and I hope my switch of firebreak was in time to spoil his aim. The people in front scatter and I ease back and hop over them, and then nudge down again until my wheels are just off the ground. God knows what those people are thinking...

I'm not sure being in the wood is such a good idea. Yes, it conceals me, and it also means the Hunters can't come down too low, but it's like being on tramlines and I cannot turn. At least one of them knows I'm here, and if he lines up on a firebreak directly from behind, he could still blast me. I snatch a glance at my map to see what shape the wood is. I'm in the longest section running north, and there looks to be another firebreak running parallel to me on my left. Look behind again, for that's where the danger is. There! A cloud of black exhaust gives his position away as he turns. It must be the first one again, and he's lining up to come in behind me. Which means at least two of them know I'm in the wood. He's coming in fast. Gauge the closing distance -- give it another three seconds – One, Two, Thr.. It's time to leave! Zoom up; over the trees, and good, there's the next firebreak.

Touch more power and stand it on its wingtip and haul back. The trees revolve underneath, and with them the new firebreak comes into line. Power off and dive back down again, heading south again. Careful! This firebreak seems to be a lot narrower, and we only just fit. The Hunter thunders past, and then pulls up into a vertical climb. Check the stopwatch, and only four minutes have passed since the start of the attack! I think I'll just stay in the wood for another six minutes; at least I've only got to watch my back. Central clearing coming up ahead, and there are those poor people again with their dog running round and round. Oh dear, he's shaking his fist... Check behind, still all clear, so ease up, quick look all round – not a Hunter in sight, and back down again into my first firebreak, going the other way.

I stayed in the wood for a long six minutes, flying up and down the firebreaks; then decided to extend it for a further four minutes, before cautiously putting my head up. I was alone in the sky. I gave the others a call, and Guy Marshall answered and said the Hunters had left ages ago, and he was well on his way back to Wallop. I was the last to land and the others were well into their second cup of coffee when I finally reached the crew room.

Only John Foster was certain he had been zapped. He flew south as we had agreed, and got caught in the open by two of them. One chased him down while the other circled round in front and then came at him head on whilst he was still trying to evade the one behind. Of the four of us, he was the only one who had not enjoyed the tussle, and he still looked pale and withdrawn. Heading east, Guy Marshall had encountered one, which may have taken a deflection shot at him before he ducked down into a valley, and Sergeant Barker didn't even see a Hunter. So working it out we reckoned there were five of them all told.

We saw the films two days later and these confirmed what we had worked out. Major Ball said that there were five attackers, two pairs working together with the Squadron Leader flying shotgun, to pick off any stragglers. John Foster was the only confirmed kill, and this was claimed by both Hunters as the films showed. His Auster looked very slow and vulnerable as it twisted and turned within the rings of the gun sights. Far from being a shark, it looked more like a daddy long-legs. There were several interesting sequences showing my Auster flying up the fire-breaks, which caused amusement all round, but I was pleased to see that the gun-sight rings never quite managed to ensnare it. But more to the point, it made me realize that a month previously I wouldn't even have dreamt of entering that wood, and it was all due to the tactical flying tuition from Sergeant Bateman that had given me the confidence to fly in without a second thought.

'Happen ye've taken some of it in, then.' Sergeant Bateman said as we strapped into the aircraft the following morning. It was to be our last flight before the Christmas break. 'If ye like flying in woods, I may as well show ye the CATO. Ye're due for your sixty-hour check straight after the break, and then we'll be doing them in earnest in Exercise Flight.'

'We? Does that mean you're going to continue to be my instructor..?'

'Aye, happen. Me and a few others. We all have a go at you in Exercise Flight. But me mostly, I expect.' He gave a disparaging grunt. 'Straight after Christmas ye'll do your sixty-hour check with Major Ball, so don't drink too much or forget all Ah've taught you. Then a few days after, ye'll fly with the CFI again for your Final Handling check. That's the big one, and he'll throw the lot at you. Oh, and on reading your dossier, ye'd best remember to call him Sir... Get those two over first, then we'll talk about Exercise Flight. Right, time to get on. Take me to that field where we first practiced field landings. The one south of Andover – large grass field with a wood along its northern border.' He jabbed his finger on my map, and I nodded. It was one of the first fields I had used with Mr Summers.

'Low level?'

'No, no... Take her up to cloud base – about 1500 feet by look of it.'

On the way there he explained that CATO stood for Concealed Approach and Take Off. The tactics were for northern Europe when we would be living in the field and operating from advanced airstrips, concealing the aircraft under the cover of trees with a camouflage net – just the same as every other army vehicle. The use of radio was to be kept to minimum, for the exact location of the airstrip had to be kept hidden from hostile eyes. The main reason for this was that the enemy would know an airstrip would be located near or adjacent to a HQ, and once they knew its whereabouts, it would become a priority target for attack – which would necessitate a swift move to a new location. Which would be a nuisance, because good strips were few and far between.

'Right, here's the field coming up now.' Sergeant Bateman said. 'The scenario is that ye've never been here before, but you know the rough location, or if ye're lucky, ye'll have been given the actual grid reference beforehand. So stay at your present height, and make out that you are on a liaison flight, just flying from A to B. The minute the enemy sees you descending or circling, they'll know there's a strip in the vicinity. Okay, you've spotted the field, and they'll have heard your engine, and hopefully the T-man will run out.'

'T-man?'

'Aye, he's not there today, obviously, but he'll be there on the day. The T-man runs out, and stands with his back to the wind, and stretches his arms out to make a T – and you treat it just the same as the T on the Signal Square at any airport. It tells you the runway in use and the wind direction. So now imagine he's just run out, and is standing with his arms out just by the hedge there. That means he wants you to touch down alongside him – make him duck under your left wing. From the way he's standing, ye'll know the wind is coming from the southwest, and he wants your landing run to be alongside the wood. Easy see? Anyway, don't worry because we'll be doing selection of Advanced Landing Grounds as part of the course, so when you do fly into one for the first time, have no fear, because ye'll know the landing ground has been picked by a pilot. Mind you, some of 'em knows how t'pick them...

'Right, you know all you need t'know, so keep on flying, but gradually alter your course so you are flying directly downwind from the landing axis. So ye need to jig north a bit onto zero-four-five. Good, now note the route over the ground for a distance of three or four miles away from the ALG, the further the better, but not too far because ye're going to come back in a minute at zero feet. So try and visualise it from that height now. Leading away from the field, there's a gap in t'hedge there, across that field to the corner, and there's a track running due north. Farmhouse and some barns and a drying silo – that should stick up. Ye want to be just north of that. Wires, leading from the farm – got them? Clump of trees in the middle of the next field. Happen ye'll remember all this, we've only gone a mile?'

We flew on in this manner for three miles, then I let down and choosing a hollow in a field, did a flat turn and started to pick my way back at zero feet. It was difficult. If it hadn't been for the grain silo I would have missed the landing ground altogether, for by the time it showed up I was about a mile south of track. I made for the silo and then remembered the wires, and then saw the gap in the hedge at the top of the hill. I pumped down full flap, remembering not to balloon up, and dragged on up the field using power and flying in the ground effect. Clip the hedge, power off and back with the stick. The AOP IX plumped down and rolled to a stop.

'Not bad, but ye'd have missed it if it hadn't been for the grain tower. Right, next you look for a marshaller who'll be flagging you from the trees, because ye've got to get under cover as quickly as possible. Now, two tips which I always found useful. It's the easiest thing in t'world to miss the ALG. Ye've only got to be a field out, and you can pass it by and keep on ground-hopping forever. And you mustn't be tempted to pop up to have a look, because you could still be near and give the game away. So, use your map and draw a thick chinagraph line of the route when you first fly over, and pick it up that way. And also write the landmarks down. Don't use your pad, it's too small, so use the window on your side instead. You can even draw pictures – like that silo, if it's easier. It's a massive window, so use it – it's easy t'wipe clean afterwards.

'And while I think of it, I always used the window to write on when I first started doing aerial gunnery shoots. The sequence of corrections can be endless, and it's much easier than using your pad. Ye'll be doing plenty of gunnery shoots after Christmas... Now, line up and take off, and do the same procedure in reverse. Wheels off t'ground and reduce your power, and low-fly out for three or four miles, before you climb away.'

We got back just before dark, and I found Roger in Room Six packing to go off for Christmas leave. He hadn't far to go, and I helped him out to his car, which was already laden up with presents. I too had contemplated leaving that night, but I had much further to go and having CATO'd in the afternoon felt too weary, so decided to stay the night and leave in the morning. I showered and changed for dinner and then wandered over to the mess. John Foster was in the bar sitting on his own, so I joined him for a quick drink and then we went into the dining room together.

'This is goodbye' he said in his staccato voice.

'Goodbye to the old year maybe, but there's a happy new one round the corner, so here's to the remaining eighty flying hours of the course!'

'No, I'm packing it in. I've RTU'd myself.'

'What? John! Why? We're nearly there.'

'We're not nearly there. We're not nearly there at all – for when we get our wings that'll just be the start. And I just can't hack it any more.'

Over dinner he told me. The fear inside him had started when we began to fly tactically. Flying itself was fine, he said, and there were times when it was great fun. And he'd enjoyed the challenge of the Chipmunk, and also the first sixty hours on the AOP IX, and was proud of his

Instrument Rating ticket. But training to become an operational pilot was another matter altogether. He was an Infantry soldier and could cope with the thought of being shot at on the ground. For on the ground there was cover, and you knew your business, and you could also shoot back. But in the air there was no cover and aeroplanes were vulnerable and made easy targets. And you were on your own. That was worst of all, and what frightened him the most. 'For weeks now I've been looking inwards and wrestling with my mind. And it's no good. I've faced up to it, and I'm just not cut out to be a scout or a loner.'

'But you won't be alone, there'll be others with you, in the same flight or whatever, all doing the same job. You're just the same as a recce-officer, only you happen to be driving a vehicle that can fly...'

'I've been through all that... so many times, believe you me. And I've watched you, and the other two; how you just take it in your stride.' He fiddled with his knives and forks, joining them together so that when you pressed the end one in the line, the movement was taken up by all the others. But his mind as usual, was far ahead. 'Remember that business with the Hunters? Well I was petrified, just waiting for them to attack, and not knowing... and then two of them just blasted me away, just like that! And do you know, I was glad! I was *glad* it was over and done with. Call it a premonition, but I *know* that'll happen to me, in one way or another, and I won't last long.' The knife-machine in front of him collapsed, and he patiently built it up again. 'And then I saw the films of you flying through that wood. How every time they lined up on you, you just waited until they were committed, and then just flipped away out of their sights...'

'Come on! That was just luck most of the time – and I was frightened too...'

'No, it wasn't luck. I couldn't have done it. I'd have hit a tree or something whilst looking behind, especially the erratic way I fly.' The waiter came with our meal, and with a flip of the hand, cleared his knife-machine away. 'See?' He said, after the waiter had gone. 'It just takes the flip of a hand, and all you are left with is a jumble of knives and forks.' He looked up and gave a sad smile. 'Perhaps I think too much to be any good at this business. Anyway, I've seen Major Ball and talked it through with him. And he's agreed to release me. It'll be good to get back to the Regiment again. Do you think I'm taking the coward's way out?'

I thought for a long moment, then looked him in the eye. 'To make a decision like that takes courage, and having got this far... I think you are one of the bravest men I've ever met.'

Next morning I drove home for Christmas.

Chapter 4

The flare reached the apex of its arc, and then fell spluttering to the earth. I squint and look into the setting sun, which is the direction from where help will come, and concentrate on blocking out all the surrounding noises; but the sky is empty and there is no sound of approaching rotors. Where the Hell was Roger? I'd heard his voice on the radio earlier in the day, so he was somewhere in the area. If he'd heard my Mayday, he'd be here like a shot... In spite of all his early doubts at Wallop, he'd turned into an extremely competent helicopter pilot. I remember when we met in our room in the evening of the first day after the course had split into rotary and fixed wing. He wasn't at all sure about helicopters then. He'd just had his first flight in the Hiller.

'The time honoured position for the captain of an aircraft is the left-hand-seat, so why have helicopter captains got to be different, and sit in the right-hand seat?' I had asked him.

'Dumbhead!' he had grunted. 'Fixed wing aircraft normally do left-hand circuits in the pattern and then they can only go round and round. Whereas we can go up, down, remain stationary, go sideways or even backwards. So in order not to confuse you, and to make allowance for your blinkered approach to flying, we like to keep well out of your way, and therefore always do the opposite circuit to you. Hence we sit on the right...'

But whichever seat he is sitting in, I wish he'd show up now.

The flare has given my position away and their fire has switched from the Beaver to my rock. Chips fly all around, and spurts of sand are gouging up on either side, narrowly missing my stretched-out legs. No wonder the colonel moved; perhaps this isn't such a sensible rock to be behind after all. I'll wait for it to die down, then think about moving myself.

'I think you'd better move' the colonel calls, echoing my thoughts. 'I'll try and draw their fire. You're stuck out on your own there, try and double back to that large outcrop behind you, then we'll have some defence in depth.'

He sets up a steady rate of fire, which immediately attracts all their fire, and my rock no longer spatters bits over me. Without waiting to think, I leap up and run as hard as I can for the large outcrop of rocks behind me. I don't think about crouching, or weaving, or whatever else a trained infantry soldier should do, but just run, head down and legs pumping. I make it and throw myself down. It's ideal – a natural parapet that would hide a whole platoon. I lie on my back, gasping the hot thin air – a fish out of water; and then look up at the sky again, and realize that is just what I am. And in two days time it will be Christmas.

The shops at home will be packed with Christmas shoppers. Stamping around in the wet. Buy, buy, buy. A frenzy of buying, as though shops will never open again; buy now, before it is too late. Too late for what? What do they know about this war we are involved with? And what do they care? 'But it's Christmas...' they'd say. So just what am I doing here, lying in the sand behind a rock in a forgotten place called the Wadi Rabwa – and away from it all?

Another Christmas in the heat. The heat never makes Christmas feel the same.

I wonder whether I'll be back in time to fly the padre around the strips for his Christmas service to the troops? I flew him last year and it had taken all day - and rumour has it, he has asked for me again. I remember we'd had a long theological discussion whilst flying between the strips. Perhaps he wants to continue with this? Well, I suppose I could tell him about how God had looked after us on our way down just now. Or rather, God and Mr Summers between them, for if he hadn't come to me in the nick of time and told me to pump down full flap, we would have hit that rock face, fair and square. I lie back and smile.

Dear Mr Summers, even then his job was running out, for helicopters were gradually taking over and there were fewer fixed wing students passing through. I remember how delighted I was when I learned that he was to be my instructor on my Beaver conversion course. He was really in his element then, with a proper aeroplane to fly, and the exactitude required for flying airways, all of which were his old stamping ground.

If I flew the padre last year, the year before – no, it must have been the year before that; I was still at Wallop, and about to start Exercise Flight on the AOP IX. That was when John Foster RTU'd himself, leaving just the three of us to continue with the Advanced Fixed Wing course. And that was the Christmas I went home to my parents, and wanted to forget all about aeroplanes and just relax. But father kept on talking about flying, and the hangar doors never seemed to shut. I remember he'd just clocked up 1000 hours in his Auster – 'And every minute paid for by myself'. And how the day after Boxing Day had been one of those bright sunny days, which suddenly make mid-winter seem like spring, and we went flying together.

* * *

'You sit in the left seat, son, I'd like to see how it's done.'

'But I've only got a tenth of your hours.'

'But I haven't got an Instrument Rating, nor have I ever used a radio...'

Although I'd flown with him since the age of eight, this was the first time I'd looked at his Auster with knowledgeable eyes, and it made me realize how basic a machine it really was. There was an altimeter; a very old turn and slip with a second needle pointing down instead of a ball; a clock; an ASI graduated in mph instead of knots; a revcounter, and an oil pressure gauge, and that was it! The compass was on the floor between the seats and was the sort you could set by twisting an outer ring. And this was the aeroplane my father flew on regular business trips to Holland and Germany?

'I don't see how you can manage without a radio?' I said in wonderment.

'You don't miss what you've never had. Sit in, and I'll swing the prop.'

It was so much smaller than the AOP IX, and the doors and windows rattled alarmingly when the engine started. Gingerly I taxied to where he told me, and was glad to see that at least it had heel-operated brakes, rather than the handbrake arrangement of the Chipmunk, which I had half been expecting. I ran the engine up, and without being prompted clicked the magneto switches one at a time, noting the drop on the rev-counter. Then he told me how to lower the flaps by pulling the lever out, to release it from its toothed ratchet by my left shoulder. Vital Actions (such as they were) complete for takeoff, I turned into wind and opened the throttle.

Used to the skip and a hop of the AOP IX, we seemed to take an age to leave the ground, and managed to use up most of the airfield in the process. Compared to the Chipmunk and AOP IX, it seemed to be terribly underpowered, and this affected everything about it. I nursed it into the air and then kept the nose low to allow it to pick up speed. The climb was agonisingly slow, and I was extremely conscious of the additional drag caused by the ailerons every time I turned. Mr Summers would not have liked it at all. Away from the circuit, by force of habit, I thought I'd see what speed she stalled at. I took a quick look round, then closed the power and held the nose slightly up.

'Here, steady on! What d'you think you're doing? You could STALL by doing that!'

'I know, dad, just what I want to do.'

'Hey, hey, hey! I had to do one of those once in a flying test, and it frightened the life out of me.'

'Don't worry, dad, I do them every day. Then I'll show you an army landing.' The aircraft gave a final judder and then dropped a wing, and I noted the speed and then fed-in power to recover. The needle of the rev-counter seemed to move in little jerks, instead of the smooth flowing motion I was used to.

'Is there anybody else flying?' I asked.

'No, no. Just us. And there's nobody in the tower today.'

'It'll be okay to land just outside the hangar then?'

'Ye-es, I suppose so... Don't you land with the engine off then?'

'Sometimes, but you have to use power for a short landing.'

'Oh. I was always taught to land with the engine off. That way you get practice at gliding it, and you'd know what to do if the engine stopped one day.'

'Yes, we've done a few of those as well' I said, thinking of my finger-strip in the wood, and resorting to a ground loop to stop in time. We flew over the house, and my mother came out and flapped a dishcloth at us and then went back indoors, and we headed back for the field.

'You see that patch of concrete just outside your hanger? Well, I'll put it down on that, and we won't have far to push it back in.' As there was nobody else flying, I did half a circuit whilst descending to 300 feet, and then swung round and set it up on the approach at five knots above the stall. With full flap I had to use a lot of power to hold the speed against the additional drag, but that was to be expected and I soon got the feel of it. I explained what I was doing and why, as I juggled the power to adjust the line, and we were approaching nicely.

'I was always taught never to speak, when you're landing, because it disrupts your concentration...'

'Sorry, I'm used to giving a running commentary, so our instructors know what we are thinking. Anyway, we're here now,' as I rounded-out over the pad and chopped the power. We rolled two or three lengths and stopped.

'I should tell them at Middle Wallop when you get back,' father said in his "thousand-hour" voice as we drove home, 'that it's better to land with the engine off, because that way it's good practice in case the engine stops. It can happen you know. Also they ought to know better to allow talking when you are landing. Make sure you tell them that. Still, I thought you did very well...'

And indeed I did tell them, for I recounted the tale to Mr Summers in the crew room the following week. How underpowered and under-instrumented I thought the Auster Autocrat was, and how, in spite of the lack of power, I managed to do a respectable short landing, the whole point of which had been utterly lost.

'Mmmm' he said. 'Isn't it time you learned *not* to show off? There is nothing wrong with the Autocrat for civilian club flying; it's cheap to run as well as being safe and reliable. And I can't think of a *better* way of learning the gliding capabilities of an aircraft than doing a power-off landing at the end of every flight, adjusting for the different wind conditions each time. You can teach a *monkey* to land using power... And of *course* he had no idea of what you were doing; you probably *frightened* the life out of the poor man. In civilian flying there's just no call to do some of the things we teach you here. He must have thought your flying was *highly* dangerous, and I have every sympathy for him. A *thousand* hours on an Autocrat? And he flies it to *Germany* without a radio, and no ADF? He must be quite a man, and quite a navigator. I should like to meet him... But what disappoints me most, is that *you* should have known better than to have even *attempted* to do what you did in an underpowered aeroplane. It was pure showing-off... and, and just *remember* that!'

I knew he was right.

But what a pleasure it was to climb back into the AOP IX, and hit the cartridge starter again! We were allowed three days to purge ourselves from the Christmas break, during which time I logged nine hours, and then Major Ball thought it was high time for my sixty-hour check.

As it was when he took me for my last check, the 'examination' turned out to be more of an additional period of tuition, with the added benefit gained from a different instructor's input. We took off and cleared the circuit to the east, and by mutual consent I climbed to 500 feet in order to do a stall check. As I recovered, he asked me how I was getting on with Sergeant Bateman, to which I replied 'Aye, happen just champion!' Then sneaking a quick look at him, added 'seriously, we get on fine, and have a great working relationship. I find him a very good instructor.'

'I understand he's done a Concealed Approach and Take Off with you?'

'Yes, we did one on our last flight before Christmas.'

'Good, you'll be doing a few more CATO's with him, and I'll be taking you for gunnery. Now, I want to check your low-level map reading, so descend to fifty feet, and flying tactically, take me to this grid reference.' He handed me a piece of paper. I read the grid reference and then copied the numbers onto the window on my side, using one of the chinagraph pencils, which I now kept in the upper sleeve of my flying suit. 'I see you've learnt that trick! Good, it's so easy to lose a piece of paper. Remind me before we start, and I'll show you how to divide the window up into useful sections for a gunnery shoot. Makes it much easier to follow the sequence.'

Whilst descending, I fished behind and found the right maps for the grid reference, and then drew a line for the route. It was new country for me, and from the map I saw there were two sets of high-tension wires to cross, as well as several villages to avoid. We got there without mishap and then flew back at a more reasonable height, with the inevitable practice engine failure on the way.

'Now, imagine it is night, and without looking inside the cockpit, place your hand on the switch for the landing light.' This was a new one! The switches in the AOP IX are placed in various groups along the top of the facia, the most frequently used being directly in front of the pilot, and working outwards to the ancillary switches which are grouped on the starboard side in front of the co-pilot's seat. The landing light switch was one of these, but which one? I made a guess and put my finger on a switch. 'No! It's the next one to the left. But never mind; the point I'm trying to make is that at night, when you may be under a certain amount of stress, I wouldn't expect you to know the exact switch. So, use the flat of your hand and turn them all on!

You know yourself that none of the switches in that group are *that* important, so why not turn them all on? It doesn't matter a fig if you turn the pitôt heat on and the downward-ident light or any of the others, for none of them are detrimental. At least you'll get your landing lights!'

Major Ball had a fund of such tips and more importantly, the thinking behind them, and I looked forward to more of this refreshing level of instruction when we started gunnery. The check lasted an hour and ten minutes, and as we taxied back he told me I was ready for my Final Handling Test with the CFI, which he had already booked provisionally for ten o'clock tomorrow morning.

I got changed, and on the way back decided to call by Advanced Rotary Wing crew room to see if Roger was there. He had gone off yesterday on a solo navigation exercise, and hadn't been able to get back and had had to put down somewhere. By the time he had got to a telephone, with the exception of Advanced Rotary who were in a panic, the remainder of the administration had all closed down, and the only number he could get through to was the Officers Mess. So he told the Mess Sergeant that he wouldn't be in for dinner, and as an afterthought wondered if he would mind contacting his Flight Commander, to tell him that he would bring the Scout back in the morning! At least, that was the tale that was going around, and I wanted to hear it from Roger himself.

Their crew room was in darkness, so I kept going, and eventually found Roger lying flat out on his bed in our room.

'Wotcher, partner,' he said, opening an eye.

'Oh, are you back? It was really quite peaceful here last night...'

'Mmmm. I didn't half catch a rocket from my Flight Commander. He took great exception to being told about my whereabouts from the Mess Sergeant. Seemed reasonable to me. At least he got the message! D'you know he threatened to put me on review...? Only he didn't think the punishment fitted the crime. Or is it the other way round? I can never remember Gilbert and Sullivan. Anyway, he's cooled off a bit now, especially as I didn't bend his precious Scout.'

'More likely he didn't dare sack you, else he and his instructors would be out of a job...' Rotary Wing had suffered casualties as we had, and three out of the eight had been RTU'd for failing the basic helicopter conversion course on the Hiller. 'Anyway, tell me all about it?'

He arranged his pillow, and sat up.

'Well, my nav. exercise took me down to RAF Culdrose at the bottom end of Cornwall. On the way back I could see the weather was clamping down, so I skirted to the north of Dartmoor to keep clear of the high ground, and then picked up Exeter all right to my south, so I just kept on heading east. By now I was pretty low, but I managed to raise the Navy at Yeovilton, but was too low for their radar, and the VHF was very intermittent and they couldn't get a fix on me. So whether I was north or south of their field I just don't know. I hadn't a clue where I was, and *nothing* seemed to fit the map. You know how it is when you are low...? I suppose I should have tooled around a bit until I found their field and landed, instead of pressing on. Anyway, after Yeovilton I couldn't raise a soul on the radio – and when I got back this morning, workshops found that the aerial fitting was loose, which I suppose accounted for it. Also it was the number-two set, which didn't help any – you know, one of those old Mickey Mouse affairs? The number-one set had been taken out for some reason.

'So there I was, partner, lost as a fart, with all my time-and-distance calculations up the spout, for by this time I was just *crawling* along at nought feet as the cloud was right down to about tree-top height. And of course, by now I was flying so slowly I was half in the hover, which sucks up fuel like nobody's business, and that was beginning to worry me. Anyway, a main road suddenly loomed out of the mist at right angles to my course, which I reckoned must have been the Blandford to Shaftesbury road because that's the only one that runs due north; so that cheered me up for it meant

Salisbury was only another twenty miles or so, and I'd be as good as home.'

'You couldn't have been far off the main London railway line. I seem to remember it cuts south from Exeter and then runs northeast to Salisbury?'

'Don't I know! And believe me, I searched for it high and low. Well, low anyway, for by this time I could only just about see straight down, and very little ahead. That road was the only thing I came across, and after that I stumbled on for another ten minutes, but it was getting worse and I was worried about the high ground – the Cranborne Chase is it? Then the Downs just disappeared ahead, and I realized the top was in cloud. I thought of turning back and finding the road again, but by now I was really worried about fuel. If my calculations were right, I reckoned I'd just about have enough to see me back to Wallop, in a straight line and at cruise configuration.

'Then I saw a house. All on its own, no wires leading to it or anything, no farm buildings, just a cottage with a vegetable patch, and a track leading off into the mist. So I lowered it down – mind you I was only a couple of feet up, but I honestly don't think I could have gone on for more than another fifty yards or so. Anyway, by then I'd had enough... You know how it is...'

'I think we need a scotch!' I got up and did the honours. 'So there you were, thumb up your bum and your mind in neutral, and nothing on the clock but the maker's name, so what happened next?'

'Well, I was winding the engine down, when I noticed a man had come out of the house, and was standing leaning against the wall, just watching. So I carried on and shut the engine down, and then unplugged and took my helmet off and just sat for a moment... unwinding, as you do... When the rotors finally stopped and everything was quiet, the man opened the gate and came into the field and just glared at the machine. Then he walked all round it, inspecting it from all angles, and then – then he walked round again! Only this time he went the other way round, and ended up where he had started. He didn't come near or anything; he just stood there glaring, and from his attitude, made it very clear that I was trespassing and not at all welcome. So I opened my door and got out and made towards him, and was about to explain my sudden presence, when – do you know what he said?'

I smiled and waited; Roger was back to his normal form.

'He said: "Huh! Down from London, I suppose?" Just that! Only in a resigned, knowing sort of voice, as though half the City invaded his wretched cottage every week! Anyway, I got over that, and then asked him where I was, and he said, "You're in my paddock, that's where you are". In his paddock! I couldn't believe it! After the strain of the flight and everything, I would have to pick his paddock. That did it, and I couldn't keep a straight face any longer! Anyway, after a while I managed to persuade him that I was genuinely lost and hadn't expressly landed in his paddock to disturb his peace, so he thawed a bit and told me he was a shepherd and lived there on his own, and mostly preferred sheep to people, and there was no telephone and no electricity, and no, he didn't have a vehicle of any kind. So I asked

Westland Scout. '...at least in a chopper you can stop and land vertically...' (*Courtesy Army Air Corps*)

him where the nearest telephone was, and he told me he thought he remembered seeing a public box about a mile and a half away, but he had never used it.

'So I asked him to keep an eye on the Scout, and walked down this track, and then on and on for miles in the mist, and eventually came across an isolated telephone box, literally in the middle of nowhere, which I don't think had been used for months because it was very reluctant to accept any money, and at first kept spitting it out, then it got the hang of it and just gobbled it up – and when I was down to my last coin I managed to get through to the Mess Sergeant and asked him to pass the message on. So then I walked back...'

'Miles and miles?'

'The same miles and miles, and got back absolutely soaked and with mud all up my flying suit, and then he asked me inside. We ate a bowl of stew by candle-light, and after that he said he was going to bed, and I was welcome to sleep in his chair in front of the fire, and – and, well that was all really! I didn't see him again; he must have got up in the middle of the night and gone off to his sheep, or whatever. When I woke up, I saw the weather had lifted, so I just fired-up the Scout and headed for home. I had just enough fuel to make it.'

'Are you sure that's all? Sure this shepherd wasn't some voluptuous, lonely widow..?'

'Those things never seem to happen to me. Ah well...'

'The Good Shepherd! Why is it always shepherds who feature in these episodes? Anyway, you were lucky that his isolated cottage just happened to be where you ran out of air... And at least in a chopper you can stop and land vertically. Flying as you were, half in the hover, meant you could carry on for much longer and in worse conditions than you could have done in a fixed wing aircraft.'

'What would you have done?'

'Climbed above it' I said without a moment's hesitation. 'Or into it, and filed IFR... Sorry, you probably don't know what I'm talking about. Instrument Flight Rules, as opposed to VFR which is visual. You can file IFR by radio if the weather clamps down.'

'Ye-es. You can do that with your Instrument Rating. That's the difference between our sorts of flying. But what if you had an intermittent radio?'

'You can still do it. Your radio would have worked better with more height, and if it was intermittent because of the bad aerial connection, you could still get down with a speechless QGH.'

'Now, I *don't* know what you're talking about. But I'm sure you do. Come on, let's go and have supper...'

But in the space of only four weeks, I would find myself in similar circumstances, and for various reasons would not be able to follow my own sound advice, with near disastrous consequences.

* * *

That night it snowed. A soft gentle snow that floated down in slow dream-like repetition of itself, and covered the airfield and surrounding countryside with silence. By morning it was four or five inches thick, but almost immediately the air became warmer and it started to thaw.

'What's the wing span?' the CFI asked, as we taxied (slowly) through the melting slush to the corner of the field where the strip was.

'Thirty-six feet, five inches, Sir.' I said.

'Hmmm. I saw the film of you flying through that wood. How much room do you suppose you had on either side?'

'Well, I don't know exactly,' I said, thinking furiously, 'but before I went in I tried to visualize an Auster flying ahead of me, and based on that, I reasoned you could get three in flying abreast, so I deemed it safe to enter. Sir.'

'Oh, I'm glad to hear that. It looked a bit tight to me...' He looked at me, and I studiously kept my eyes ahead. 'Off the cuff, that's a pretty good answer ' he said after a pause, 'but I think you're a bloody liar! From what I saw, there couldn't have been more than twenty feet on either side. Three abreast? That's a load of codswallop!'

'The second firebreak was a bit tight, and had it got any narrower I was going to lift up so that my wings were just above the trees,' I said, hoping he wasn't going to ask me to take him there so he could assess it for himself. 'But in the event there was enough room. I kept to the wider ones after that...'

'Hmmm. You did well to escape from two of them working together. I saw their Squadron Commander the other day, and he asked me to pass on his compliments. They're using that film as an example to modify their tactics, and have asked to have another go at you. I said no...'

We arrived at where I thought the end of the strip should be, and swung the aircraft round so that it faced ninety degrees to the runway and I could see the approach. I then applied the brakes and ran the engine up. I thought for a moment that it might slide forward on the snow, but the soft, fat tyres found enough adhesion to maintain a grip.

'I won't ask you to take me back there. There's no point now, and you got away with it – and you achieved what you set out to do, which is to your credit. But I would give you a word of friendly advice. It is a well-known fact that between 100 and 200 hours, trainee pilots often reach a stage when they become over confident. We instructors have to tread a delicate line; initially we try to build your confidence up, and then suddenly it's out of our hands and you think you know it all, and we've got to hold you back. As I said, statistics show this happens time and time again, and all we can do is to make you aware of it. So be careful, and always remember that aeroplanes must be treated with the utmost respect.

'Right, let's get on with the business. Nice snowy landscape, things will look very different this morning, so we'll start with some low-level navigation...'

His words had their effect, and to dispel any signs over confidence I made sure to let him know what I was thinking at all times throughout the flight. I found it difficult to judge my height accurately over the snowy landscape, and so told him that I was allowing myself a little more height to be on the safe side.

By now we had reached Salisbury Plain and there was a large tract of open country to cross. I took a glance at my map; we were on course and I would just have to use natural ground cover to see me across. There was a hedge running up the hill to a wood at the top, so I jigged left and followed its line, flying as low as I dared. Once again I couldn't help but marvel at the AOP IX's performance for this sort of flying. With ten degrees of flap and at sixty knots she was perfectly balanced, and responded instantly to every thought. On that first morning, Mr Summers had never said a truer word when he described her as *'quite remarkable'*. The map showed a valley on the other side of the wood, running roughly in the direction we needed to go and I hoped this would see us across the next open patch. I was glad to ease up again when we got to the cover of the wood, and skirted round its edge, explaining every thought and action. Since the trees offered plenty of cover I could keep a safe distance out, which would allow room to turn the final corner.

We banked around the corner, and came face to face with a Scout helicopter doing the same thing from the opposite direction.

We both saw each other at the same time, and in the same split second took avoiding action. But it was a near thing, and if I hadn't eased away from the wood, or gained those few extra feet, there wouldn't have been any room to manoeuvre. As it was, I was able to stand the aircraft on its wing and flick past.

I found the valley and carried on, and in spite of my bumping heart, tried to keep my voice as casual as possible, as though a near miss at zero feet was a normal occurrence, and to be expected in the Low Flying Area. But I could see that the CFI had been severely shaken by the incident, and was mopping his face with a trembling hand.

It is always worse when you are not in control yourself.

I made a point of mentioning that I had been taught always to keep line features on my left, and although arguably not a line feature, I had kept the wood on my left for this same reason. But he made no response, and other than calling for the items on his check list, sat in silence and as though no longer part of the proceedings. I found this disquieting and tried not to let it effect my flying, but all the time couldn't help wondering whether there was anything else I could have done, or maybe had neglected some safety aspect, which would have avoided the situation in the first place?

The items on his list took an hour and forty minutes to complete, by which time I was certain the incident had marred any chance of passing, and my confidence – let alone any question of over confidence, was now all but eaten away. Also it had suddenly got colder and had started to snow again. In the reduced visibility I left the ten degrees of flap down and picked my way back at sixty knots. We rejoined and were told that no other aircraft were flying. I waited for the CFI to tell me what manner of landing he required, but still he sat silent, so I left it until we were down wind, and then told him I was going to opt for a short landing in order to keep the length of the run to a minimum, for by now the runway conditions could be freezing slush covered by a layer of snow. We landed without further ado and taxied back to the dispersal.

I got changed and sat despondently in the crew room, pretending to read a paper whilst waiting to be called in for the de-briefing. There was no sign of Sergeant Barker or Guy Marshall so obviously flying had been cancelled, and they would not be taking their tests today. After about forty minutes Major Ball poked his head around the door and asked me to come in.

'Sorry to keep you waiting,' he said, offering me the only other chair, since the CFI was sitting in his behind the desk. 'We've been talking about the safety aspects as a result of the near-miss you had this morning.'

'Yes, I was wondering about that too, I've been thinking about it ever since, and I honestly don't think...'

'You did very well,' the CFI interrupted. 'But I don't mind telling you that it shook me up. I too have been thinking about it ever since, and I'm a long way from getting over it yet. Especially as it's part of my job to make sure that it doesn't happen again. Which is what we've been talking about just now. But your reactions at the time were excellent, and for that, I thank you.' He then went through all the points on his checklist, and I discovered I hadn't done too badly, in spite of my misgivings. He ended by once again warning me about the dangers of becoming over confident, and said I had passed, and was clear to continue with the remaining tactical side of the course.

I hardly noticed the snow as I walked back to the mess. It was as though a great weight had been lifted. I couldn't help reflecting that only an hour ago I had been in despair and now my spirits were at their highest, and how short a time it took for the pendulum to swing from one extreme to the other.

Another new Chipmunk intake had arrived and the mess was full of laughing people. Only nine months ago I had been one of them; but as it is with young children, when nine months represents a gulf of indeterminate proportions, now the difference between us was measured in flying hours – as well as nine months knowledge accumulated at ground school. With this morning's Final Handling under my belt, I felt quite the seasoned pilot, and with a pang of guilt, realized I was regarding them with a jaundiced eye, and picking out the monkeys. Perhaps I had crossed the gulf, and although still wingless, now regarded myself as part of the establishment – which, nine months ago we had all fought so hard against.

'You've got *dirty fleish*!' a voice said from behind.

'Tristan!' I swivelled round, and there was my old friend, looking as debonair as ever.

'I heard you were here, so I thought I'd better try this flying lark, and see what you were up to...'

We had lunch together and then he had to go and collect his flying gear, and I was running late for ground school, so we arranged to meet for an early drink at six in the bar. It was good to know he was here. We had met on our first day as Officer Cadets, and had remained friends ever since. We usually sent Christmas cards, and I had told him that I was at Wallop, but he had not mentioned anything about flying in the card he had sent me. Dirty fleish indeed! I remembered the incident well, and it had all been to do with his bayonet...

'Your Bayonet is DIRTY, Sirr.' The Irish bastard had said to Tristan, who was standing to attention next to me in the front rank.

Tristan, who had spent most of the night burnishing his bayonet, decided it was time to take a stand. Looking the Company Sergeant Major straight in the eye he took courage.

'It is NOT, Sir.'

There was a stunned silence. The atmosphere in the ranks became electric as everyone strained to hear. Nobody had EVER answered Company Sergeant-Major Rudd back before. The first lesson you learned in the army was to take insults and injustice on the chin.

As an officer cadet this is especially so, for an officer cadet has neither rank nor status. If you want to pass out with a shiny star on each shoulder, you keep your nose clean and try not to be noticed. It is all part of the 'moulding process'. Someone had told us that the army had a deliberate policy to break a person down to nothing, then, when they could see that you could survive the indignity of being a *nothing*, they would build you up again, only this time, they would build you the way they wanted. Nobody knew if this was actually true, but then again nobody was prepared to find out; for if you delved too deeply into the system it could be fatal, and you could be deemed to be a trouble maker, and not at all suitable to hold Her Majesty's Commission.

We were young, and it was all rather confusing, especially as we soon discovered there was another quality, which was loosely termed as *form*. Form is totally different, and is but a fine line away, and furthermore is definitely what they *are* looking for. To steal the colonel's shirts from his washing line for a bet would be considered showing *form*. To steal a lump or two of his coal from his garden bunker to supplement the meagre amount allocated to keep your barrack room warm, would be considered a criminal offence – and subject to instant dismissal!

Tristan was on the borderline, and his career at stake.

'And what's more, Sir,' he had drawled, still holding the sergeant-major's eye as the latter stepped forward and thrust his bull-like face inches away, 'I would like to see the Company Commander at his earliest convenience – on a *personal* matter.'

Checkmate, in one! It was the only move Tristan could have made to outmanoeuvre him.

Company Sergeant Major Rudd had been the first person we had met on the day we assembled. He was a towering figure of a man and his turnout was absolutely immaculate. In his hand he had what looked like a split walking stick, which opened out like a large pair of dividers. The ends were pointed and had highly polished brass caps. This, we learned was a pace-stick, an appendage which no self-respecting drill-sergeant would ever be seen without. He was dressed in impeccable service-dress uniform with a glittering Sam Browne belt, with the shoulder strap hanging loose down his left side. Later we were to learn that only Officers and WO1's were allowed to wear the shoulder strap over the right shoulder.

'My name is *Rudd*' he had said, 'and my Regiment is the Irish Guards, and I'm your Company Sarn't-Major for the duration of your stay here. Therefore we'll soon be getting to know each other quite well.' He fixed us with a piercing eye. 'So let's get one thing straight from the start. As Young *Gentlemen*, I calls *You* "Sir", an' you calls *Me* "Sir", only you *means* it, an' I *don't*! Sirrs!'

Nobody said anything.

'UNDERSTAND, Sirrs?'

'Yes, Sir!' we had chorused.

'That's better, we'll all just be getting along fine... Now in a minute you will be given a piece of paper to sign, which excludes you from all your normal rights! If you refuse, I regret you will be unable to continue with your education at this establishment... Understand?' He stared at us one by one, and paced the barrack room clicking his stick, as though he was on Guard Duty outside Buckingham Palace. Then as if by magic, produced a clipboard from behind his back, and settling it on his chest, called the roll. Each name he pronounced with open distaste, and laboriously licked the tip of his pencil before ticking against it, as we solemnly confirmed our presence, each one unable to resist the mono-tone of the one before.

And thereafter, life had been Hell. They had shaved our hair off and given us baggy denims to wear, and we were marched as a squad everywhere at double time, swinging arms straight until our armpits and body sides became raw. But we had survived – as countless others had before, and soon discovered that you can do anything and be subjected to any injustice, so long as you are with like minded people; and together can somehow manage to laugh or cry at the system. It is of course, deliberate and the army calls it *Building a Team*, and reliance upon one another. Reliance upon oneself and solitary strength, determination and survival are taught much later.

Until the occasion of Tristan's dirty bayonet, some three weeks on, and the first parade in our newly fitted uniforms. We had spent all night pressing and cleaning. Our webbing belts and rifle slings were blancoed white, together with the georgette patches with gold buttons on the upper lapels, denoting our rank as *Nothings*. And Tristan knew that although his bayonet was clean, he had been picked on as just part of the pantomime. But being Tristan, he wasn't having it.

'Very well, Sirr,' CSM Rudd had gulped, turning purple. 'I'll arrange an appointment for you to see the Company Commander – that is your privilege – but I'll be seeing him *first*, Sirr, and your reasons had better be good...'

But a sergeant-major cannot be allowed to be seen to lose face, and he had turned to me with a vengeance.

'And you, Sir...' Scanning my immaculate turnout up and down until his eyes fixed on my cheek.

'You, Sirr, have *dirty fleish*!'

'Fleish, Sir?'

''Tis Answering *back*, you are, Sirr. I'll not have it in my Platoon. *D'ye hear*, Sirr? Fall Out! 'Tis the Guard Room for you Sirr, until you learn *good order* and *discipline*! Slee-ope *Arms*. Quick *March*. Ef-Eye, Ef-Eye, *Smartly Now*, Ef-Eye, Ef-Eye.'

And so from the sunlight I was marched into a cell, and the door shut with a clang. *For what? Where am I? What the Hell is happening? This is ridiculous. I am supposed to be training to become an Officer! This is outrageous, to be treated like this...by this...Pig Shit, Bullying Irish Peasant!*

There was no official charge. My crime, I discovered was that I had a spot of white blanco on my cheek.

I had to put on filthy denims, and was then given a bucket of water and a toothbrush, and told to scrub the whole of the guardroom floor and adjoining cells. I had an essay to write which had to be in by the next morning, but that bore no weight and was deemed to be just another excuse, and bordering on further insubordination.

It had taken all night.

That had been seven years ago. Tristan had managed to talk his way out of the situation with the Company Commander by inventing some sort of family crisis, and had actually managed to obtain three days compassionate leave from the incident. Only he could have got away with it, but thereafter, Mr Rudd had made life difficult for him until the day we had passed out.

We both went to our regiments, which by chance were stationed next door to each other in Germany, so had seen quite a lot of each other, and had once gone skiing together. And now here was Tristan again, looking just the same as ever, and still with that boyish air of enthusiasm about him.

Thinking about it, he had the temperament to make a good pilot, but he had never been one to suffer fools gladly, and would have to guard his tongue to endure some of the pettiness found in Elementary Flight.

* * *

For once, ground school finished early and Roger and I walked back to our room, and then changed and went over to the mess, for I dearly wanted him to meet Tristan. Guy Marshall was at the bar and wanted to hear all about my Final Handling Test. If the weather cleared, he was due to take his tomorrow, and so to help him, I gave a blow-by-blow account. I had nearly finished and had just got to where the CFI had said nothing – even to the point of testing my judgement to select the most suitable type of landing for the snowy conditions, when Tristan came in and caught the tail end.

'I saw an Auster landing in the blizzard just before lunch, was that you? We could hardly see you across the field, but my instructor pointed it out.'

'Who have you got?' We wanted to know.

'An ex-Transport Command pilot called Williams...'

'Good, stay with him. He saw me through all right – he's a good instructor.' Guy said.

And then Tristan wanted to know all about it. And more to the point, what made flying so special? What was the mystic that surrounded aeroplanes? Wasn't it just learning to make a machine do what it was designed to do – rather like a car, only there was one wheel missing? What made men like his instructor, who had flown all sorts of aircraft all over the world, take a puny little job teaching novices to fly, when they could be earning real money away from flying, by doing almost anything else? To fly, obviously needed a little more intelligence than driving a bus, so why didn't these intelligent men put their brains to work elsewhere, instead of homing in to the nearest aerodrome? And it wasn't as if Chipmunks were proper aeroplanes anyway; if you could fly, why not go and fly real aeroplanes, and go places in them?

The three of us looked at each other. These were all

129

perfectly valid questions, and ones that, at one time or another we had all asked ourselves; but they were questions that a pilot did not ask, for a pilot could not give the answers. A pilot just knew.

Guy looked up and smiled. 'Do you ski?'

'Yes, I'm not very good, but...'

'Do you sail?'

'Yes, again I've done a little bit and...'

'...And? And, given the opportunity you'd like to do more skiing, and become really good at it? And, likewise sailing? If you were taught properly, and given the time to perfect the techniques – in all the different kinds of weather and conditions, you'd like to become more proficient? Okay, flying is a sort of mixture of both, only it's not really a sport, it's a useful job as well. If you can sail a dinghy, it doesn't take much to learn how to sail a large yacht – or a sailing ship for that matter. Sure there are more ropes to know about, but the technique is the same. If you held a Master Mariner's Certificate in sail, but got fed up with being away from home all the time, I think you'd make a very good dinghy instructor. And you'd do it because you know how, and not only that, you'd do it because you've got the sea is in your blood! Funny, but people understand that, but they're not nearly so ready to accept a bloke if he says he's got air in his veins!

'And don't denigrate the Chipmunk. It may be only a two-seater, which by definition will obviously restrict the amount of fuel it can carry, and therefore limit its range. But it is just as much a proper aeroplane as the largest airliner flying, and certainly is worthy of the same respect. Sure, it can't climb up halfway to the moon and catch a jet stream. Nor does it have four jet engines and all the systems and fuel transfers that go with them – but an airliner has a crew to help look after all that, just as a large ship does. The Chipmunk was *designed* to be a training aircraft. That's its role in life. And to train people to fly properly you've got to have all the right gear. You can't train people to do an instrument letdown without the proper instruments. And you'll find the Chipmunk has got exactly the same number and type of flying instruments as any airliner; and if you've got an instrument rating which qualifies you to use those instruments properly, you can fly a Chipmunk – or any other aeroplane for that matter, in exactly the same conditions. It's all a matter of horses for courses. You couldn't run a large ship onto a beach as you can a dinghy. So the dinghy sailor has got to know about breaking waves and surf. No more could you land an airliner in a grass field in a blizzard with no radio aids – as he landed his Auster this morning. I don't imagine an airline captain would ever be crazy enough to want to do that, but the point is they're both *aeroplanes*. They just do different jobs, that's all.'

Guy found his walking stick and prepared to go. I thought he'd done rather well, and had had no idea that under his Guards facade he harboured such deep feelings for the subject. But then, why not? Why should I think I was any different? Or, as Mr Summers would have put it, perhaps it was because I recognized Guy as a true *aviator* at heart.

Over dinner Roger and I primed Tristan all about the course as we knew it; the system of review, and the importance of keeping abreast of the learning curve, as well as turning in good weekly marks from ground school. It gave him a lot to think about, and it wasn't long before he was knocking at our door in the evenings, with all same questions and doubts that we had been through. As Roger remarked, life in Elementary Flight would have been a lot easier had one of us had a like mentor on the previous course.

And we were busy enough as it was, for the tempo of ground school was hotting-up with the introduction of gunnery and tactics.

The aim of the tactical instruction was to give army pilots' detailed knowledge of Army Air Corps techniques, as well as sufficient military knowledge to enable them to use their aircraft correctly in support of other arms. Which covered an awful lot, and meant as well as learning the roles and organization of army aviation at the various command levels, we also had to know the organization, together with the communication network of the Infantry, Armour, Artillery et cetera, when employed at Brigade or Battle Group level. Thus, if we were on air observation duties and saw an enemy target, we had to know the radio frequency and call sign of say, the recce-troop commander of an armoured regiment, or whoever else may be in the best place to deal with it. But where was this person likely to be at any point during a battle? This meant learning the tactical roles of all the teeth arms during the advance, the attack, the defence, or the withdrawal. And then in the event of nuclear weapons being used, the battle roles and tactics of all the above were likely to take a subtle change...all of which we had to know about, and what's more had to remember without resorting to the bucket technique, for at the end there was to be a final exam...

On the practical side, flying took on a new purpose. We learned how to read a battle map and how to observe the battlefield to be able to give an accurate report either by radio or at a de-briefing afterwards. We learned about flank reconnaissance, engineer reconnaissance, route reconnaissance and traffic control. We learned how to drop messages rolled up in a little bag with a streamer, and how to drop leaflets effectively, without blowing all over the countryside. We learned how to select landing strips from the air, and then to fly into them with replenishment, and out again evacuating casualties. We spent a lot of time taking air photographs with a special camera attached to a bracket on the fuselage, and then interpreting the results afterwards. The roles seemed to be endless, and every time we flew there was something new.

As it used to be with forced landings, now we practised CATO's on every sortie. For they were the culmination of all the techniques learned so far, as well as needing a lot of practice to perfect. The three of us worked together, and one would select an ALG, and radio the grid reference to the other two, and then land to act as T man as well as observer.

The other two would arrive overhead, but rarely together, and then fly away before commencing their letdown. We ran a book by way of competition and if the T man observed the descent, the CATO was declared null and void and a forfeit payable from the miscreant. This motivation proved to be far more effective than any tactical tenet, and soon we could find the field and hit the spot from a range of five miles at zero feet. And it was here Sergeant Barker came into his own and invariably won the kitty. Guy or myself would stand and wait as T man, and he would suddenly appear without warning; a popping from the engine, a shadow and a swish, and we would have to duck down to avoid being hit by his wing. It was he who introduced a dogleg into the approach, which foxed us for a long time, and he reckoned that as well as being more effective, was a lot easier to accomplish than a five mile straight run at the field.

Then there was gunnery.

As if all these new airborne roles weren't enough, gunnery was still treated as the primary function of the army aeroplane. The AOP IX was after all an Air Observation Post, and had actually been conceived for this specialist task. Moreover, was it not this battlefield role that had largely been responsible for the survival of army aviation as a whole? We were not to know that the first zephyrs heralding a wind of change were already stirring. The Beaver was proving to be an admirable maid-of-all-work, being able to fulfil most of the tactical roles of the AOP IX, as well as having the advantage of being able to carry seven people; or as an ambulance, two stretcher cases and three attendants or sitting casualties. Moreover it was a lot faster and had a range of 800 miles, as well as the power to operate in hot and high conditions, which the AOP IX was never very good at. With the Beaver setting new standards in the liaison role, there was also a new generation of helicopters in the pipeline, soon to follow the American lead and to be armed as gun-ships. Army aviation was about to undergo enormous change and expansion, and to develop from what was largely an unarmed and passive role, to one, which would become a major and aggressive force.

'But whatever weapons the future may have in store, there will always be a place for conventional artillery, which is why I am here, and in the first instance will instruct you how to become an observation officer, which arts you will then be able to employ in an airborne role.' The Royal Artillery major paused and handed out numerous sheets of paper, pausing before Roger who was the only other gunner in the room, before deciding that he too, may as well learn from the beginning along with the rest of us.

It was a whole new language. But as with most things military, the language was based on first principles, and the logic was clear and concise, having stood the test of time as well as countless engagements; and as generations of gunners had before, we soon learned the sequences as well as the jargon.

First we would have to identify the enemy and be able to describe it as well as their location by way of a grid reference. Then we would have to establish a flyline, which would be out of sight of the enemy, but obviously in a position where you could observe the fall of shot. This usually meant selecting an obstacle-free path, to enable you to low-fly up and down at tactical height and out of sight of the enemy, and then just popping-up for a matter of seconds for a quick look-see, before diving down again. Much like a hare in a field of long grass. The other essential thing to know was the exact position of the gun battery, together with their radio frequencies and the type of guns they were using.

'Then we gunner's use a triangulation method called OTBT the gunner major continued. 'If you draw a triangle on the piece of paper in front of you, mark the apex of the triangle with a T and the two points at either end of the base line with O and B, you have a triangle T-O-B. Right? All done that? Now T at the top of the triangle is the Target, and O at one end of the base line is you, because you are the Observer, and B at the other end of the base line is the

Battery. So the line O-T is Observer to Target and the line B-T is Battery to Target. Simple, see?' We looked, and we saw.

'So the sequence of orders to the Gun Position Officer, who we'll now call the GPO, are likely to be as follows: First you identify the nature of the target and alert the gun position by calling "Battery Target". Then you tell the GPO the position of the target using a grid reference, and the number of degrees from you as observer to the target – or the line O-T. So you'd call "Grid Reference 749263 OT 72 degrees". So he can now mark the enemy position on his map, and he knows your angle to the target is seventy-two degrees. Now if you're good, you'll try to establish your flyline on the BT line - that's the Battery to Target line, which will save a lot of time and working out. So you'd call "Grid Reference 749263 OTBT." It makes it a lot easier for you too, because once you start ranging, you can go left 500, or up 500, and know it's on the same line as the guns, and you'll quickly get the feel for it.

'You then tell the GPO what method of ranging you want. If it is in rocky ground, for instance, it's best to use smoke. Otherwise you may want a salvo, or one-round gunfire – a lot depends on the conditions and nature of target. And if you've got time, this is the point you can tell the GPO what he's firing at. He likes to know, and also it could affect his charge. So tell him "Enemy machine gun post, now firing", or something of that nature. You then fly up and down and wait for the GPO to call you back. When he's ready, he'll call "Ready, time of flight twelve seconds", or whatever it is, but he'll always tell you the time of flight.'

'Now, at last I see you are beginning to appreciate the nicety of the timing! When you are ready, you order "Fire", and he'll come back to you "Shot One" when he fires, and immediately you start counting the seconds. How much time d'you need to zoom up - five seconds? So you've got to be in the middle of your flyline after seven seconds. It's no good your being half way through a one-eighty turn at one end of the line. So, count seven seconds, and then zoom up and watch the target for the fall of shot. Also the GPO will help by calling "Stand By", five seconds before the fall of shot. Now, the procedure for ranging...'

There were dozens of variations to this theme, all of which needed precise orders and in the correct sequence. We did a number of classroom shoots, and then went out for the day to Lark Hill gunnery ranges, and fired real guns from ground observation points.

Then came the day when Major Ball took me for my first airborne shoot. He showed me his way of dividing the window up into squares, so that it was just a matter of writing in the numbers as they came.

'What sort of watch have you got?' he asked, half way to the ranges. I showed him my wristwatch that I'd had for years, and had a full sweep second hand.

'Yes, that'll do' he said. 'You'd be amazed at the fancy watches some people seem to think it's necessary to use.' The memory of the Skeeter pilot in Germany suddenly came to me. And his complicated watch with the moveable dial and lots of buttons. '*It's useful for timing the time of flight*' he had said, and I knew now what he meant. But all the same I was glad to hear that Major Bell thought my old ordinary timepiece would do just as well.

'I never use a watch for counting seconds at all now,' he went on. 'Not only in gunnery, but when you're flying there are so many times you need to count seconds. A rate-one turn, when you're on instruments; so many seconds on a leg; when you're doing an ADF letdown... Or how about if you're descending through cloud to break the ground, and you're at your minimum limit? You know there's an obstruction ahead, but you can also feel a break coming, and you know you're safe to letdown another fifty feet, but only for ten seconds. Your eyes would need to be outside then, and it would be fatal to be clock watching.' He let that sink in for a moment. 'So, try raising your tongue to the roof of your mouth and then bringing it back into place again whilst counting. As if you were saying "Tut", only with your tongue further back. Go on! Time it on your watch now, you'll find each cycle is a second – and it's a lot more accurate and easier than mouthing the one-thousand-and-one, one-thousand-and-two method.'

I tut-tutted all the way to the ranges, and by the time we got there had perfected the rhythm: which was to remain ingrained in my mind, to be used again and again, and in so many different circumstances. It was one of those things that once learnt, you wonder how on earth you ever managed without? Much the same as the dimensions of my hand had become, for I could now span my fingers over a map and know the flying time to the minute.

That first time the enemy obligingly put down red smoke, and I managed to pinpoint their position on my map and wrote the grid reference in its box on the window. Still flying straight and level I then found the gun battery, and marked their position likewise. Next, to find a suitable flyline on the BT line... There! A cleft in the ground suddenly materialized. I had the feeling this ground had been used many times before. Whilst descending I tuned the army radio into the gunner frequency and gave them a call and established communications with the GPO. I settled into the valley with ten degrees of flap and trimmed for sixty knots, and flew up and down a couple of times to get the feel of it, whilst tut-tutting the length of the run between the turns. I took my time and then tried a zoom to make sure I could find the target instantly, again tut-tutting the time it took.

'Battery target, grid reference 587392 OTBT' I called, and the shoot began. I made a hopeless mess of the ranging and it took an age, and the window on my side was soon covered with 'Up 800's', spilling out of all the boxes. But eventually I managed to bracket the target, to the relief of the long suffering GPO who by this time must have been despairing at my efforts, as well as using up precious ammunition. But I found the tut-tutting worked a treat, and I soon got the hang of zooming up five seconds before the fall of shot, as well as allowing enough room to descend again before the turn at the end of the line. I had been so intent on the zoom up and focusing onto the target, I had forgotten about the dive down again, which if anything is more important, as well as taking more distance over the ground.

Major Ball sat through the roller-coaster of a ride without saying a word, for which I was grateful, although extremely conscious that he could have bracketed the target after only a couple of ranging shots. But on the way back he seemed pleased enough, and said that with a bit of practice, my ranging was bound to improve.

So we practised.

I had difficulty in finding a natural flyline for our next shoot. In the end I went for one that wasn't really long enough, and the nature of the ground made it impossible to extend. But at least it was free of obstructions, which had made me discard the only alternative, and also this one was into wind, which meant we didn't have to crab into it at nought feet. The target was also further away than I would have liked which made it difficult to spot. But I had fired the first shot whilst flying into wind, which at least...

'Stand By!'

Start the clock. Tut – Tut – Now, zoom up! Tut - There's the target. Tut – Wow! A flash and black smoke. Miles out! Over and to the right. Throttle back and push down. I'll do one correction at a time, else I'll get in a mess. Scribble the correction on the window.

'Go left, four hundred!'

Back down to zero feet, speed falling back through seventy, and feed-in power to meet it. There, just right! And it's the end of the line. Steep turn to the left, I'm well down in the dip and my wing won't stick up. Oops! Nearly clipped that bush. Must remember it next time. Straighten up and back down the line. We got blown downwind in the turn and our speed over the ground is noticeably faster.

'Ready!'

That was quick! Now, wait until we are almost at the end...

'Fire!'

End of the line, round we go!

138

'Shot, three!'

Tut – Tut – Tut. Come on, we're falling behind, tighten the turn. Tut – Tut – Still not round, touch more power and tighten it up. Tut – Tut - At last! Roll out and get onto line. Tut – Tut – The wind...

'Stand By!'

Shit, I'm not nearly in position! Too late, must zoom up now! Tut – Tut – And I can't see the target! Fly on. Tut – Tut – Where's the target? I'm exposing myself for too long. Tut! That's it! No more Tuts. I've missed it! Now what...?

'The target's over there, you want to go down 800 feet,' Major Ball said, saving the situation. 'And *use* the wind, don't fight it. Next time order "Fire" when you've completed your turn. With this wind there'll be plenty of time – it's almost strong enough to stand still...'

No two shoots were ever the same, and we soon learned the value of establishing an intellectual link with the GPO. This only took a few words on the radio, but was essential if the shoot was to be a success. You'd never met the person, but suddenly you were to become his eyes. You could anticipate on his behalf, and he could anticipate on yours, but to do this you had to *know* how the other thought. You both had the common objective to destroy the target, and you could only achieve this by working together as a team. In many ways it was similar to the relationship formed between pilot and ground-controller on an instrument letdown, only then the positions are reversed, and he becomes your eyes. But either way, it is remarkable how quickly a bond can develop, and by the time whatever objective is achieved, you feel you almost have a duplicate of yourself, who has shared the same experience whilst understanding your every thought. And then suddenly it is all over, and it is with genuine reluctance that you have to turn your back on your newfound self and sign-off. And all that remains is a small flame, which is left burning in the chance that maybe one day you'll be able to work together again.

And we practised.

Until the targets no longer put down red smoke to mark

their position, and flylines were no longer conveniently to be found on the same line as the Battery, and the whole business became realistic, and with it professional. When we landed, our windows were no longer covered in a mass of blue chinagraph numbers, and one day I noticed that the other two were no longer using them as a message board, and had reverted to using their kneepads. Which seemed a far more professional way to go about it, so the next shoot I resolved to do the same. For the first time we began to meet our rotary contemporaries when flying, and joined with them for gunnery shoots as well as for some of the other tactical roles, and it was interesting to compare the techniques and performance of the two types of aircraft. One evening Roger told me that we had now conducted more live shoots than the average young artillery officer completes during the whole of his training when on their young officers course. This in itself, I thought was significant and showed what store the AOP role was regarded by gunners and the army as a whole.

Having mastered the gunner technique, we then learned how to fire naval guns, which meant a new set of frequencies and call signs, as well as coping with the knowledge that the BT line could be on the move! We only had one day of this, but we found it was fairly easy to adapt once we knew the expected rate of fire from their various guns, as well as allowing for the vast increase in the time flight.

Major Ball had by now ceased to accompany me, saying that the gyrations of zooming up and down, followed by too many tight turns at zero feet were bad for his constitution, and he had far better things to do in the office; and anyway by now I knew what was required and could practice just as well on my own. Which meant staying with it until the target was obliterated, and only then could you come home. But however well my shoots went, I usually found the other two had pipped me to it, and managed to get home first, so it was just as well we hadn't thought of extending the forfeit-book to include gunnery.

Tristan came round after dinner and told us he was in

serious trouble.

'What about?' I asked, 'I thought you were doing okay... You must be nearly at your thirty-hour check on Chipmunks?'

'That's just it,' he said gloomily 'I've been done for train-rocking...'

We had all done it, for when you are first let-off the leash, it often proves too tempting to pass up. Nor does it help when the main London line runs straight through the newly discovered low-flying area. There are various ways of playing with trains – and cars too, for that matter. I remember 'Arry 'Arrison's party trick had been to fly against the traffic on the Winchester by-pass, with flaps down and his landing-light on as though attempting to land, and howl with laughter as he watched the cars scatter in front of him. Train-rocking was not nearly so antisocial, and merely meant finding a train – the best place was on the long straight between Andover and Salisbury where the line ran on top of an embankment; and matching its speed – which at that place was usually just right at about ninety mph, and then letting down beside the carriages so you could look up into them. Passengers would notice, and the theory was that they would rush to the windows to have a better look. Once there, you flipped over the top, and peered in again from the other side. So they would then rush to that side... and if you got it right, you could get them rushing from side to side so that it rocked the train...

Only Tristan had been reported by one of the passengers who happened to be a retired wing commander, and knew all about it.

'When are you due for your thirty-hour with Major Walsh?' Roger asked.

'Well, I've been told to report to him tomorrow, but the thing is I'm also scheduled for my thirty hour check with him tomorrow...'

Roger drew himself up and looked at him in a benevolent way. I recognised the stance and couldn't wait for what was coming. 'Mmm. In aviation terms you are but a *child*...' he said, '...and all *children* do naughty things, and the only way they learn is to get a *slap* every now and then. I think you'll get a slap and be watched *very carefully* from now on.'

Tristan looked hopefully at me.

'Yes, I'd agree – but I'd get in first and come clean with him' I said, remembering the time Major Walsh had given me a second chance with the ground school exam. He'd said he had found some of it difficult when he'd done the course, and I wouldn't mind betting he'd done his fair share of train-rocking too! 'The crime you've actually committed is unauthorized low flying. If they want an excuse, they could kick you out for that. But if you're doing okay... well, I'd own up and admit that your behaviour was totally irresponsible, and tell him it won't happen again... A lot will depend on your attitude and also how you do in your thirty-hour check.'

The weather the next morning was forecast to be bright in the morning, but clouding over with snow showers later in the day. Tristan was due to fly his check in the morning, and Guy and I were scheduled for a joint gunnery shoot starting just after midday. A joint shoot meant we would each be given a target, but would both have to use the same gun battery, which would prove to be interesting. We took an early snack lunch, so I did not see Tristan in the Mess, and by 1200 hours were on our way to the ranges, flying in loose formation. The overcast was pretty low over Salisbury Plain and the battery position was at its furthest point, but we managed to scrape under the cloud with about 100 feet to spare, and made contact with the GPO. In the event there was no question of dividing the battery to shoot at both targets together, for one target was south of the battery and the other almost opposite and to the north east; so Guy went first with the near target, and I made off to locate the other one and then wait somewhere suitably out of sight.

Guy's shoot went well and he completed in about twenty minutes and then signed the guns over to me. In the meantime I'd been busy and had found a perfect flyline, concealed in a deepish valley, and I'd had time to practice and also to time the run. And it turned out to be my best shoot ever. Everything went right, just as though it was on the model we used in the classroom and I managed to bracket the target with a minimum of ranging shots, followed by one full salvo which hit bang in the middle, and it was time to pack-up and go home. I'm sure the gunners were pleased too, for the weather had turned very black and cold and it couldn't have been much fun for them. I signed-off with the GPO and disconnected the army radio and reconnected to Air Traffic.

And found I was trapped.

I'd been so busy with my shoot, keeping down in the valley, and only zooming up high enough each time to see the target; I had not noticed how the weather had closed in. I tried both ends of the flyline, and the cloud was down to the top of the moor at both ends and suddenly it was black as pitch. We were into the third week of February, and only a couple of days ago I had remarked to Roger how the evenings were beginning to draw out... but now it was still only early afternoon and... The blackness suddenly exploded into a solid wall of snow. Not just a few horizontal flakes, but a thick mass, instantly reducing visibility to zero. Instead of being soft and wet, it was the large sticky variety, which quickly coated the leading edges of every surface as though they were covered in glue. Soon all the surfaces I could see had a thickening layer – especially the wings and wing-struts, which were growing forward even as I watched. It was uncanny, and within seconds the wing-struts had doubled their normal thickness. Then it started to build on the front windshield, starting at the top edges by the wing-roots, and once gaining a hold, working down over the Perspex. Normally the prop-blast would have dislodged it, but now in the forced air it quickly froze, and having established a firm base, allowed more to accumulate on top.

There is only one way out and that is up.

I'm still at sixty knots with ten degrees of flap, and roughly half way down the flyline - about the position where

I had been zooming up; which leaves about twenty seconds before the end of the valley.

Throttle wide open, and build the speed up to sixty-five and ease into a climb. *Tut-Tut-Tut...*

I hardly notice when we enter the overcast, and hold the heading until the twelfth Tut, and then start a gradual turn to the north, away from the high ground. We are climbing sluggishly and automatically I start to bleed the flaps off, little by little, gradually increasing the angle of climb whilst holding the speed steady at sixty-five. I reach across and click the Pitôt heat switch on. This heats an element in the tube that protrudes forward like a stick from the port wing, and will stop the aperture from freezing up, thus denying air to the wind-driven instruments. At 2000 feet I start an easy turn to the right, to bring me onto 120 degrees, which is roughly the direction of home. At 2100 feet we can climb no more, and although still on full power and in the climbing attitude, we just mush along on at sixty-five. I glance at the outside air temperature gauge, and it stands at twenty-eight degrees. This is not looking good. I ease forward a fraction and the speed builds to eighty knots, still on full power. I leave it where it is, and then tune the radio to Boscombe Down and give them a call.

'Boscombe Approach, this is Army, Mike Zero-Six, do you read?'

Nothing! There is just a hissing in my earphones. The hissing then starts to build and turns into an abrasive squealing, like fingers scratching along a slate. I flick through all the frequencies, only to hear the same noise. The window on my left still bears traces of blue chinagraph pencil marks from a forgotten sortie; they're probably mine, although I did use my pad for the first time on this occasion. I focus beyond and onto the port wing-strut. It is now grotesque; no longer covered with snow, but a bar of solid ice. I try the rudder pedals and they are immovable. The rudder, far back and out of reach is frozen solid. I try waggling the stick, and then stirring it round. The aircraft responds sluggishly; so we are still able to turn, and at least the elevators are still working, but I must remember to keep stirring.

'Boscombe Approach, this is Army, Mike Zero-Six, do you read?'

A queasy sensation passes through my stomach, and suddenly my cheeks feel on fire and I am gripping the control stick too hard, to stop my hands from shaking. They are sweating, and have stained the kid-leather gloves black – and I catch myself still mouthing 'Boscombe, do you read? Please, d'you read..?' For I need a Ground Controlled Approach to get down, and Boscombe is the only airfield that can help. And although I can see myself doing it, I cannot stop my mouth from working.

Come on, get a grip! I concentrate on my hands and the stained gloves, for they are real. It just needs something to steady my mind...

It all happened so quickly. And how much ice can an Auster..?

I don't normally like wearing gloves, but we were told to wear them as part of our flying kit at the very start. In case of fire... And now I put them on as a matter of course; in fact I'd feel naked without them, and I would no longer dream of touching the controls of an aeroplane with bare hands...

Flying is a mixture of such apprehensions, and I hadn't realised about the gloves until now. But it seems to have done the trick, and my hands are steady and the fire gone from my cheeks.

But even with steady hands, they are no longer capable of holding an altitude of 2000 feet, for we are slowly sinking. The propeller starts throwing off chunks of ice, which crash into the side of the fuselage somewhere behind. *Of course, the propeller must also be accumulating ice, which is retained only until centrifugal force whirls it off. It is an aerofoil section just the same as a wing, and needs a clean edge to enable to bite.*

But it does not shed the ice evenly, and the carefully balanced blade is balanced no more, and sets up a wicked vibration. The panel in front of me shakes and the delicate needles jump in their clocks. To stop it, I need to reduce the revs. But this aeroplane needs every revolution it can get in order to fly. I leave the throttle where it is, and after a pause the altimeter starts to unwind again.

Come on, think!

Haven't we been through all of this with Mr Avery? The only difference is that he's not here to boom at you; and at least we've got a full panel. Okay, the synopsis is that we are IMC in cloud, and are carrying a load of ice, which is still accumulating. The radio does not work, though why this should be, I don't know. Probably the aerial is a block of ice, but you'd have thought it would be better positioned, and the one time you need it most...

'Boscombe Approach, this is Army, Mike Zero-Six, do you read?'

No, nothing! It doesn't work, so forget it. That means a GCA into Boscombe is out, a QGH into Wallop is out, and this aircraft is the only one which hasn't a radio compass, so even if that aerial was free... anyway, so that's out. Most important, we cannot hold our altitude and are now descending through - check, 1600 feet. But the engine is still working. I only hope the air scoop doesn't ice up, for without air the engine... Our present speed is seventy knots on full power, but I am slowly sacrificing height to maintain this. I shudder to think what shape the wing is, so God knows what the stalling speed is likely to be... I could try easing back, sacrifice some more speed, and see if we can hold altitude; but it's a no-win situation, for if we stay at this height we'll only carry on collecting ice. So it's best to continue with a slow descent, and hopefully we'll find a layer of warmer air. Our position is over Salisbury Plain – probably right in the middle by now, near Tilshead again, so we've still got about 1000 feet clearance over the top of the moor. The snowstorm was probably localized, and once the other side of the high ground there may be a gap under the weather.

And I cannot use the rudder.

This is new to me, and the one thing we were never able to practice. So turns will have to be done very carefully using aileron only, and even then they will be limited. So it's no use flying a triangular course, in the hope that Boscombe Radar will pick us up. They couldn't do anything anyway, so we'll just have to get out of this ourselves. I could fly south for about forty minutes by which time we'd be over the sea, and I could try a letdown then, and sneak back in underneath. But I've only got about an hour's fuel, and I don't think it would stretch to doing that. Anyway, with this weight of ice I don't think we'll still be flying in five minutes, let alone forty...

FIVE minutes? It's time to stop kidding yourself.

This aeroplane is no longer flying. You know how well it can fly, it's normally like a bird - no, it is better than that, it's like a seagull amongst birds. A delicate, beautiful and sensitive flying machine. But a seagull cannot fly if it is smothered in oil; and we cannot fly with all our aerodynamic surfaces encased in ice. We are gaining weight every second, and power alone is merely prolonging our descent to earth. No, we are not flying; we are merely a propelled projectile in a semi-controlled descent.

The aircraft trembles, and every instinct tells me we are on the brink of a stall. I ease forward and the trembling stops as our speed increases, but with it we sacrifice more height, and I watch the needle of the altimeter pass through 900 feet.

Unless we can find a warm layer of air to burn some of this off. If there is a gap the other side... I wonder what the ceiling is at Wallop? If only I could talk... I wonder..? Damn, it's worth a try...

I de-select from the Air Traffic, and switch back to the army radio, which is still set on the gunner frequency.

And it's talking..!

'...Zero-Six, Mike Four-Niner?'

That was GUY's voice!

'Mike Four-Nine, this is Mike Zero Six, were you calling?'

'Zero-Six! Where the devil are you, we've been going bananas here?'

'Four-Nine, it's *very* good to hear you. I can't seem to

raise anybody on Air Traffic. I'm IMC somewhere over Salisbury Plain, and I'm carrying a load of ice, and cannot maintain altitude. Where are you?'

'Zero-Six, I'm on the ground outside the Tower. I just managed to sneak in – conditions are a bit marginal here... I've been up to the Tower, and they've been trying to contact you – oh, and they've also alerted Boscombe and have got a line open to their radar. What's your altitude? Hang on, I'll just shout up and tell them I've raised you...'

Thank God! Who'd have thought the short-range army set would have worked when the main set was useless? I can't think what they can do to help, but it's good to be in contact. Good old Guy!

'Zero-Six, Four-Niner, d'you read?'

'Four-Nine, Zero-Six. Go.'

'Zero-Six, Boscombe Radar had a very weak signal on what they thought may have been you, but you're outside their keyhole and then you disappeared off their screen. If it was you, they last placed you just north west of Amesbury, about four minutes ago...'

At that moment we fall out from the overcast at 400 feet. The ground is covered in a light blanket of snow, but on hearing Guy say Amesbury, I straightway recognise where we are.

'Four-Nine, thanks for that. I'm Victor Mike again at 400 feet and can see where I am. Now listen, my rudder's frozen up and I can't turn very well. Could you alert the tower and tell them I'm going to try and make the field? I'd like a straight-in approach from the west, in about – Ah, seven minutes? I'm just a flying ice-cube, so it will be a flapless landing and wherever I can dump it down. I'll need a bit of room, so are there any choppers messing about? Oh, and what's the wind? Zero-Six.'

'Zero-Six, got all that, I'll make sure the field is clear. Wind is gusting from the northwest, about fifteen knots. See you soon! Four-Niner.'

That is if we can make it. I glance at the outside air temperature and it now shows thirty-three degrees. Not exactly a thawing temperature, but at least we shouldn't accumulate any more ice. The propeller shakes itself free and throws a few more lumps. Nothing changes on the panel, but I sense the aircraft straining for another knot. *Now, if we're where I think we are, Bulford camp should be coming up on my left, about there. Good!* I pound the rudder pedals with my feet, but they are still solid. It's an odd to fly without a rudder. At least the damn thing froze when the ball was in the middle, but it is unnatural not to be able to *feel* the balance. Next I slacken off the throttle friction nut and thump the sliding throttle knob with the palm of my hand. It moves a fraction forward and I tighten-up again. Again nothing shows on the rev-counter or on the ASI, which shows sixty-eight knots, but I sense a minute increase of power. I ease back a touch and immediately the aircraft begins to shudder again. But now I dare not sacrifice one more foot of height. *Come on; Fly!*

We flick over the A303 at 300 feet, just west of where it crosses the Tidworth road and I very gently try a bank to the right to head towards Wallop. It doesn't like that much and the shuddering increases. It seems to ripple in waves around the whole aircraft. But I can do nothing and so try to ignore it until we settle onto the new course. The wind will now be coming directly from behind – and if Guy's estimate of fifteen knots is right, our ground speed is about eighty-five knots. I can't see ahead at all, for the windscreen is opaque covered in God knows how many inches of ice, but if I sit well back, I can get a slight forward angle out of my side window. And there's the railway line, running along its embankment – this must be near where Tristan played with the train. The line is empty, which is just as well; it wouldn't do to have the retired wing commander complaining about being beaten up by a flying ice cube...

We are down to 120 feet, and I cannot keep this aeroplane in the air for much longer.

Shit, shit! And I can't even turn into wind, so when we hit, whatever we hit, it's going to be close on 100 mph. Dare I try some flap? It worked before, it will give more lift, and also slow us up, but it'll increase the drag too, and I dare not risk that. Should have tried it when we had more altitude, but not now. Come on, Fly, I need just another minute!

If I'd been able to see out of the front windshield, I would have seen the hangars of Wallop fast approaching on the skyline. But instead I recognised the clump of trees that bordered the corner of the field where the strip was. Like an errant pigeon the AOP IX had homed in to its favourite stamping ground. *Oh you beauty!*

I lowered the nose and aimed for the boundary.

Our wheels brushed over the hedge and I chopped the power and hauled back as we hit the ground. We cut a swathe through the light snow, running diagonally across the whole field. I just let it go, and hoped it wouldn't ground-loop or nose-over. With the rudder frozen, I couldn't have done much to steer it anyway, even if I had been able to see, which I couldn't. God knows what speed we touched down at, but eventually we slowed and finally came to a halt not far from our dispersal, and two mechanics came running out and took hold of the wings to steer whilst I gingerly taxied the last few remaining yards, and then switched off. Guy arrived, having taxied his aircraft over from the tower, and swung it alongside. We looked at each other through our windows, and in the end I gave him a weak grin and a thumbs-up. Then the door opened amid a shower of ice and it was Mr Summers who unclipped my harness and helped me down.

'Well *done*, Lindbergh!' he said. As usual I was wondering what I had done wrong, and it was good to hear the warmth in his words. As well as Mr Summers, Major Ball was there, walking around the aircraft.

'Call this an aeroplane?' Major Ball said, 'I've never seen anything like it!' and went back to find his camera.

I turned and looked, and stood staring for a long time, as the others had been doing. It was almost unrecognisable, and every surface was covered in a layer of glittering ice, in places three and four inches thick. The two air scoops on either side of the engine cowling, as well as the main air-inlet under the propeller boss were almost completely glazed over, with only a tiny hole left in the centre of each aperture. Another minute? Maybe two? And the engine would have stopped, starved of air.

A Land Rover drew up and I saw it was the CFI, no doubt having been alerted by the tower. He didn't get out, but just sat there, looking at the aircraft. He'd bound to want a post-mortem, but I really couldn't cope with it now. Major Ball came back with his camera and went over to talk to him.

'Come on Lindbergh, and you too, Guy,' Mr Summers said, seizing the opportunity 'let's get you back to the crew room, I think you *both* could do with a coffee...'

I turned away and followed Guy and Mr Summers to the crew-room.

✽ ✽ ✽

That was the last of the snowy weather, and the last week in February had a touch of spring about it. It started well, and we hoped that it would end well, for this was our final week.

Roger and I spent the whole weekend in our room, swotting for the ground school Final Exam. Every subject was to be included, and our programmes showed that the whole of Monday was to be devoted exclusively to the exam. So to be on the safe side we decided to revise everything, starting at the very beginning and methodically working our way through. Which turned out to be an interesting exercise, for in spite of the variety of subjects, many of them slotted nicely together and followed a natural sequence, hitherto unseen. Also by now much of the theory had been backed up by practical knowledge gained from flying, so a lot of it suddenly began to make sense. By Monday morning our buckets were full to the brim, and we took our places in class and scribbled the day away. We would not hear the results until the end of the week, by which time we would be back from Exercise Orbit.

Exercise Orbit was a concentration of practical and tactical flying. Four days and nights in the field, under simulated battle conditions, putting together all that we had learned.

The week became a blur with sortie after sortie calling for all the tasks that could be expected. Every day or night a move to a new field location; CATO in, refuel and CATO out again, off on a photographic sortie. Waylaid on the radio on the way back and diverted for a gunnery shoot, then, switch back to the Squadron net, and could you manage a route reconnaissance, which will take you up into the Welsh hills? Return to find the ALG has gone and there had been another move whilst you'd been away. Fuel really low now, should I try to find the new position, or fly to the nearest RAF station and refuel first? You're on your own; no longer a student, but suddenly an army pilot, so do as you really would.

We landed back at Wallop at last light on Friday, and slept for most of the weekend. There was no ground school on Monday, so Guy and I had a leisurely breakfast, where we fleetingly bumped into Tristan, and learned that he was still with us, having talked his way out of the train-rocking incident, and then we strolled down to the crew room.

'And where have you two been?' Sergeant Bateman wanted to know. 'The course doesn't end while Wednesday, so go and get changed. Happen an hour on't strip won't come amiss... Sergeant Barker's already there...'

So we found an aircraft each, and joined Sergeant Barker in some strip bashing. We placed a handkerchief ten paces in, and ran the book to see if we could land with our starboard wheel on it, which being on the offside made it difficult to see. As usual Sergeant Barker won the kitty, but it was a near run thing.

Major Ball asked me into his office for a chat in the afternoon, and he told me I had passed the course, and would I like to go and fly Austers in Malaya, or Austers in Kenya, or stay at Wallop and do a Beaver conversion course? And to let him know by Wednesday? That was quite a difficult choice to make, for Austers in Malaya would mean going on to Borneo where there was a war going on, and Austers in Kenya would be terrific fun, and was considered to be one of the peach postings. Or to spend a further two months at

Wallop on a Beaver conversion course also appealed, as well as being a feather in my cap, for there was a queue of Auster pilots waiting to convert to the Beaver, and only the best were chosen – and hardly ever a student fresh off the course. He then asked me if I would fly to RAF Manston in the morning to deliver an urgent package containing some spares for a Scout that had been stranded there, and then to be here at 10 o'clock on Wednesday morning when we would be presented with our wings.

Roger too had heard that he had passed, and that evening told me he was going to fly Scouts in Aden. But he also told me that on the helicopter side, three more had been RTU'd within the last two weeks. From the eight that had started, two failed the basic rotary conversion, and the last three had failed the final ground school exam. These three had been placed on review and told that they would be re-assessed during Exercise Orbit; but none had done sufficiently well for this to be rescinded.

So there were only six of us on parade on Wednesday morning.

Chapter 5

Nothing seems to be happening. They've obviously got bored with turning the Beaver into a colander, and there hasn't been a shot for about three minutes. At least it stops us from firing back, for we haven't got much ammunition to spare – especially the RSM who has been chattering away with my SMG. I roll back onto my stomach and check the number of 9mm rounds in the box that the RSM had given me. There are twenty-five, plus a fully charged magazine. Also I have another seven flares left for the Very pistol. Enough to hold them off for a time if they attacked, and a lot would depend on how much ammunition they were carrying.

What I ought to do is to crawl back to the Beaver and see if the army radio is still working. If there's a patrol on the way, they'd bound to be listening on the Brigade net, and also if Roger were still about, he'd be listening-out too. But I'm not feeling very brave at the moment, and anyway the batteries are probably shot to hell. The door to the battery compartment on the port side is conveniently marked with a white square in the middle, which would have made a perfect bull's eye for them to aim at, especially as most of them are in the rocks on that side...

Best to keep our heads down and wait it out... and I bet those Air Traffic boys aren't discussing their fishing right now! With any luck they're trying to persuade the RAF Belvedere crew to off-load and fly a search and rescue mission. Ho ho! – I can just imagine it, with the Belvedere pilots in a quandary because they aren't authorized! That's probably it! Most likely they think they're still running an airline, rather than supporting troops on active service. Avoid any issue that may mess up their safety record on the number of accident-free miles they have flown! Still, it's not their fault, and I shouldn't blame them, for the pilots can only fly to their rules.

Although not their fault, the RAF pilots are severely restricted by the policy of their Service. This being an operational theatre, the army – as well as the navy when a warship is in the vicinity, are based on a wartime footing; but for some reason the RAF still seem to be hampered by the rules of peacetime accounting. Or at any rate we assume this must be the case, for in most instances their restrictions make for gross operational inflexibility. As army aviators, we are governed by the same set of RAF rules and paperwork; but here the difference ends for as an army officer one is expected to know what is happening on the ground and thus we authorize our own flights according to the tactical requirements. The army tend to regard aeroplanes as 'jeeps that fly', and the Army Air Corps is encouraged to think and behave in this role, thereby ensuring full ground co-operation.

Although our roots stem from the Royal Flying Corps of the First World War, we are still young in our present role – and possibly can be likened to the RAF between the wars, when they too were less rule-bound and their aircraft less technical. Our aircraft and helicopters are relatively simple compared to the heavier and more sophisticated types the RAF now operate, and the pity is, their operating procedures have had to keep pace with the technological advances of their aircraft, and often to the detriment of what the aircraft were actually designed to do. Working by the book, invariably means the RAF pilots have to have their heads firmly inside the cockpit and sometimes we feel they lack awareness of the operational necessity of their mission.

Only last week I listened to an extraordinary exchange on the radio between the pilot of an inbound Belvedere and the Duty Officer on the Brigade net. The pilot identified himself and said he was authorized to drop stores and ammunition at a grid reference – this being the mountain top location of a section of infantry who could only be supplied by air. The Duty Officer explained that the section had moved forward *during the night and could now be found at grid reference so and so, being the next mountain top in the range and they had marked the DZ and were ready to put down smoke. The pilot replied that he was not authorized to extend his flight and would drop the stores on the original position. Which is exactly what he did, and then returned home, mission accomplished. No doubt had he crashed or had some mishap at the new location, being unauthorised it could have been the end of his career; but the real fault lay with the system, and the RAF rulebook which, when followed to the letter could result in such appalling action. I later learned that the pilot concerned was the squadron commander, and when the issue was questioned by Brigade, his Service fully backed him and justified his decision. So what chance of initiative, from their younger pilots?*

The CFI at Wallop certainly tried to impose those same rules... Like the time I addressed him as Wing Commander and he told me to call him Sir! Tristan told me he'd done exactly the same on his Final Handling, and had got a dressing down for it! Only being Tristan he'd taken it a step further, and with wide eyed innocence had said 'Oh excuse me! Have I got it wrong? You ARE a wing commander aren't you? The same as a half-colonel? Oh thank goodness! I thought for a moment I'd made a gaffe...' to which there had been no answer, so he'd gone on calling him Wing Commander! And as he said afterwards, 'the ruddy man IS living with the cavalry, so he ought to TRY to learn how we behave'.

Then there was that other time – when I landed that Auster covered in ice, and he'd driven over in a Land Rover. And how he hadn't said a word to me at the time, and had waited until after the enquiry, in case he'd jeopardize his position. Major Ball was furious and had told me later that the only concern the CFI had had was to ask why it had been ALLOWED to happen? And had I been authorized to fly? Because there COULD have been an accident, and then it would have been his responsibility!

I didn't think much of him for that.

Long after the enquiry – about the time I was ready to leave for Aden, I was with Tristan in the Mess, and we bumped into him at the bar. He'd said that with the enquiry over, he could now talk to me and that he thought I'd done a good job to get that Auster home...

I remember saying something like 'Wing Commander, you may be responsible for overall safety here, but I would have thought your responsibilities would also have extended to pilots and particularly to student morale?' And he'd just snorted and turned on his heel and walked out. Much to Tristan's amusement, who couldn't resist baiting him at every opportunity. He left soon after that, and I never met the new CFI, but Tristan wrote and said that he was a totally different person and fitted in much better. Whatever that meant... But it was lucky Tristan had the new CFI for his Final Handling on the AOP IX, for as always seems to happen, he was by that time a marked man!

God there was some snow that last winter at Wallop. From November right through to February, it seemed to snow on and off just about every day! It would be nice to see some of it here; it would be really good to wake up to a fresh frosty morning, instead of this perpetual heat and humidity...

Hello! Something's moving out there. Was that someone darting behind that rock? There he goes again! He's well out of pistol range, but I wonder if the Very gun would give him a fright? At least it would deter him from coming any nearer, for he's obviously trying to work round and outflank my position. I wonder if any of the others have seen him? So, if that's what you're trying to do, you'll probably make for those rocks there next...

I load another flare into the pistol, and then steady the blunt barrel onto where I think he'll appear next. The sweat keeps dripping into my eyes, and there's a thirsty fly that won't leave me alone...

There!

The gun coughs in my hand, and a red flare streams out and bounces off the ground, and then rebounds up and into his chest. He screams, as the flare, still halfway through its burn, seems to attach itself to his body and instantly sets his clothes alight. He twists away, trying to shake it off and then turns and runs back towards the main outcrop behind the Beaver. The SMG chatters over from my right, and spurts of dust follow his feet as he runs, and then he is hidden again. I want to be sick. Did I really do that? It was though he was doused in petrol, for he was a mass of flames as he ran, and I can still see a whisper of smoke coming up from behind his position. And he is still screaming, a high-pitched keening, on and on, almost like an animal.

'Nice-one, sir!' That was the RSM. I still want to gag, and can think of nothing to say. 'Secret weapon! That'll make the bastards think twice...'

'Watch your front!' The colonel shouted, 'I think they're about to attack...'

I eject the spent cartridge from the pistol and load another flare, and then peer ahead again. They are up, a whole line of them running forward in a ragged attack, mouths open, screaming as all infantry are taught to do in the attack, and have done throughout the ages. It's supposed to put fear into the enemy, and I must say, it works. Obviously these are not local tribesmen, but trained soldiers. The brunt of the attack is away from me and over to my right, and I am conscious of the penetrating crack-crack-crack of the high velocity SLR on steady fire. That must be the cook doing his stuff. He sounds steady enough... One of them drops, and the rest hesitate for a fraction, and then are rallied on by their leader. I fire another flare, which passes diagonally across their front and then lodges under a cleft still burning. I'm too far round to get a proper angle.

There is a thump on the ground as the Political Officer lands beside me. His white suit is dishevelled and covered in sand, but his straw hat is still in place.

'I thought it might be safer here...' he says, rolling into position beside me. Then, 'here, give me that pistol; you seem to be managing quite nicely with that flare gun. This is the sort of situation that no longer calls for diplomatic status, and I'll feel happier with a gun...' He checks the magazine with

practised hands, and then takes up the proper stance. 'I used to be a soldier...'

That's just it! I used to be a soldier too. Once you start off down the specialist route, it's so easy to forget. Flying the AOP IX one could never really forget, because its roles were all tactical and you were never very far away from the mainstream activity. But at Wallop, the Beaver was always regarded as something else. It was the largest aircraft the army had and was stuffed full of instruments – all of which had to do with a very different sort of flying; and once you'd mastered it, you were already a step away. The Beavers at Wallop were actually better equipped than most airliners, and consequently those who flew them soon regarded them as just that...

* * *

With wings on my chest, Wallop became a different place.

But it also meant that this large impersonal mess, which had been fine as a temporary measure was now to become my home; for the letter had come telling me that I had been accepted by the Army Air Corps, and that I should change my regimental badges forthwith. Just that. There was no interview, no welcoming committee or anything of that sort; just a slip of paper attached to the official letter informing me who the Corps tailors were so that I could order one of the light-beige uniforms and a new mess kit, together with an estimate for the cost of these items. After the exhilaration of passing the course, it was quite a letdown, and it had been very different when I had first joined my regiment. And when I saw the price of the mess kit, I resolved to make-do with my old regimental one, or at least until such time that it was noticed, and I was ordered to do otherwise...

Or maybe there was more to it than that, and perhaps deep down I still wanted to retain a last link with my regiment – for at heart I felt I still belonged. I had been so occupied with the turmoil of the course, day by day, stepping from one stone to the next, until finally the coveted wings were pinned onto my chest... I had had little time to think of where it was all leading. For a regiment is a family, and no matter where you are or what you are doing, you still belong. And it was only now, with the tailor's estimate in my hand, that the full significance of the step I had taken came to me. The realization hit me like a blow. Utmost in my mind was the incongruous thought that I had never been dined-out properly, and because of that, all my friends would think that at sometime or another I would be back. Sure, I could always go and visit them – but it would never be the same, for I would no longer be one of them.

Carefully I placed my badges and regimental fore-and-aft dress cap into a box, where they were to remain forever more.

But there were compensations. The Mess sergeant said I could now park my car at the front of the mess; the sentries suddenly started to salute me at the gate, and best of all, the day I walked passed Elementary Flight and Mr Avery came out and stopped for a chat, during the course of which he said 'Oh, and by the way, my name's Bill!' Now I knew I really belonged! But even that came too late. Sometimes when I'm flying he still comes to me, but he always comes as Mr Avery... for some things cannot change.

Also, Wallop seemed empty without the rest of the course, although we had ended up with only six. Guy went off on long leave prior to being posted to Malaya; Sergeant Bateman somehow got reclaimed by the REME, and went to the workshops in Detmold where he was to have a joint role, primarily as an aircraft engineer, but with the dubious responsibility of being able to test-fly the finished products. But most of all I missed Roger and room six, for now someone else occupied our room, and I had been elevated to a single-officer's room in one of the wings of the main building.

Roger had been posted to 653 Squadron in Aden, where for some time there had been unrest and some local skirmishing in the Radfan – which was the mountainous area between the coast and the Rub'al-Khali desert or Empty

Quarter. Now we had formerly taken sides, and the whole thing was fast developing into a war. The helicopter flight in Aden was in the process of being equipped with Scouts to replace their Allouettes, which had been found to be not powerful enough for the hot and high conditions of the interior.

Meanwhile, I had elected to stay at Wallop to be initiated into the mysterious ranks of the Beaver pilots. They were a race apart, and you could spot one a mile off. Their badge of office was a bulging flight bag, which contained strange green and blue coloured charts that were best understood when consulted with the aid of a fancy flight computer. These computers could only be obtained through some airline or other and were vastly superior as well as far more complicated to use than the service-issue sort, which were mere 'toys' by comparison. Of course Beaver pilots didn't look the same, for no two aviators ever do, but there was something... an air of aloofness about them, as though they were removed from other earthlings, and they all had that same faraway look in their eyes. Also they talked their own language, which nobody else could understand.

And neither could I, on that first windy March morning.

It must have been blowing thirty knots or so, and enough to have blown an un-tethered AOP IX away, but the Beaver just sat there on the concrete pad outside the hangar, unaffected by the gale. I stood and looked at it for a long while, indifferent to the wind that was channelling around the corner of the hangar and beating against my flying suit, making the emergency-knife (which I had yet to take out from its sheath) bang against my leg. Of course I had seen plenty of Beavers whilst I had been at Wallop, but I had always coveted them from afar, and never really studied one close to.

The general layout was on the same lines as an Auster: a high wing and a single wing-strut and... but there it ended. She was so much larger, with a wingspan of forty-eight feet and standing over ten feet high, as well as being some ten feet longer than the Auster. Most aircraft of this size would have two engines, but she had a stubby round nose, which moulded round in just the right shape to contain the single 450 hp Pratt and Whitney radial engine. From the centre of this protruded a large aerodynamic propeller boss, which made the whole of the business end look extremely purposeful. At the rear of the aircraft the tail fin swept up in a graceful curve from the tapered box fuselage, which somehow balanced the whole effect, and it couldn't have been any other way.

There were two small doors for the pilot and co-pilot, with steps on the undercarriage legs to climb up to them. Then, aft of the wing-struts were two large passenger doors which had trapezium-shaped windows, and behind these two porthole windows set into the fuselage. Not much attention had been given to streamlining for there were aerials and chunky protrusions everywhere you looked, as well as two fixed steps hanging down under the passenger doors for easy access. Inside, behind the cockpit seats were two passenger seats and then behind those a folding bench-seat arrangement, which would seat another two or maybe three

De Havilland Beaver. '...She had a stubby round nose, which moulded round in just the right shape to contain the single 450hp Pratt & Whitney radial engine...She was like a Land Rover...a powerful workhorse, designed for the job of work...' (Courtesy Philip Jarrett)

people at a pinch. Behind and under the bench seat was a space for luggage. By pulling a little knob the seats could quickly be removed, which left the interior as a cavernous box for cargo.

I don't suppose many people would call her a pretty aeroplane, for everything about her was large and chunky and designed with practicability in mind. She was like a Land Rover in that way – a powerful workhorse designed for a specific role.

I thought she was pretty – but then she was my sort of aeroplane, and I couldn't wait to fly her!

'Is she *calling* to you?'

I didn't need to turn round. 'Oh yes!' I said.

'Well, let me show you around, and then we'll see if we can make it *go*...' Mr Summers said.

The first thing I noticed on clambering up the steps into the pilot's seat ('No, no, please you sit on the left, I'll just come along for the ride...') was the control column. It was an enormous Y affair, which grew out of the floor in front of the two pilot's seats, on the end of each appendage was a half-wheel, which the Americans call a 'cow's horn'. The whole column was hinged to rock forward and back, and both wheels were connected to each other and turned through a 180-degree arc. On the tips of the horns were various buttons, on the left a two-way switch, which you clicked one way to talk externally on the radio, or the other way to talk internally to whoever was plugged in. The right hand horn had a red button encased within a guard, and was the bomb-release button – which I would learn all about in due course.

The six flying instruments, grouped in their usual T directly in front of the pilot I recognized, but not a lot else. Also there was a stranger tucked away in the corner of the flight instrument panel labelled 'homer'. This consisted of a vertical needle, pinned at the top so that it swung like a pendulum through graduations on either side. This, Mr Summers told me, was called Green Salad, and it was very simple as well as being extremely useful. If somebody called you on the radio – whichever radio you were using and there were four of them, the needle would swing to the side the transmission was coming from. Just that! So if you were on Wallop Approach frequency, all you had to do was to ask them for a long transmission and then steer the aeroplane towards the side the needle was pointing until it centred, and then follow the needle home. More important was the tactical significance, for it would home just the same into an army set transmitting from somebody's backpack.

He then showed me the location of the radios. There were two 360 channel VHF's on top of each other; an HF set, which was in the roof, with an adjoining panel containing a switch for the electric motor that let a trailing aerial wire out, together with a meter, which showed when you had the optimum tuning. Finally there was the army radio, and the only place they could find room for that was between the seats. To monitor all the radios there was a selection panel set into the port wing-root. At first sight, just to look at this was enough to put you off, but in fact turned out to be quite easy to use, and if you wanted, you could run all four radios at once and route them to four different headsets, or any other combination you chose.

'But look, instead of *darting* about all over the cockpit, lets run through the pre-start drill, and that will cover most things as well as running in a *logical* pattern. It may look complicated at first, but this is a serious aeroplane and as such needs all these instruments. Also the Pratt and Whitney is an old-fashioned engine and they always did have a *plethora* of manual pumps and levers, and these alone take up most of the room. If you use your checklist, you won't forget anything. And remember, the more clocks and dials you have, the better you can *diagnose* what's going on. You'll find all the instruments and controls are grouped in their own panels, and once you know where the panel is, you'll be able to find the right switch...'

We started on the far right of the facia where there was a circuit breaker panel containing twelve switches, which all had to be up. Then to an electrical-switch panel, which contained an ammeter, a voltmeter, the generator switch, the bomb-master switch and the navigation light switch; and then underneath eighteen round fuse holders all neatly labelled. Our fingers then swept to the centre of the fascia, at the top of which was an ADF neatly built in, and directly underneath, three magnificent levers in a row. The right-hand one had a red knob and was the mixture control and fuel cut-off, the centre one had a yellow knurled knob and was the lever to control the propeller revolutions, and the left one had a round yellow knob and was the boost lever.

By way of explanation, Mr Summers told me the engine was supercharged, and you couldn't just wack the throttle open as I had been used to, but could only open it to a maximum of twenty-eight inches of manifold pressure, else you would blow the cylinder heads off. As you gained altitude, so the air pressure decreased, and you could then gradually increase the throttle opening to keep the needle up to the mark, until you finally reached 'full-throttle' height, which was normally about 9000 feet.

Likewise, he explained the middle knob, which controlled the propeller revolutions to the constant-speed propeller. When flying, you selected the revolutions best suited for the purpose. Thus if you were in a hurry, you could increase the revolutions – at the expense of greater fuel consumption, or if you wanted to fly for endurance you could reduce them and thereby fly slower, but save fuel. Normal cruise setting was between 1850 and 2200 rpm and your fuel consumption would then be between 18 and 20 gallons per hour. If you set 2000 rpm and pushed the nose down, instead of the engine speeding up, as it would with a fixed-pitch propeller as fitted to the Auster or Chipmunk, the revolutions would remain at 2000 and the propeller would automatically coarsen its pitch to compensate. The reverse happened in a climb, and instead of the engine slowing, the propeller pitch would gradually change to fine, with the revolutions remaining the same.

'It's much the same as a car with an automatic gearbox. If you selected D for drive, and then held the car stationary with the brake on, then you revved the engine to a certain level and kept those revs constant. On releasing the brake the car will accelerate and then work its way up through the gears at its own comfortable pace, and will eventually settle at whatever speed your pre-selected revs will give you.'

Having digested this, we then looked at the gauges on the engine-instrument panel, which was directly below the three levers. There were six in all, set vertically in three pairs, as well as a number of warning lights. The top two were the manifold pressure and the RPM, so you could read them both together. The centre pair of gauges were both divided into three, the one on the left with separate needles for monitoring oil, fuel and engine temperatures, and the one on the right containing three small dials, showing the contents of the three main fuel tanks. The bottom pair of gauges showed the carburettor mixture temperature and the cylinder-head temperature.

'How on earth did we manage to fly an Auster without all these things?' I asked.

'As I said before, it does no harm to *know* what's going on. Flying a jet is easy after one of these; you've only got half the amount of engine instruments to bother about. Anyway, as you've seen the fuel gauges, I suppose I'd better tell you about the rest of the fuel system. The main tanks are in the belly of the aeroplane, and the front and centre tanks hold twenty-seven and a half gallons each, and the rear tank holds twenty. In addition to the main tanks there are also tanks in the wing tips and they hold another thirty-six gallons. There are two selector taps, the one for the main tanks is in front of you, and you simply switch it to front, centre or rear, and the other selector is up here in the starboard wing-root, and this drains the tip tanks. You do it little by little and it drains into the front tank, so first you've got to suck enough out to make room. And keep an eye on the front tank gauge so as not to overfill it. Right, that's explained the fuel, so come on, we're over half way there, and the rest is easy...'

Under the engine-panel was another row of large levers, so placed that they fell to hand without having to look down. There was a fuel and oil shut-off lever, a starter-bush release lever, a fuel wobble-pump lever, the carburettor hot-air control lever and the parking brake, which was an incongruous T shaped knob.

The flaps were controlled by a hydraulic pump with an up and down selector alongside, much the same as the Auster, only located conveniently between the seats and in front of the army radio. The actual flap setting was shown by an indicator-arrow, which moved over graduations marked in degrees, and was located on the top of the facia, along with a lot of other warning lights.

Up to now we had studiously ignored a totally alien panel situated directly in front of the co-pilot, which consisted of four multi-coloured dials, together with a roll of grid paper and an automatic marker, much like a barograph. This, Mr Summers told me was the Decca navigator, and was worked in conjunction with another panel in the roof, but he wasn't going to explain it now, for we had already spent the best part of forty minutes, and hadn't even started the engine yet!

So we skipped that, which led us to the trim wheels, which were also in the roof. As well as an elevator trim, there was a rudder trim, which was necessary on this aircraft to counter the considerable amount of torque put out by the engine. The roof also housed the bomb-aiming and selector panel. This was a panel with four switches – inner and outer left, and the same for the right, and each turned its own light on to show when it was armed. Underneath were four more release switches under guards, which you could either operate from here, or more conveniently transfer to the little red button on the control wheel. There were two bomb racks under each wing. They could either carry explosive bombs, but were more usually put to use to carry external containers, which could be jettisoned, or good old jerrycans, four strapped together in a bundle with a parachute. Each rack could carry one bundle of four jerrycans containing fuel or water, which the pilot could then release all together, or one at a time without having to use the services of a dispatcher.

By this time we'd worked from the back of the roof to the front, and were now just above the split windscreen, where there was a good old-fashioned roof-mounted compass with a graduation ring you could turn and a mirror, which you could angle down so both pilots could use it. I was pleased to see this, for here was an old friend and I had been dreading to find one of those small wobbly compasses that swim in a glass globe and only show one degree at a time, which the Americans and French seem to favour in their light aircraft.

Which then brought us to the starting-panel, directly in front of the pilot and under the flight-instrument panel. This contained the battery-master switch, the ignition switch for the magnetos, the three switches used for starting, and then another row of ancillary switches for landing lights, anti-collision lights, cabin lights, radio lights, emergency lights, downward-ident light, engine and flight-instrument dimmers and most important, a large stopwatch, just where it should be. There still seemed to be the odd handle and light that we had missed, but by this time Mr Summers was impatient to start, and said I'd have to familiarize the rest myself, using Pilot's Notes.

With the aid of the flip chart the engine started, and then by pressing down on the toe-brakes and pushing the small T handle, we were free to roll.

'This is the best *bush* aeroplane in the world' Mr Summers was saying, as I got the feel of taxiing. The tail wheel steered with the rudder pedals, and the aircraft just ignored the thirty-knot crosswind. 'So God knows why the army insist on treating it as though it was an *airliner*. Sure it's got all the bells and whistles, and most of the conversion course will be spent flying on the airways, but frankly we're an *embarrassment* up there trundling along at 120 knots. Her place is *away* from airways – she's just as happy on skis, or floats – and I've seen them in Canada with canoes strapped to the floats... Yes, first and foremost she's designed as a *bush aircraft*, and there is *nothing* in the Beaver, which is not essential for reliable performance of hard work. So try and remember that, and don't join those other spoofs who go around with flight-calculators hanging out of their top pockets and talking Decca jargon to each other...

'You're going to *love* her, because this aeroplane can really *fly*... You enjoyed the AOP IX – well she'll do everything an AOP IX can and then a whole lot more besides. Just *listen* to that engine!'

We took our time going through the pre-takeoff checks, and then when he was sure I understood about the propeller revs, and how not to over-boost the engine, I lined up and with the palm of my hand covering all three levers, advanced the left one with the heel of my thumb and watched the boost gauge creep up to twenty-eight inches. The noise was wonderful! Compared to the other aircraft I had flown, the power was enormous with acceleration to match, and before I knew it we were airborne! You didn't have to do anything with the control column; she just seemed to gather herself and fly. I decreased the RPM to 2000 and brought the boost back to twenty-four inches and then pumped up the flaps. We left the circuit and I did a few tight turns to get the feel of her, and then rejoined downwind and set up for landing. We flew down the approach as though on tramlines, and then, again with hardly any movement of the control column, she just landed herself. She was the easiest and most docile aeroplane anyone could ever wish to fly.

'Told you you'd like her' Mr Summers said. 'I'd just like to show you her party trick – if I may?'

'You have control,' I said.

We taxied back and swung round into wind again. 'I'll just show you her short takeoff and how to climb an obstacle... Ten degrees of flap and stand her on the brakes and fire-up. Now, let her roll and watch your speed... Forty-five knots, and haul back smartly! The tail wheel will thump the ground – there! Feel it? And she'll now lift-off in her own propeller blast! Hold the speed at forty-five, and pray you don't have an engine failure...'

The takeoff run had taken less runway than an AOP IX, even though we were three times the weight, and now the Beaver was standing on its tail, virtually going straight up, with the engine bellowing in fine pitch. I couldn't believe it, and watched the altimeter jump up to sixty feet. Then it slowed and we just hung in the sky.

'She won't keep on doing it for ever' Mr Summers was saying, 'so don't let the speed drop back, and push forward, quite firmly like this...'

We resumed the normal flying attitude, and just sat, seemingly stationary with the engine still howling and bellowing. Then the propeller started to bite, and without loosing any height the speed gradually increased. At sixty-five knots, Mr Summers eased the propeller and boost levers back and we resumed our normal climb.

'Not bad eh? She'll almost out perform a *helicopter* if you ask her nicely!'

There were only two Beavers available for the conversion course. The war in Borneo was by now in full swing, as also was the war in Aden, which was beginning to look serious. Together they demanded every resource, which in turn had drained all the surplus aircraft from the training pool. Beavers and Scouts were fast replacing the ageing Allouettes and AOP IX's, neither of which were suitable for the hot and high conditions of both these theatres. Especially Aden, which was real Beaver country, and the Flight there needed all the Beavers they could lay their hands on.

The course was to last approximately sixty hours, and the only other member arrived two days later, by which time I had gone solo. Mike Anderson was a major in the Highland Light Infantry and about to start his second flying tour. He had flown AOP V's on his first tour some years previously, and as a result was very rusty. Since we were already out of step, it was decided that Mr Summers would continue to be my instructor, whilst Mike Anderson would follow on at his own pace with Staff-Sergeant Mercer as his instructor.

I soon learnt my way around the cockpit and spent the next three weeks taking the Beaver to all my old haunts, as well as learning to use the bomb racks and adapting to all the other tactical roles. As Mr Summers had foretold, although larger and slightly more ponderous, the Beaver managed to perform these equally as well the AOP IX, but she definitely had her own style, which took a little getting used to. The best thing about her was the enormous amount of power available, and this would always get you out of trouble.

Then I put my maps away and we started to explore the upper-world of the Airways, which used their own charts and reference points and totally ignored topographical features; for up here one could rarely see the ground. We started to use the Decca navigator and were able to follow our progress as a spidery line inked across the chart that rolled through the instrument. We flew from beacon to beacon, reporting our position at each stage, and our world was the cockpit and our place was time and wherever the needles said we were. We would takeoff from Wallop and climb into the overcast, then wait for the appointed time, finally to descend and land at an airfield under an identical overcast; only now we were in Germany. It was a totally different sort of flying, and in spite of being the best bush-aircraft in the world, one that the Beaver was equally at home in.

By this time Mike Anderson had caught up, and we sometimes flew some of the long trips together, taking it in turns to sit in the left-hand seat. I never felt very comfortable with his flying. He was a big man with a bluff manner and treated aeroplanes much as though they were errant horses with a hard mouth. But just as horses are all different, so it is with aeroplanes and some – like the Chipmunk, need firm handling, whilst others are docile and will respond to the merest thought. A jockey or any professional horseman will know instinctively how to treat a horse, and so it should be with a pilot; and the Beaver – the most docile of aeroplanes, did not respond kindly to being kicked and shoved. But how do you tell another pilot this, especially when he has many more hundred hours than you have?

Sharing the confines of a cockpit with someone over a long period of time can often induce an ambience to what I imagine exists between priest and parishioner at a confessional. Although you are sitting only inches apart, you sense rather than see the other pilot, for your head is encased in a 'bonedome', your eyes are ahead on the instruments, and you can only hear each other through the remoteness of your headsets. And it was here I learned about Mike Anderson. Being English, how he had felt out of place in his Highland Regiment, which had made him go flying in the first place. I heard about his experiences flying Austers in Malaya together with his doubts and aspirations. He loved flying, but was innate enough to realize that he was not a very good pilot – and certainly not a natural pilot, and therefore knew his limitations. But having tasted it once, he could not leave it alone, which was why he was leaving his regiment for a second time and chancing his luck with a second tour.

But the confessional only existed when we were aloft, for once on the ground he became a totally different person and it was as if his shared confidences had never happened, or the recipient acknowledged as such. Which, I suppose, is the very reason priests like to remain anonymous.

But mostly I flew with Mr Summers – where the same cockpit ambience served to strengthen and deepen our existing relationship, with the notable difference that our understanding remained constant wherever we happened to be.

'Better wrap up warm tomorrow, because I regret we're going to have to fly with the *doors* off!'

'Whatever for?'

'Parachutists. There's a tattoo going on at Aldershot, and they want to do a free-fall jump.'

There were five of them, so we removed all the passenger seats, and somehow managed to bundle them, together with their parachutes, into the back. We also took the starboard passenger door off, which would enable them to jump straight out. The drop is timed for 1430, so we decide to leave at 1355 which will allow us time to climb to 10000 feet, which is what they need to give them the 'magic minute' of free-fall, as well as to allow some extra time over the target. The only trouble is, there's a solid overcast at 1500 feet. We confer with the jump leader, and he says that if we can guarantee to get them over the target, they will jump through the cloud. Mr Summers lifts an eyebrow, and then says that that should pose no difficulty, and so the matter is settled.

We take off and climb through the overcast, emerging on-top at 5000 feet and continue to climb on track. The wind whistles in, blowing dust everywhere, and it gets colder as we continue up.

'Right, time to put the Decca into bottom-gear' Mr Summers says, producing a large-scale Decca chart of Aldershot and fitting it into the machine. 'Would you mind doing the business in the roof?'

I click the switches to set the decometers to the new co-ordinates, then select the new chain and key, and position the pen on the chart. Then it's a matter of fine-tuning, so switch the receiver to standby, and set the decometer fraction pointers to zero. Receiver back on – check, green light back on, and set the flight log to agree with the decometers, and finally cancel the no-torque warning. The pen on the chart gives a jerk and the roll resumes its turning, only now at high speed. It shows we are just on the edge of Aldershot.

RPM up to 2000, and reduce the boost, whilst feeding in flap, and we're nicely set up at sixty-five knots and at 10000 feet. In the meantime Mr Summers has been twiddling with the army radio between the seats, and then announces that we should be on net with the tattoo controller. I reach up to the selector box and deselect the Air Traffic, and patch into the army frequency. The commentary from the tattoo booms into our ears, and I turn the same knob on the selector panel, which reduces the volume. It is 1420 and we have ten minutes to wait.

The Decca pen now shows us to be over the sports ground, which is our dropping zone. I set up a racecourse pattern and time the legs. The second time round, the pen shows we have drifted to the east, which means there is quite a strong wind at this altitude. I readjust the timing of the legs, and the next time round, manage to keep the drop-zone within the penned circle on the chart.

There is a pause in the commentary, and I jump in and give them a call. There is relief in his voice as he answers, and he tells me to stand-by. Mr Summers has already given the wind information to the jump-leader, and they make ready to go.

The tattoo controller comes back and tells me that he is ready when we are. I wait until we are on the up-wind leg and then give a thumbs-up to the parachute leader. Within seconds they have gone and the aeroplane is empty, and we turn for home.

Mr Summers looks at me and smiles. We are both thinking rather them than us, but neither of us needs to voice the thought.

'Come on, I'm freezing. Let's see how quickly you can get this propeller driven icebox back to Wallop, so we can thaw out? It's occasions like this when I wish we were flying something quicker, like a jet...'

'You couldn't drop parachutists from a jet.'

'Mmm. That's an interesting thought. It's also interesting that RAF students never learn to fly on a propeller driven aircraft any more. They miss out on a whole *concept* of flying by doing that. I suppose what they never know about, they'll never miss – but they do miss an awful lot! "Low and slow" is such a *special* sort of flying it should be included in every pilot's training; you can learn so much about basic flight from it.

'Every *other* person aspiring to become a pilot will learn to fly a light piston-engine training aircraft. And the *extraordinary* thing is, the aircraft themselves have hardly changed since the very beginning! They've shed a wing maybe, and the cockpits are now enclosed, and they've probably grown wheel-spats and a fancy paint-job, but the fundamental dimensions and their operating speeds and ceilings – and in many cases even their engines have hardly changed at all! *And low and slow* means you can operate from small fields and rough pastures, which no jet can ever do. That's what they miss.

'And have you also thought, that since their conception, and within the span of *one person's* lifetime, aircraft have developed almost beyond recognition? It's so *exciting*, if you think about it! In a mere *fraction* of time, aircraft have developed from virtually a powered kite, barely capable of lifting the pilot, to supersonic fighters that are no longer aeroplanes, but fast becoming *weapon systems*; and airliners that are now capable of carrying *hundreds* of people halfway across the world! And just think of what made it possible – the step-by step progression of all those aircraft that came in between..? It's like motorcars from the same era; one could actually *recognize* them by the shape of their wings or fuse-lage; and each made its own distinctive noise!

'The Sopwith Camel of 1916, do you know why it was the most successful fighter of its time? It was because it was so aerodynamically *unstable* it couldn't fly in a straight line, which made it almost impossible to hit! Then all those *pretty* Hawker biplane fighters between the wars... And amongst all this development, there was a whole *era* of airships, until it suddenly came to an end as the result of one disaster, which was fed by *public opinion*! What did the *public* know about them? It's such a *shame*, for with today's technology, I'm sure there would be a place for airships still. Then take the much longer era of the flying boats – some of them the *prettiest* of aeroplanes. The Short Scipios and the Sandringham, and then the Catalina, with its *perfect* plank wing – only for the whole era to come to an end as a result of *saltwater* corrosion! Ships don't corrode, the pity is that technology has always been a step behind, and so often comes too late to save them...'

We are still in a dive at 140 knots and about to enter the cloud. I decide to keep the speed as it is and give Boscombe Radar a call and advise them of our in-flight conditions. But Mr Summers doesn't seem to notice, and is still musing about aeroplanes of long ago. I love it when he opens up like this, for he knows so much about all things aeronautical, and it is almost a privilege to sit next to him on these occasions.

'The DH 89 or Rapide' he was saying, 'that *beautiful* biplane with the tapered wings – and coincidentally of a size and performance not dissimilar to this aeroplane we are now flying, but so *different* in every other way and unmistakably from its own era. Then compare the sheer *beauty* of line of the Spitfire against the *brute force* and ruggedness of some of those US Navy fighters – like the Bearcat and the Corsair? Yet in *spite* of their differences, they all managed to do much the same job. Designers didn't have computers then, and they could develop and expound their own ideas. And do you remember our own ultimate piston engine fighter the Sea Fury? Now *that* was an aeroplane... And then the good old DC 3's and later the DC 6's – and so into the early jets – the Hunters, those *huge* SAC bombers, the Vulcan and of course the beautiful and ill-fated DH Comet... Did you know the pilot's seat in the Comet was exactly the same as fitted into the old Rapide? *Very* uncomfortable, but a beautiful aeroplane nonetheless...

'Each aeroplane was an improvement on the last, and in its time, became the ultimate flying machine... But now all gone,' he sighed, 'save a few cherished *classics* still on display or still flying to remind us when *they* were the Monarch of the Skies...I no longer even bother to look up at an airliner anymore. It will only be climbing up to the nearest jet stream, and it looks and sounds like any other... You know what the computer has done? It's made all aeroplanes into aluminium *tubes*!'

'You could hardly call this one an aluminium tube!'

'Oh you silly man! That's the point I *thought* I was making. This is a *light aircraft* and just as the mouse survived the dinosaur, light aircraft *have* managed to survive, and what's more, they've remained virtually the same.

'You should regard yourself as extremely *fortunate* having the opportunity to fly the last of the army fixed wing aircraft – for their end is in sight, and in a few years helicopters will make them all but redundant. But these aeroplanes, although they are still light aircraft, they are the top of the range; at the ultimate stage of their development – just as the Sea Fury was the *ultimate* piston fighter, before the jets finally took over. And people who fly light aircraft – and we've already established that light aircraft will continue in much the same form as they always have; these pilots would give their *back-teeth* for the opportunity to get their hands on an AOP IX or a Beaver. The army *developed* the AOP IX and adapted the Beaver for their *specialized* role. In real terms this meant fitting the largest possible power plant that would fit into their airframes.

'Take the AOP IX for instance. It looks much the same as its civilian counterpart, and in spite of being fitted with an engine of almost twice the power, its *speed* is still determined by the high-lift, high-drag configuration of its airframe. Only the army's requirement was for an aeroplane that could takeoff and climb fully laden out of a *cabbage patch*, which is why the large engines were fitted – and the army couldn't give a fig about running costs, which is what makes them such fun to fly...

'There are *dozens* of different light aircraft, all with different engines varying between 100 and 140hp, and they will all cruise comfortably at around 120 knots and consume between six and eight gallons per hour. The Beaver cruises at much the same speed, but its 450hp engine will consume between *eighteen* to *twenty* gallons an hour, and up to *forty* gallons an hour in the climb! Which is hardly an economical prospect for any civilian organization, let alone a private owner.'

By now Wallop was in sight, and I joined downwind, slowing my speed to slot in with the Chipmunks, forever going round and round, and joined the queue to land. Mr Summers broke off from his reverie and I realized how fortunate I was, not only to fly an aircraft like the Beaver, but also to have a man like him to teach me.

There was an official looking letter waiting for me in my rack, and with some trepidation I opened it to learn that I was now a captain, and I could put my third pip up.

My first day as a captain was also to be the last

cross-country of the conversion course. We were to go to the French Air Force base near Lyons, flying airways both ways, and Mr Summers would come as a passenger and be there merely to observe. I worked out the route and saw it would take us right through the middle of the Paris Control Zone, so built in a dog-leg to take me to the west of this and then filed a flight-plan. The forecast was not good, but by now this did not matter, for I was a Beaver pilot – although I had still not managed to get hold of one of those nifty flight-calculators, which were only half the size of the issue ones, and fitted so nicely into the top pocket...

The flight went according to plan, and we had lunch with the French and also delivered an official looking package, which we had been asked to drop off with the adjutant, before setting back in the afternoon. Shortly after takeoff I received a call informing me that it was impossible to return by the same route, and would I divert to the east, via Pithiviers, Toussus and Pontoise...? This would now lead me firmly into the Paris Controlled Airspace, and involved a lot of bookwork from the family bible known simply as Jeppesen.

Elrey Jeppesen had been an early American airline pilot for United, in the days when they flew DC 2's and 3's, and had kept a methodical record of all the airfields, beacons, letdown procedures and en-route navigational aids. Somehow his notes had been used as a general pattern and were added to, soon to outstrip the bounds of his United route and eventually to become a worldwide institution for the use of all aviators. The only drawback about Jeppesen was that it now contained so much information it had to be contained in a bulky metal-cased file about seven inches thick, and you also needed to know your way around it. Most aircraft flying airways will have a navigator, or at least a co-pilot to help in such situations, but today I was on my own, and Mr Summers studiously looked out of the window, muttering that I should be thankful for small mercies, because it could have happened at night.

The Paris Control Zone is a jungle of conflicting routes, all of which had to be found, then plotted, together with the distances and frequencies of the numerous beacons. Of all Control Zones, Paris has never been known to be the most helpful, and although English is the universal language used by all aircraft, they insisted in talking to me in French, or in such heavily accented English it made little difference. Once settled on their suggested route to take me through the maze, they gave me another call and said this route would now no longer be possible, and would I re-route again via Bray, Coulommiers and Montidier?

I re-plotted, and noted it would take me even further off my course, and wasn't the whole purpose of flying airways to avoid this sort of thing?

Then they called again, and denied further penetration on the latest route, and gave me yet another combination of beacons to follow. By now I'd had enough of flicking through Jeppesen, good chap though he must have been, and decided to call their tune and so replied 'Negative. Plus tard! It was now impossible for me to divert and I would continue on the route I was on...' This evoked a tirade of voluble French, which was then joined by several other excitable voices, but I kept stubbornly on until I eventually left their airspace, and switched to the more measured and laconic tones of the London Controller.

Mr Summers opened an eye and said 'Well, you seem to have bluffed your way out of that one alright, but in spite of your new awesome rank, I'm not sure if it was the *correct* procedure...' and settled back to finish his nap.

Half way across the Channel Mr. Summers stirred himself and came to life.

'Right, it's time you showed me how *well* you know this aeroplane. We're at 15,000 feet, and according to this chart we've got sixty-five miles to run. I want you to set the boost and RPM to give a gradual descent, and then trim the aircraft to fly hands and feet off, and without touching the controls I want us to be at the circuit height at Wallop on an extended finals to the active runway at a range of two miles.'

'I seem to remember doing just this one night in the AOP IX..?'

'Ah yes, that was a *glorious* night. But then we could see, and also there was an element of *luck* involved. Now we are above a solid overcast and there is no question of luck. This is precision flying and it's for real...'

I radio for clearance to start a descent, and then, thankfully without having to refer to Jeppesen, tune the ADF to the Beacon at Wallop. I then set the figures on my circular computer; distance sixty-five miles, less two for the approach leaves sixty-three miles, at a speed of say, 120 knots, and through a height of 15000 feet. Deduct 800 feet for the circuit-height, which leaves 14200 feet, and that will mean a rate of descent of – turn the computer round, ah, 451 feet per minute, and this other little window shows it will take thirty-one and a half minutes.

So, decrease the boost to 18 inches and reduce the RPM to 1750, and set the pointer of the stopwatch to thirty-two and a half and punch the button. Trim the rudder and centre the ball, and then fine-tune the elevator trim so that the ASI remains steady at 120 knots. Wait for a moment to see if she's balanced, and then take hands and feet off.

We start to fly down the line and then momentarily brush through the tops of the cloud at twelve thousand feet, before becoming totally immersed.

Ten minutes gone on the stopwatch, and we should just about be in range of Wallop. I dial their frequency and give them a call. They come back loud and clear so I give them my ETA and ask for their weather. They confirm the active runway, and tell me the cloud base was last reported at 900 feet. I then have an inspiration and dial the frequency for Boscombe Radar, and tell them my intentions and ask them to monitor my progress.

Mr Summers smiles, but says nothing.

Another eleven minutes and Boscombe Radar call and tell me I am on line for the active runway at Wallop but beneath their estimated glide path, and I should decrease my rate of descent. Also they can no longer guarantee coverage as I am falling off the bottom of their screen.

I am conscious of the grey outside becoming lighter, and

glance up from the instruments just as we break free. We are at 1200 feet. I call Boscombe and tell them we are VFR and thank them for their help and then reselect the Wallop frequency.

'Decca says you've got five miles to run.' Mr Summers says looking at the chart. 'Let's see, 1200 feet, which leaves another 400 feet to descend to circuit height. Say another minute, in which time you'll travel two miles, which will leave you three miles on the approach instead of two! Still, not bad. How did you know what boost and RPM to set?'

'I didn't – I guessed... it just sort of *felt* right.'

'Mmm. Good, I'm glad you said that. It's all to do with feel. If we'd had a full load of passengers and fuel, the settings would have been different – but not by much. I usually keep 1800 RPM on – but I can't give you a reason why. There's a chart somewhere which gives all the settings against weights, but really it's all to do with feel... like so much else is in flying. Anyway, keep setting yourself these little tasks and learn to enjoy the mathematics of flying. To hit something like that, dead on, and not having touched the controls from 15000 feet, should give you far more satisfaction than hare-arsing around the *pylons* at nought feet with all the other monkeys. And I'm glad you involved Boscombe to monitor the descent. Always use every available service; that's what they're there for.'

That was the last time we flew together.

The following day I had my Final Handling test for the conversion course and then was told I could have a month's leave before flying out to Aden. I totalled my logbook before leaving Wallop and found I had 54 hours and 16 minutes on the Beaver, and an overall total of 253 hours and 50 minutes.

Then one day Tristan rang me at home and told me that Guy had had a car crash on the day before he was due to leave for the Far East. He was in a London hospital and alive, but only just, and they didn't think he would ever fly again.

Two days later Tristan rang again, and said Mr Summers had been killed. A student had been flying and they'd hit some wires when low flying.

Chapter 6

*The SMG stops them. That RSM Fowler certainly knows his
stuff. The leader tries to rally them, but the élan of the attack
has evaporated, and they turn and run back to the rocks,
leaving their one casualty lying face down in the sand.*

*'Is everyone okay?' the colonel shouts. We all answer in
turn, and nobody has been hit. Then, 'I don't think they'll
try another frontal attack, and will probably try to work our
flanks, so keep a good look out.'*

*The Political Officer – once more thinking like a soldier,
decides more coverage is needed on the left flank. He makes
off at a crouching run, taking my pistol and the box of 9mm
ammunition with him, leaving me with only the flare pistol.
Still, it's proved to be pretty effective up to now...*

*Two shots crack out from up in the hills and away to the
right. Surely that's a SLR? Only they make that distinctive
high velocity crack, I wonder..? There! Isn't that a soldier
standing on a rock waving his arms, and I can just see a
Land Rover behind him. Thank God! It must be one of the
fighting patrols that Air Traffic told me about. I don't know
how they think they can get a Land Rover down there, for
there's no track; and it'll take them a good half-hour to get
here on foot, but at least they're on the way.*

*But more to the point, our friends behind the rocks will
now know help is on the way, so I wonder if that will effect
their tactics? What options do they have? Assuming the situation remains status quo for the next thirty minutes, they
could either attack again straight away – and hope that our
ammunition is nearly spent, or they could move to outflank
us and then attack from another direction, say, in about ten
or fifteen minutes time. Then it's possible they may think of*

taking on the patrol – and the best way to do that would be to ambush them. Or, they could cut their losses and just melt away. Personally I'd be quite happy if they did just that, but that's not being very responsible... After all they are the very reason we're here – and they're an elusive enemy, trained in guerrilla tactics, and it's a relatively rare occurrence to have a positive contact, like we have now. Anyway, so far as it effects our immediate situation, I think I go along with the colonel's appreciation, and assume they'll try to outflank us. I daresay he worked all that out even before I began to think about it! Ah well, each to his own... I don't suppose he'd be very good at flying through the Paris Control Zone...

God, it's hot in this valley – I feel as though I'm burning up.

* * *

That was the first thing that hit me, when I arrived in Aden. The door of the aeroplane opened and the heat just seared in, like a bush fire, burning up the air-conditioned cabin, so much that it took your breath away and you wondered how anybody could live in such heat? Mind you, it was mid June, which is the hottest month. June 10th – a year exactly from when I had my first air-experience trip with Mr Avery in the Chipmunk; and a year since I first met Roger in room six.

I remember waiting for my bags outside the Customs Hall, and looking around to see if the Squadron had sent any transport for me; and suddenly, there was old Roger, large as life, picking up my bags. He was in uniform, and although all the other military were milling about in short-sleeved khaki-drill tunic and shorts, he was wearing a cream shirt with a pair of wings pinned above the breast pocket, and long beige corduroy trousers. He was also wearing a pair of sand-coloured desert boots and he told me that this was the rig the Squadron had adopted for working-dress, and they did not fly in flying-suits. And it was no ordinary transport he had either, for he had a Scout on the pad and we were going to travel in style!

The Squadron, he told me, was based at Falaise, which was at Little Aden and a few miles northwest of Aden itself. BP had established a community there surrounded by a tank farm that stored crude oil. From there it was pumped into tankers and shipped away to be refined elsewhere.

We flew over the tank farm, row upon row of large silver tanks shimmering in the heat, and then on a few miles further to the camp complex, where he told me we shared living quarters and messed with the 16/5th Lancers, who were on a one-year tour of duty, which was due to end in about three months time, when they would be relieved by the 10th Hussars. The airfield was to the north of the camp, and comprised of three runways set in a triangle, which appeared to be only slightly larger than the strips at Wallop.

'You'll find it's home from home here, partner, because we're in a hut just like room six! I've put you in with me, but it'll only be for a few months, for there's a brand new mess being built, which will be quite something when it's finished!'

The next few days went by in a whirl.

The Squadron's normal routine was to start work just after first light, and work through to about one o'clock, and then take the rest of the afternoon off. Which was handy, because the next day Roger borrowed a car and we drove into Aden in the heat of the afternoon. What had taken only a few minutes by air took about an hour in the car – a long dusty road that eventually led across a causeway and skirted the aerodrome at Khormaksar where I had landed, and then continued into the town.

We parked in a back street outside the door of an Indian tailor, who having measured me, said he could fit me up with some uniforms if we called back at about eight o'clock that evening. The white Mess Dress tunic together with a white dinner jacket would take a bit longer and would be ready in about two days time! I also bought some casual shirts and shorts, and changed into them in the shop.

We then drove to a large modern garage, which looked totally incongruous in that quarter of the town. There were white flat-roofed Arab buildings on each side, and the road outside was heaped with piles of cardboard boxes, which seemed to be the staple diet for numerous goats. The only other traffic seemed to be camels pulling rickety carts, or the occasional old lorry draped all over with colourful blankets, to keep off the heat.

Roger said he'd had his eye on a Mini Minor, and thought it would be a good idea if we bought this together and shared the running costs. It was sandblasted nearly silver, but the engine sounded okay and it only had about 30,000 miles on the clock. So after the requisite amount of haggling we bought it, and then drove the two cars to the Club at Steamer Point, where we lazed on the beach, and caught up with the last three months.

I told him I had been to see Guy in hospital, and how he had been swathed all over in bandages, and how it had been like talking to a mummy. He'd broken just about every bone in his body and was lucky to be alive. Other than that, it was still too early for the doctors to be able to tell what the permanent damage was likely to be, but in any event he would never be able to pass another flying medical.

I then told him about Mr Summers' funeral. How packed the church had been, mostly with people from Wallop, the majority of whom would have hardly known him – or at least would never have never flown with him, and how I had only managed to find a seat at the very back. I told him about his widow, whom I had never met. How frail she had looked; yet what poise she had possessed, standing between her two daughters, both in their teens, and how like Mr Summers the younger one had looked, with every move and gesture the same. The final hymn had been Onward Christian Soldiers, which had been his favourite, but that had been too much for me and I'd cracked-up and could not utter the words, but only gulp. After the service they were all going on some-where, but I'd felt I could not face any more and just wanted to slip away. Then, how by chance, I had come face to face with his widow just as I was leaving; and I'd mumbled some-thing, and she had said 'Which one are you?'

'Sometimes he called me Lindbergh' I had said.

'Ah yes,' she'd said, ' he often talked about you. You were very special...' We had both looked at each other, she searching my face, and then she had smiled. And we had both understood.

It was good to be able to talk to Roger again, for I hadn't enjoyed my leave very much, and had felt very much away from it all. Now that I was here I couldn't wait to get into harness and asked Roger all about the Squadron.

He told me 653 Squadron administered three flights, but at the moment only two were based at Falaise. These were 15 Liaison Flight, which exclusively operated Beavers and 13 Recce Flight, which had just changed over to Scouts, but also still operated a few AOP IX's. The other Flight was 8 Independent Recce Flight and was based in Kenya. They operated a mixture of Allouettes, Beavers and AOP IX's, but they were due to re-equip with Scouts, after which the rotary element of the Flight would come over and join us here. Also 653 Squadron was about to change its nomenclature and be re-designated as 3 Wing AAC.

The Scouts, he told me, had at first given a lot of teething troubles, which had left the Beavers with the brunt of the work, and the Beaver pilots were averaging over 1000 hours a year. The AOP IX's were just not powerful enough for the climate, and in order to fly without overheating had had to be modified with an extra oil cooler stuck on the outside of the engine cowling.

'What about the tactical situation?' I asked.

'God knows, it's just a muddle... It's basically tribal and they've been fighting amongst themselves for years. Now it's reached the stage where half of them are being trained and equipped by the eastern block, so in order to stop the slaughter, we thought we'd better step in and support the other half – I suppose it could be likened to a modern version of the old North West Frontier. Anyway, the main war is going on in the Radfan, which is where the Scouts are employed. The Radfan is in the mountainous area halfway between the coast and the Rub'al Khali desert – or the

Empty Quarter. Helicopters come into their own when it comes to supporting troops on the top of mountains. But as well as supporting the Brigade in the Radfan, you'll be flying all over the place because you also support the FRA and they've got out-posts throughout the remainder of the country. We haven't really got the range to go way up-country...'

'FRA – who are they?'

'Federal Regular Army – sort of Arab Levee, made up from tribes all over. They're very good and dead smart – they've been policing the place for years.'

At about six, it suddenly got dark, with hardly any twilight to speak of, so we gathered our things and went in for a drink. The night air was incredibly humid, but the club inside was air-conditioned which made all the difference. I felt very pale amongst all the other bronzed faces. We went back and collected my uniforms at eight, and they fitted perfectly. Roger then showed me some of the nightspots around the town, but it was too early for most of them, so we had a bite to eat in a little restaurant near the airport, and then decided to call it a day and head back.

Besides, I didn't want to be too late, for I was flying in the morning.

* * *

Perhaps it was because Mr Summers was still very much in my thoughts, but when I met my Flight Commander, I couldn't help thinking that he reminded me of him in many ways. There was no physical resemblance; in fact the reverse was the case, but he possessed the same quiet manner and unassuming air, which I immediately found familiar and one that I could associate with.

His name was Arthur Prescott and he was a major of considerable seniority from a respectable county regiment, which had long since lost its identity when it became absorbed into the vast Royal Anglian Regiment. Possibly he had been misplaced during the reshuffle, for he was now on his third flying tour. He was of medium height and stocky, and had not the slightest trace of bearing or turnout expected from a military man. Which was probably why he was still a major. There was evidence of corpulence about his waistline, emphasized by the manner in which he wore his belt – which was so low that his trousers seemed to remain in place without reason. His head was nearly bald and had a large round face that contained two sorrowful eyes, which he had a habit of closing, as though in a prolonged blink, and everything about him would stop until he opened them again. To accompany this he had a mannerism of blowing down his nose, in a sort of 'knuff-knuff' reversed sniff, which emitted a noise not unlike cymbals crashing, and until you got to know him could be somewhat disconcerting.

I had already heard about him from someone I'd met at Wallop, who had told me about Arthur and the propeller.

They were in Malaya flying Auster V's, on the early versions of which there had been a defect to do with the fitting of the propeller boss. On occasions the bolts would shear, allowing the propeller to spin-off into the blue. It needed but a simple modification to cure this, and thereafter there had been no further trouble.

A new pilot joined the Flight, and Arthur, who even then was an old hand, volunteered to fly the new man around and show him the strips. There was only one aircraft available, and inevitably this was the only one that was still waiting to be modified. So they took off and climbed to about 2000 feet, and were flying along over a solid mat of jungle, when after about five minutes there was a bang and a whine and the engine started to scream, prior to revving itself to destruction.

Undismayed, Arthur shut the engine off and trimmed the aircraft to glide.

'Knuff-knuff! Oh dear, oh dear, I think we've lost our propeller. How very annoying. Knuff. I suppose I'd better put out a call...'

There are three sorts of distress calls. If you have an emergency that threatens loss of life – like loosing your one and only propeller over the jungle, you send a Mayday. The next category is a Pan call, and this you give to alert the controller should you have a situation that could develop into a full-blown emergency – for example, a flickering oil gauge: it could either be the gauge that was faulty, which event would be harmless, or it could indicate that the oil pump was about to pack-up and the engine about to seize. Upon receiving a Pan, the controller is immediately alerted and will be ready to activate the mayday procedures should the situation deteriorate. The third category is rarely used, and never in an emergency. It is called the Securité call, and exists for training purposes, or sometimes to test communications.

By the very nature of their profession, pilots are ever reluctant to declare a full-blown emergency – especially when one may not exist, which is the very reason this three-tier system has been devised. It is simple and covers all the eventualities and has been found to work very well.

'Securité, Securité, Securité.' Arthur called in his tired voice. 'Situation: Knuff-knuff, my propeller has fallen off. Intentions: I propose to glide back to the airfield, and execute a dead-stick landing. Factors relating: I may have to knuff, land downwind, and therefore would be grateful if you could relay this to any other aircraft movements you may have. Admin and Logistics: I'll endeavour to land on the grass outside the Control Tower, so it won't be necessary for the knuff, fire engines to leave their shed. Securité, Securité, Securité.'

He had then wheeled-about, and with great dexterity managed to stretch his glide to alight in a perfect dead-stick landing on the patch of grass outside the Tower, just as he had said he would do!

Today, as he had that other time, he was going to show the new pilot the local area and some of the landing strips; and where better place to start than the Radfan? We were in his office, and he made as if to get up from his chair. Then a better idea came to him and he thankfully sank back down again. For here was a man who hated any form of physical exertion, and did not care who knew it. Maybe it was his way of combating the heat, but whenever possible he would remain absolutely still, except for the occasional prolonged lizard-like blink of his eyes. Then, when he had to move, he would flounder to the nearest supporting object, and there he would remain until absolute necessity compelled him to move again.

'Can't seem to find my, knuff-knuff beret. You'll find the Form 700 under the details-board in the corridor. Just sign us out, and then go and pre-flight the aeroplane, and I'll knuff, join you in a minute... Oh and by the way, I've allocated your permanent call sign; it's Five-Zero-One.'

I finished the pre-flight and was about to climb up to the cockpit when he emerged from the small side door of the hanger. He was still without his hat. He paused in the shade of the hangar and frowned at the glaring strip of concrete he had to cross to reach the aeroplane. Rather than a direct line, he elected to sidle along the side of the hangar, where there was still a strip of shade about a foot wide; every crab-like step its own calculated movement. When at the nearest point he made a dash for the aircraft, and heaved his bulk into the right hand seat beside me. I was studying the map, which apart from the sea, was coloured various shades of yellow and brown, and had large areas overprinted with 'Relief Data Unreliable' in red capitals.

'Habilayn – that's the knuff, main airstrip in the Radfan and it's about forty-five minutes due north from here. Just follow the trail of oil – those AOP IX's are still chucking it out. We'll reach the mountains then, and I'll show you the route in. The maps are only good for outline reference. Flying is all about time and distance here. You'll soon get to know the main features and the shapes of all the mountains, and the way the desert lies. The other thing is the wind, and you'll see how it blows off and shapes the dunes. We're in the monsoon here, so it blows from the south in the summer and from the north in the... Knuff-knuff.'

He saw me looking at the large hole in the facia in front of him, where the Decca should have been.

'No Decca chain here, of course. Makes a useful glove compartment to put your beret... I wonder where I did put the damn thing...? Just hope we don't run into Colonel Mike at Habilayn. Never mind, knuff, as I was saying, the only nav-aids we've got are the ADF and Green Salad. There's one ADF beacon at Khormaksar on frequency 218 and that's your lot! The ADF – and also the VHF radios only work when you're south of the main mountain range. Obviously, line of sight. A lot of our flying is in the interior, and once over the mountains, you're on your own.'

'What about the HF set?'

'The Sunair? Knuff, well you can always try it. Sergeant Baker always seems to get through. Over desert, the skip distances are very long, and they vary at different times of the day. You can sometimes raise Nairobi, and they can relay back to Khormaksar, or you can try to raise an Aden Air flight on the Air Traffic – they're always good for a relay...'

'What do they fly?'

'All sorts – including a few old DC 3's; they're the only aircraft that can cope with the rough strips. With a tail wheel they don't pick up the stones with their props. They've tried others, but keep going back to Dakota's. The RAF lent them a couple of Andovers last year, and they wrecked the props on their first takeoff from Ataq. The DC3 and the Beaver are the only two aircraft that keep on going out here – knuff, you'll see...'

As directed, I flew north, and then he showed me the entrance to the Wadi, which we followed until we came to Habilayn, a large north/south strip situated in the centre of the wadi, and surrounded on three sides by a tented camp. There was a Twin Pioneer as well as a Beverley in the circuit, so Arthur told me to overfly, and showed me the current troop positions on the battle map, and then all the other strips in the area, on two of which he asked for a landing.

'Habilayn should be okay now, got to wait for the dust to settle...'

'Dust?'

'Damned Beverleys. There's no need, but they will,

knuff, put them in reverse-pitch when they land, and it blows up a dust cloud to about 1000 feet, and takes half an hour to settle. Always try and beat them in if you can. Unless you want to knuff, land IFR.'

We landed at Habilayn and walked over to the tent that the pilots used as a crew room. There I met my new Commanding Officer, Lieutenant-Colonel Mike Staverton and some of the other helicopter pilots who had flown up that morning. The Scouts could only digest so much sand in their engines and still needed a lot of maintenance backup, which was not available in the field. By careful management they could usually find one to leave at Habilayn overnight together with a duty pilot, and the remainder flew up on an 'as required' basis during the day. There was also one Beaver left on permanent station, on call to the Brigade for operational duties and this was then backed by another Beaver flying one or sometimes two Air Dispatch flights per day, fetching and carrying around the strips and returning to Aden in the evening. Thus two were permanently engaged in the Radfan, leaving the remainder free for the longer liaison flights throughout the rest of the country.

The Colonel then took me across to the Brigade HQ tent where I met the Brigadier and most of his staff – who all

Beverely and Beaver at Habilayn. '...always try and beat them in if you can...'

192

Radfan Country (above and below)

seemed a friendly lot, and I was immediately conscious of a relaxed and professional working atmosphere.

'That was a useful morning' Arthur said on the way back. 'You'll be flying a lot of those people, and it's very impor-

Scount and Twin Pioneer at Habilayn

tant to be part of the team. This is not like soldiering in BAOR or the UK, knuff, and it's important that your face fits. There's no room for incompetence on active service, and if you make a ball's-up, they'll send you home. The Brigadier's sent whole regiments home, and he's got a damn good team about him now...'

I had to fly another thirty hours by way of a 'theatre conversion' course before I was allowed to carry passengers. This took twelve days, during which time I visited the majority of the airstrips, and began to recognize the position and shape of some of the more prominent mountains that stood out from the rest of the range that divided the whole country.

Flying was fine first thing in the morning, for in the quiet air one could see as far as the eye could reach; but by midday the desert air became a turmoil and the sand haze rose to about 5000 feet, reducing visibility to 'straight down', or at best to half a mile. At first I found it unnerving to fly for hours over the desert with only a compass and a stopwatch, and I would catch myself glancing towards Arthur's beret-compartment in the facia where the Decca used to live. I hadn't realized how much I had come to rely upon that little pen, scratching its spidery line across the chart and constantly updating our position to within a few metres.

Used to the pinpoint accuracy required for tactical low flying, together with the precision required for flying airways, this was altogether very different. It required thinking in a much larger perspective and trusting your own judgement – with the knowledge that should you become hopelessly lost, you could always turn south for an hour or so, and eventually you would find the sea...

Many years would pass before I would again find myself flying over similar desert terrain in another type of bush aircraft. Only then I would have a box called a GPS as a companion. Once again this would constantly update and pinpoint my position, only this time it would tell me wherever I happened to be in the world by way of orbiting satellites. The aeroplane had hardly changed at all, but no longer would its roof be filled with dials and switches, nor half its facia filled with coloured gauges and a revolving map; for the complete size of this world-wide navigational system would be portable and able to fit into my pocket.

But for now I had a very good compass, a Direction Indicator which I could set to it and a stopwatch; and it was just a question of brushing up your dead-reckoning and having the confidence to see it through.

Some of the trips I flew with Neville Bamford, who was the QFI, others with Arthur Prescott and through his fascinating insight learned much about the background of the country and also of its people, which time had not changed since man had first learned to live in the desert. Occasionally I flew in the right-hand seat with the other pilots of the Flight, all the time absorbing the routes, and learning their philosophy and approach to this kind of flying. For as Mr Summers had told me all those months ago, the Beaver, first and foremost, was the best bush-aeroplane in the world, and at last I was learning to be a bush pilot.

Arthur Prescott set a demanding pace, for the Flight was desperately short of pilots, and the sooner I could pull my weight the better. Also, Paul Aston's tour was about to expire – which would leave us desperately short again.

I was to fly with Paul on his last long trip, for he was due to leave at the end of the week, by which time Arthur wanted me to have finished my theatre conversion and be qualified to take his place. It had the makings of an interesting sortie, for we were to resupply a party of sappers who were way out in the Empty Quarter doing a survey. Arthur didn't know exactly where they were, but he gave us the general area and said that they would be listening out on their frequency, and hopefully we would be able to home into them using Green Salad.

Before we left, Arthur caught my eye and gave the merest of frowns, which had the effect of standing out like a beacon in his otherwise immobile face. I didn't quite know what to make of it, so I lifted an eyebrow and left it at that.

We took off with a maximum fuel load and four bundles of jerrycans containing water hanging from the bomb racks, and Paul in the left-hand seat. It didn't take long to discover Arthur's warning; for Paul was the roughest pilot I'd ever flown with. I'd thought Mike Anderson on the airways course had been rough, but his was nothing compared to Paul's flying. Maybe it was because Paul was the old hand trying to impress the new pilot, for not only was his handling rough, but his whole attitude was lackadaisical and his actions slapdash. He gave an airborne flight-plan, which just didn't tally, and this doubt was echoed in the voice of the controller at Aden Centre. More worrying was the fact that he didn't seem to notice we were climbing some fifteen degrees to the south of our course, which error was burning precious fuel. We levelled off at flight level nine-zero, and then he reported overhead the Boundary at fifty miles. This was a compulsory reporting point, but he did it according to the time he'd noted on his pad – and the same he'd given on his flight-plan; when

'...ahead the sky took on a yellow hue, heralding the edge of the Empty Quarter...'

even to my inexperienced eyes I could see we were far short of the boundary and still had a considerable distance to travel.

The RPM was still set at 2000 and I waited for him to reduce them and then lean-off the mixture. By my reckoning there would be little enough fuel as it was, especially carrying wing stores, and leaning-off now would make for a considerable saving. But he left the levers alone, and we continued on in the same fast-cruise setting...

We had full wingtip tanks, so during this time we had correctly been using fuel from the front tank, and when it showed nearly empty I pointed a finger to it and offered to flick the transfer tap which was on my side in the wing root by my right shoulder.

'Yes, okay, may as well...' Paul said, and I turned the handle to 'Both' and watched the front tank needle with satisfaction as it started to fill again. Once full, the correct procedure would be to select the rear tank, and thenceforth burn fuel from the three belly tanks from rear to front, thus bringing the centre of gravity forward.

Paul left the fuel selector where it was, and I watched the needle of the front tank start down again.

We crossed the escarpment and the ground leapt up six thousand feet, and with it the knowledge that we were now beyond VHF radio range. After another thirty-five minutes I spotted the ancient town of Khora set like white blobs amongst the mountains, and Arthur had told me this was the landmark to change course to the north to skirt the Yemen border.

We flew on.

Ahead, the sky took on a yellow hue, heralding the edge of the Empty Quarter.

'According to Arthur's last known position, those sappers should be about there.' I pointed on my map. 'Touch to the left, d'you think?'

'Mmm. Might as well...' He jerked the aeroplane round and we headed north. The front tank now showed just under half full. I twisted round and tuned the army radio between the seats. The numbers were upside down for it had been positioned for the captain to use from the left-hand seat. I thought of Mr Summers and how he had done the same for me when we had dropped those parachutists over Aldershot. The dials would have been upside down for him too, and I hadn't thought at the time.

'*Mr Summers, what can I do about this man sitting beside me? I am not at all comfortable, and I suspect he is a monkey...?*'

I set the frequency; maybe it was too soon, but it would be worth a call.

Paul ignored it. It was impossible for me to operate, for the selector box was on his side. *Ah well, perhaps it is too soon to try...*

We reached the beginning of the sands of the Rub'al Khali, ridge after ridge of huge dunes, forever shifting with the wind, seemingly stretching to infinity. What a place to do a survey...

'What course do you think..?' he ventured.

'Well, we're pretty far over to the east now, so I suggest we fly thirty minutes northwest, and then start a bracket search to the west?'

'Yeah, might as well...' He didn't bother with the stop-watch, so I made a note of the time on my pad.

We flew on, boring into the unknown. Half an hour came and went. I left it for another three minutes, and then made a point of looking at my watch.

'Why not give them a call..?'

He ignored me and did nothing for another full minute, eyes fixed firmly ahead. Then, after sufficient pause to have made the point, reached for the selector box and transferred the radios.

Perhaps he's resenting my perpetual interference? Best to leave him alone and just sit it through...

'Holfast Survey, Holfast Survey, this is Army Five-Two-Three, do you read?'

'Army Five-Two-Three, this is Holdfast Survey reading you Fives.' The answer came straight back, clipped and professional. Paul gave me a triumphant look and swung the aircraft to the left, and then asked for a long transmission. I couldn't see the Green Salad from where I was sitting, but he centred the aircraft due west and then asked the sappers to give another call when they could hear our engine.

The needle of the front fuel tank now stood at zero.

'Army Five-Two-Three, we can hear your... in fact we can now see you, you're heading straight for us.'

We both saw them at the same time. Two sand-coloured Land Rovers and a one-ton truck, with what looked like rolled-up track sections spilling out of the back.

The fuel gauge is on zero, and this engine is about to stop...

I casually flicked my finger at the gauge.

'What? Oh, that's alright for a bit...'

He asked the sappers to put down smoke and then armed the bomb panel. Somebody was on the ball down there, for almost immediately there was a red smear, which soon thickened to a dense cloud. He set the RPM and boost for slow flying and then turned and ran into wind with twenty degrees of flap at sixty-five knots.

Why won't he change the fuel tanks? What perverse logic is making him deliberately prove his point? It's becoming like a game of Russian roulette...

We overflew the target and when upwind he released the stores. I saw the parachutes open just before they hit the ground, some 100 paces from the lead Land Rover.

'Nice drop! They're all okay – and thanks, we were running very short'

'Roj. You're welcome – see you next time' Paul replied, and then increased the boost and cleaned the flaps up. The engine responded with its normal bellow, then gave a cough and stopped.

Give him his due, but he was onto it in a flash, although he must have been half expecting it. He twisted the selector to the rear tank, flicked the fuel pump on and then changed hands and wobbled the yellow fuel pump. The propeller was still wind-milling, and after a few turns one cylinder coughed, and then the others caught one at a time, with a lot of spluttering and banging.

He didn't look at me, and I didn't look at him and neither of us said a word.

We flew back in silence... which, after a while became deafening, for what else was there to say?

I saw Arthur next morning and he asked me into his office. Paul was flying the ADS to the Radfan – this, his last sortie before returning to the UK the following day.

'How did you get on yesterday, knuff?' he asked.

'Oh, okay – we managed to find them and deliver the goods.' I wasn't going to elaborate.

'Hmm. You knew Bob Summers, didn't you?'

'Yes – he, ah, *tried* to teach me to fly...'

'Mmm. I saw that in your logbook... but did you know him?'

I looked at him for a long while, matching the stillness of his stare, and then quietly said 'Yes, I believe I knew him.

He influenced my way of thinking a great... and he's still very much a part of me, if you know what I mean. It was almost as if he had his own creed about flying... and, and well, it's such a *terrible* waste...'

'Yes, he effected a *few* people that way. Knuff, me included. He taught me for a period – when I converted over to the Auster IX. I can always tell his disciples by the way they fly... and more to the point, by the way they *think* about flying. More's the pity he knuff, didn't teach Paul to... Ah well! At least Paul has managed to complete his flying tour and he managed it out here. It hasn't always been easy...'

I wondered whether Paul had seen Arthur and had mentioned about the fuel, but I didn't like to ask.

We were interrupted by the telephone.

Arthur answered it, his face immobile and only his mouth moving to utter the occasional grunt. He put the receiver down and stared at the harsh sunlight outside the window for a moment, then looked back at me. 'That was Colonel Mike at Habilayn. Paul has crashed. He was taking off from the strip at Ajra, and hit a down-draught... The Beaver's a write-off, but he and his three passengers all managed to walk out from it. Colonel Mike went up there in a knuff, chopper and has just brought them back to Habilayn...

'So here's what we'd better do. Neville Bamford is waiting to check you out on your final handling. There's only one aircraft, so go and knuff, do that and then get off to Habilayn as soon as you can and finish the remainder of Paul's ADS sortie. Then you can bring him knuff, back with you. We're dining him out in the mess tonight... Can't have him missing that...'

I flew for an hour with the QFI and then after the final landing taxied over to the fuel bowser and asked the ground crew to top up the belly tanks. Arthur sidled out from the hangar and made his way over, dodging from patch to patch of shade. He arrived just as Neville finished his debriefing and was unstrapping his harness. They talked for a moment under the shade of the wing and Neville told him I could now start earning my pay. Then a hastily assembled crash team arrived, and asked for a lift to Ajra so they could assess the damage and take photographs.

'Better not drink too much tonight, I want you to take this aircraft to Habilayn tomorrow at first light, and you'll be the duty aircraft and relieve John Mercer. Knuff, better pack enough kit to stay for about ten days...'

They walked back together, and the four members of the crash team clambered in, and without further ado I took off and headed north for the Radfan.

I went straight to Ajra and landed on the makeshift strip there. At 6500 feet it was one of the highest strips in the area – a flattened-out area on the top of a ridge, marked by four white painted rocks at each corner. At the end of the strip was a valley with a sheer drop of about 400 feet, and then another, slightly higher flat-topped ridge beyond.

Paul had taken off fully laden, and by the time he reached the end of the strip had not gained enough height to avoid the downdraught of rapidly sinking cool air caused by the shade of the valley. He had sunk into the valley and still on full takeoff power and nose high in the climb attitude, had not quite managed to clear the ridge beyond. His tail wheel had caught the edge of the ridge which had smacked the aircraft down, shearing the undercarriage off and shedding a trail of bits, as well as all his fuel from the belly tanks, for a further fifty metres. For some reason, the aircraft did not burn.

It was a very different Paul who climbed into the back of the aircraft when I finally finished going around the strips and was making ready for the flight back to Khormaksar. He'd walked away from the crash without a scratch, but gone was his gung-ho swagger, and he was still very shaken and subdued.

We dined him out that evening, and although I had been in Aden for over two weeks, it was the first time I met most of the 16/5th Lancers and whose mess we shared, for I had spent most of the fortnight either in the air or in my bed. I found it an exhausting climate to work in. Roger was not at the mess night, for he was doing his stint as resident helicopter pilot at Habilayn, where I looked forward to joining him in the morning.

* * *

'Habilayn, Habilayn, this is Army Five Zero-One, good morning!' I called halfway up the wadi, and still self-conscious of my new call sign. Why Arthur had allocated me the zero-one digit I had no idea, for it was usually reserved for commanding officers and once revealed on the air could have startling results. Already I was aware that radio procedures from all the other aircraft flying would suddenly sharpen up, as well as a certain amount of deference from all those who had to reply to me. The downside was that everyone listening was just waiting for you to make a mistake, which I think had been Arthur's little joke in the first place. That, and the fact that he had awarded the revered handle to the most inexperienced pilot in the theatre! Knuff-knuff to you, Arthur, but at least the call sign commanded instant attention!

'Five-Zero-One. Good morning' they said politely, and gave me the altimeter setting and the weather.

I'd already been to Khormaksar on the first leg of the ADS, and every seat was taken. On landing at Habilayn I would hand over to John Mercer who would continue with the ADS before flying back to Aden, whilst I would resume his duties as resident Beaver pilot to the Brigade.

I made my way across to the HQ marquee and the corner where the Operations staff worked. Roger was there talking to the G2, who signalled me over.

'Good, you're here' the G2 said, and handed me a list. 'It's a busy time right now, and we're preparing for a bit of a push. These are your jobs for the day, try and do them in the order we've set out, and remain on frequency in case we need you... Oh, and try to be back here by six and join the Orders Group – we hold one every evening.'

It was a formidable list, a condensation of all the air requisitions from the supporting companies, and put into a rough priority by the G staff. It involved resupply of ammunition and water to various outposts, troop movements, replacement of a generator, a leaflet drop and a number of air reconnaissance requests.

I went to the G3's desk and he updated my battle map, and then I got going.

I flew all day, and time and time again, just when I thought I was getting on nicely with the list, I would receive a radio call that diverted me to another more urgent mission. It was dusk when I finally landed and made my way back to the HQ, where the 'O' Group was already in progress, outside the tent under a kerosene lamp with the Brigadier presiding. All the Teeth Arms were represented – Infantry, Armour, Gunners, Sappers – all at Colonel or Major level, with Roger and I the most junior ranks, representing Air. Tomorrow was to be the big day, and all were given the Plan and their individual Orders for the day. My task, I learned, was to drop water and ammunition by parachute onto set positions – mostly mountaintops, and in a set sequence. I was then to remain airborne and ready to act as Observation Officer and maybe direct artillery fire to cover the advance.

I marked the positions and sequence onto my battle map and saw with concern that during the parachute drops I would be exposed to just about every known enemy position. I had to wait until "Any Questions?" before I could air this.

'Brigadier, from a flying point of view, I would like to reverse some of this sequence for the parachute drops. The wind in the morning will be from the south, and it would be more practicable to approach all these positions from the north – which will give me a far better chance of hitting the targets?'

'No, I want you to do it in the sequence laid out conforming to this Plan.'

'But Brigadier, these targets are just pinpoints; they'd be difficult enough to hit in still air – there'll be about twenty-five knots of wind aloft, and this totally distorted by the mountains, if I could approach...'

'No. Too late to change it all now; just do your best. Any more questions...?'

Takeoff was timed for 0700hrs. We took the rear doors off the Beaver and loaded the stores that were going to be dispatched by Corporal Frazer from the cabin. Then we bundled the jerrycans into fours, and with their parachutes lifted them into place in the bomb-racks under the wings. We had flack jackets to wear – sort of chain-mail affairs over our shirts. I folded two of these and put them under my seat – a forlorn notion to protect my bottom from bullets coming up. God knows why, because they'd have to penetrate the fuel tanks first...

We staggered into the air on time, and I set a wide turning climb to obtain altitude and positioned the aircraft upwind of the first target, and waited.

'Five-Zero-One, are you in position to start your run? Over'. From Brigade.

'Zero-One. Affirmative.'

'Roger. Commence now! Out.'

I took my time in trimming the aircraft properly, and then took my feet off the rudders and curled my legs up under my seat to present as small a target as possible.

Above the noise of the engine I was aware of three slight 'thunks' and looking out saw three small holes in the starboard wing. The bastards really are shooting at us! Already we were in position for the first drop, which would be dispatched from the cabin. I gave Corporal Frazer the nod, and he heaved the bundles out, one after another. The wind wasn't as bad as I'd feared, and the parachutes drifted down and landed not far from the DZ.

The wing drops onto the next three targets were not so good. The targets were smaller and the Plan decreed that I could not drop into wind, which made it almost impossible. It made me very angry, and why had they to interfere in something they knew little about? To recover the water, those troops would have to do a lot of clambering. We remained airborne for the rest of the morning as instructed. It was difficult to determine exactly what was going on, for there was little evidence of a battle, and I was not called upon to direct ground artillery.

I was still angry when I landed, and with Corporal Frazer examined the bullet damage in the starboard wing. Corporal Frazer said he could patch them up, but the point was, it shouldn't have happened in the first place and there had been no need to fly over their positions, all of which were clearly marked on the battle map. I donned my beret and walked determinedly to the HQ marquee.

'Thank God you're safe' the G2 said as I entered, which immediately took the wind from my sails.

'Why did you have to expose me to ground fire, when I could have achieved exactly the same result by dropping from another direction?' I countered.

'Well we actually needed to know where the enemy was hiding. We knew about one position, but were uncertain about another – so the thought was, that whilst you were dropping those badly needed stores, it was just possible that you'd make an irresistible target for them, and...'

'What? You mean you sent me up as a decoy?'

'No, no – not really, but there was just a remote chance – and as it was, you flushed them out nicely. We were ready for them; the minute they moved to get a bead on you, we clobbered the lot! But that was just a sideline. The main attack went very well and we've gained a lot of new high ground...'

'I don't believe this! I thought this sort of stuff only happened in second-rate war films. Why didn't you just tell me, I'd have routed them out for you a damn sight better if I'd known what I was doing? And it needn't have risked the life of my dispatcher as well?'

'Hey, hey – Steady! That water was desperately needed, so it *did* warrant the use of a dispatcher. That *was* your primary mission. We merely thought it would be *extremely* useful if you could do both jobs at the same time. We're on wartime footing here, so certain risks *have* to be taken. I'm sorry if we didn't put you fully in the picture – but that was the Brigadier's decision. You *are* new to the theatre and he didn't know what you were made of, and therefore thought it better this way. I'll make sure he *does* know in the future – and well, all I *can* say is, welcome to the team...I heard you got hit?'

'Three small holes in the wing, nothing vital and nothing we can't patch up.'

'Well done, that's more like it! A lot of decisions get made in this corner of the tent, and sometimes they are *difficult* decisions, and more often than not the *reasoning* behind them gets lost, which is why, thank God, we have orders and discipline to uphold them. I'll tell the Brigadier about our conversation, and I'm sure he'd like to have a drink with you – say about seven-thirty, after the 'O' Group?'

I walked back to my tent, and decided to have a shower. On the way I suddenly thought about the toothbrush episode all those years ago. When I was marched to the Guardroom with 'dirty fleish' because of a spot of blanco on my cheek. It wasn't the blanco at all, I realized, nor the ridiculous punishment of scrubbing the floor with a tooth-brush. It was all to do with taking orders. Unwittingly or not, CSM Rudd had demonstrated that however unjust an order may seem at the time, you are expected to carry it out – and the army does not expect you to question an order. Moreover you are rarely in a position, or at a sufficient level to be party to the global reasoning behind an order...

But against this, at what stage should the intelligence of the individual be taken into consideration? What exalted rank do you have to attain before you are given credence to have intelligence as well as experience? Obviously Nelson had had the same problem, and he got away with it when he put a telescope to his blind eye, and he went on to become High Admiral... The military system could be extremely frustrating to a thinking person. The trouble is, the army trains you to take orders blindly, whereas flying teaches you to think... unless, I suppose, you are a monkey.

I found the shower – a makeshift arrangement of a tank set on a tower and heated by the sun. But it worked beautifully, and washed the morning away. It had taken too many years of searching, I reflected, to find a moral behind that toothbrush business, and anyway, it had all been Tristan's fault in the first place...

That evening, Roger and I decided it would be fun to lay on a small impromptu flying display. It needn't be a very long affair, and would best be demonstrated one evening during a 'quiet' period, and also when the air was cool. It would be good for the troops' morale, we reasoned, and started to plan a routine. The main difficulty was to find the time for a practice, for we wanted it to be a professional performance, but were both busy flying from dawn to dusk.

The following morning I had to fly back to Aden to pick up three officers from Staff College who were visiting from the UK and had been called to the Brigade for a conference and a battlefield tour. I flew down empty and what better occasion to see how aerobatic the Beaver was? I had not done any aerobatics since my Chipmunk days, for both the AOP IX and the Beaver were strictly off-limits and designated as non-aerobatic aircraft. But, I reasoned, all aeroplanes are stressed for positive loading, and so long as you know what you are doing and keep within these bounds, surely they are all capable of aerobatic manoeuvres?

I tried a loop, and she went round beautifully – as if on rails, and just as you would expect from the docile beast she was. What's more, the constant-speed propeller was ideal for aerobatics, and there was no question of over-revving or anything going out of limits. I tried a stall turn, and the weight of the engine pulled us round in the most graceful of curves, and it was as though she had been waiting a long time to show how this really should be done. I was delighted! Should I try a barrel roll? This could be tricky, because you can fall out of these, and inadvertently over-stress or go into negative loading. Anyway, I was too low for safety and nearly at Khormaksar, so I would restrict my display to a short takeoff, when you stand it on it's tail; then some tight turns on half-flap and you can spin like a top; a couple of loops, maybe a roll-off-the-top and then a stall turn or two. Put together with Roger's manoeuvres and a few deliberate near misses, should be enough, if performed with sufficient panache.

I returned with the visitors and then had another sortie to fly, so after their conference Roger flew them around the battlefield positions and then returned them to Aden. That evening I told Roger about my discovery and we revised our program, and then decided to meet by radio arrangement at Dhala the following afternoon for a short practice. Dhala is the ancient town at the head of the wadi. If you follow the wadi north from Habilayn, the mountains close in on you from both sides until the valley is only about a quarter of a mile wide. Then, you fly round a final blind corner and are confronted with a mountain wall some 3000 feet high – and Dhala is situated on the plain above where there is also a long empty airstrip, which would be ideal.

We met as arranged; both in-between sorties and clicked to our prearranged frequency. For a first attempt it wasn't bad, and then we spent some more time on the near-miss routine until it was wholly realistic, and left knowing where we both needed to brush-up our individual displays. The secret, we discovered, was to be in constant communication and to know precisely where and what the other was doing.

Our chance came that very evening. We didn't tell anybody and met halfway down the strip as though by accident, he rearing up to do an emergency stop, and me doing likewise with a stall turn, and then disappearing and both going round so that we met again and had to repeat the performance. We did this a couple of times by which time the whole camp was out wondering what was going on and everything came to a standstill. Roger then entertained them by doing all the things a helicopter can do, including flying a circuit backwards and covering everything in dust, whilst I climbed out of sight. Then it was my turn and I went through my routine, slowly loosing altitude with each manoeuvre and ending up just above the ground in a tight turn on half-flap trying to catch Roger's tail. On an impulse I decided to end in a low pass, running downwind and flat-out over the camp and then pulling up into a stall turn, whilst dropping flap, and landing off it the other way.

It all went down very well, so much that the Brigadier came up to us in the mess and asked whether we could repeat it the following evening, only this time could we take some of the clerks and cooks with us, as they did such a stalwart job but received little thanks, let alone any excitement?

Of course we had to agree, but decided to modify our program considerably, especially the near-miss routine.

The following evening when I climbed for altitude, I had an aircraft full of nervous passengers. Should I try a loop? On the ground they would be expecting something, but I wasn't sure about it. Then someone said 'Can we loop the loop, sir?' But I still wasn't sure. We were heavy, and our height above sea level was about 8000 feet; sure she would go round, but in the thin air I would need a lot of speed and a lot of room. I wasn't really high enough, for some of the mountaintops still looked very close. The temptation would be to tighten it up too much, and that could result in a high-speed stall. How would Mr Avery have tackled it – dive first to 140 knots? No... more likely he would have quoted his favourite ditty: 'There are *bold* pilots, and there are *old* pilots, but there are very few old, bold pilots.' I circled around once more, then gave Roger a call. 'Chopper Eight-Niner; Zero-One. I think I'm going to take my lot round on a battlefield tour...'

'Zero-One, Chopper Eight-Nine. Yes, I've been thinking along the same lines myself. We've got about forty minutes of light remaining, so let's do two fifteen-minute trips each. I'll call Brigade, and get them to rustle-up another load for us both.'

I set course for the main battle area, and gave Mr Summers a smile...

* * *

That night the weather changed. Roger and I were both woken simultaneously by the tent, which gave a tremendous crack and then started to flap and bang. He got up and inspected the guy ropes on his side, and then came in and suggested that I did the same, as the whole thing was about to blow away. There was a full gale blowing, funnelling up the wadi and making an eyrie moaning sound, and the air was full of sand. I wrapped a cloth around my face and went down to the strip to see if the Beaver was all right. Corporal Frazer was there with a couple of his lads, banging in pegs and securing the aircraft to the tie-down rings under the wings. I gave them a hand and then also helped with the cover that fitted over the nose, in a forlorn hope to keep the sand out of the engine. By this time it was almost light, and the whole camp looked a shambles, caught out by the freak storm.

As abruptly as it had started, the wind suddenly lost its fury and the anemometer on its post outside the Air Traffic tent ceased to be a blur of whirling cups, and resumed more sedate revolutions, finally settling for thirty-five knots. The two controllers were inside.

'Who's Five-Zero-Six?' they enquired, 'Beaver inbound with the ADS?'

'Zero-Six – that's Arthur Prescott, my Flight Commander...'

'Well I hope he knows what he's doing. I told him we'd had a sand storm in the night, and the visibility at the moment is not much better than zero.'

'What time is he due?'

'He said he'd be overhead in six minutes, and landing in thirteen... At least, I think he said overhead, his radio was a bit distorted and making odd snorting noises. Must have been static I suppose...'

I smiled. 'That's Arthur all right; his radio often makes those noises. But overhead? That's odd; if I were attempting to come up the wadi in this dust, I'd enter low down, and creep up on half-flap...'

'I'm sure that's what he said... listen, isn't that him now?'

I went outside and cocked my head, and sure enough could hear the distinctive thrub-thrub-thrub that only a Pratt and Whitney makes. It gradually diminished to the north, and then there was silence.

We waited.

Seven minutes went by, each second shown as a lingering pause from the hand on the clock, as it swept round.

'Habilaynknuff, Five-Zero-Six on short finals.' The radio announced.

From our position halfway down the strip we could not see the end of it, let alone any aircraft on short finals. The other controller grabbed the microphone. 'Zero-Six you are cleared to land. There is no other traffic and the wind is gusting from the south at thirty-five knots. Caution, visibility is severely restricted with blowing sand...'

There was the seductive whine the supercharger on a Pratt and Whitney makes when you finally reduce the boost, followed by a metallic rumble as the wheels met the stony surface, and the Beaver emerged from the yellow mist. It finished its run just opposite the Air Traffic tent, and then swung off the runway and taxied up, stopping neatly alongside mine, and then shut down.

The passengers got out, and finally the small pilot's door opened and Arthur's bottom appeared, the rest of him still inside as though he was searching for something. Then he heaved his bulk backwards through it, and sauntered over to us, minus his beret.

'Morning, knuff' he said. 'Almost as bad as landing behind a Beverley...' then he saw me. 'Ah, just the man! Thought I'd drop in and see how you were getting on, and I've brought you some knuff-knuff, mail...'

It was a letter from Tristan and I slipped it into my pocket to read later. We didn't have a lot of time to talk, for his arrival released a flood of air requisitions which the 'G' staff had been sitting on, thinking the weather was too bad to fly, and both Roger and I had to be briefed. By then the dust was beginning to settle and soon after I heard Arthur take off to resume his ADS.

The weather was still misty and very humid, but good enough to fly and I cleared most of the local sorties by mid-morning. Then I was asked to do a gunnery shoot – the first live shoot against a real enemy, and also the first I had done from a Beaver. It was difficult to see the ranging shots falling in the rocks and I had to use a lot of smoke, but at least I didn't have to zoom up and down, and managed to conduct the affair from a flyline selected at a comfortable height. On the way back I received another call; would I fly down to Khormaksar to pick up four members of a bomb-disposal team together with all their equipment? Apparently during the storm last night, one of the company positions had been infiltrated and their vehicles booby-trapped, which was altogether a new development and one that could have far reaching implications.

I have an empty aeroplane and enough fuel, and so abandon any further thoughts of lunch and maybe a short nap in the afternoon to catch up on last night, and increase boost to over-fly the field and head south. South of the mountains the desert is like a boiling cauldron and the air above thick with sand. I manage to tune the ADF to the Khormaksar beacon, but it is not at all positive and continually hunts from side to side. I keep thinking about Arthur's approach and IFR landing this morning; obviously he has charted his own letdown procedure into Habilayn, and I resolve to do the same. With enough height you could do it with a back bearing from the ADF at Khormaksar and then... well it gives me plenty to think about. Then Khormaksar Radar comes on and informs me I am ten miles, and I change to the Tower frequency and ask for a straight in on their runway One-Four, which is a little used dirt strip, but ideal for the Beaver and reasonably into wind.

I land and ask for clearance to taxi over to the fuel enclo-sure in the corner of the field, and then have to fill in a lot of forms before the RAF ground crew can top up the tanks. This all takes about forty minutes, and has made me very late. It would have been much quicker to have landed and topped up at Habilayn, which would have only taken a few minutes and no bureaucracy. I climb back in and prepare to start up, but am then stopped by the Flight Sergeant in charge of the fuel compound.

'This aircraft is in an un-airworthy condition, and I cannot permit it to leave my area' he announces, adopting an aggressive stance with his hands on his hips, and one foot firmly on one of the chocks he has placed in front of the landing wheels.

'I beg your pardon?' I call down from my side window.

'I am in charge of this area, and any aircraft within its bounds come under my jurisdiction. Having inspected this aircraft, I am duly authorized to restrict any further movement until such time that the various faults have been rectified.'

'Various faults? Un-airworthy? I'm afraid I don't know what you're talking about...'

'Just look at the state of it! The tyres are cut to ribbons, there is evidence of structural *damage* to the tail-plane, and as for the propeller, it's way out of limits. It is therefore my duty to ground this aeroplane.'

I sigh, and clamber out again. He points to the dents on the leading edge of the tail-plane and then at the tyres. I walk round to both wheels and remove the chocks.

'Here! Those are my chocks, you can't do that! I cannot permit this aircraft to...'

'Flight Sergeant, the so-called damage you see, is caused by stones. We get that every time we take off...'

'Be-that-as-it-may, I don't seem to have made myself clear! This aeroplane is grounded and is not leaving my...'

'Flight, this is not your aeroplane; it is mine. Nor does it belong to the Air Force – it happens to belong to the Army. I think that lets you off the hook, doesn't it? Now be a good chap and stand aside, I'm halfway through a sortie.'

'Any aircraft that enters my...'

'Also I happen to be an officer, and therefore I am now obliged to give you a direct order to stand aside.' I smile at him and then climb back in and activate the inertia switch, leaving him standing with a perplexed expression on his face as though trying to categorise the conflicting priorities of his situation.

The G2 was right, I think to myself as I taxi the half-a-mile to the pick-up point, *sometimes you have to resort to a direct order, to penetrate the military mind. And on this occasion it certainly seemed to work...*

I finally arrive at the pick-up point over an hour late,

where there is an impatient looking major and three subalterns from the of Royal Engineer bomb-disposal unit waiting to board.

I leave the engine running as they stow their gear and strap themselves in, and then ask the Tower for clearance to take off from runway One-Four again. I complete the vital actions on the move, and swing onto the runway at the halfway point and without stopping, power-up into a short takeoff. Even using only half the available runway, we are airborne well before it crosses the main Zero-Eight runway, and I clear to the right and head back into the cauldron.

Perhaps it's the recent confrontation with the flight sergeant, which was unnecessary and upset me, or maybe it's because I'm tired; but I am uneasy. Something is niggling, and it's enough to alert the sixth sense, which is never far away when you are flying. Okay, this I will accept, so what's wrong?

Again I check around the cockpit. A glance is enough, for one needle out of place or even the slightest flicker would have registered; everything is normal with the aircraft, and well I know it.

I look behind to see if the passengers are aware of my unease. The major is pale faced and obviously just out from England. He is peering intently out of the window, but with the air full of sand and the visibility barely above half a mile, his first impressions of South Arabian 'up country' would be somewhat limited. The three subalterns have a more seasoned look about them – or at least they are a healthier colour and they don't seem too alarmed by the queasiness caused by the superheated air. One is asleep and the other two are reading, so obviously nothing amiss has been transmitted through to them.

I hotch irritably in my seat and make a minute adjustment to the RPM lever. The needle drops to 1750 RPM and I adjust the trim to allow for the corresponding reduction in airspeed and mentally add another minute to my ETA.

We drone on in silence, save the occasional crashing of static in my headsets. The Beaver feels heavy and sluggish and I mentally liken it to a tramp steamer ploughing through a typical Conrad oily swell. I check the stopwatch and peer ahead. Good! Through the haze I can just make out the contours of the Jebel Manif, which is the first mountain and stands some miles south of the main range, directly on line with the entrance to the pass. The period of dead reckoning across the desert is over; we are on track and now have a landmark to work from.

Abeam the Jebel the drifting sand of the desert ends in an abrupt line, and sparse vegetation of the wadi takes its place. There should be an outcrop of rock showing through the last of the sand – There, good! It's a useful pointer and I know is dead on the centreline of the wadi. Now, zero the stopwatch, and carefully reset the DI to the compass. If I can keep to the centre of the wadi, the strip will eventually show up. Away from the blowing sand, I had hoped that the visibility would have increased, but if anything it is worse and the proximity of the unseen mountains has turned the yellow haze to grey.

The altimeter shows steady at 4000 feet on the standard altimeter setting. Ground level at this point is 3000 feet above sea level, so we have 1000 feet clearance above the ground. Over the next thirty-five miles, the wadi bed will rise a further 700 feet – which will leave 300 feet clearance at Habilayn, and just right for a straight in approach. There will be a downwind element in the landing, but the strip is long enough. Or maybe there'll be enough room for a tight circuit – I'll just have to see what the conditions are like further up... Without one of Arthur's homemade letdown charts, a low level approach is the only way in – and then it all hinges on maintaining contact with the ground. Even though I can now only see vertically beneath me.

In spite of the fix, my unease has not left me. I feel we are low. I stare at the needle indicating 4000 feet. With this restricted visibility it is impossible to obtain any perspective. Does the haze create a magnifying effect? Maybe, but I could swear that there is not 1000 feet of clearance beneath us. We are now screened by mountains and too low to raise Aden Centre on the radio to obtain an area altimeter setting, but Habilayn should now be just about in range.

'Habilayn, Habilayn, this is Army Five-Zero-One, do you read?'

Nothing, but the crash of static. I turn to the selector panel and disconnect the Number One VHF and select the army radio, which is still tuned to the Brigade frequency. To ease my growing disquiet it is suddenly very important to contact somebody.

Again my only reply is static.

The alarm bell, which for some time has been ringing in my subconscious, increases volume and becomes too loud to ignore. Somewhere, somehow, something is amiss.

'Come on, Lindbergh, surely you don't need me now, to tell you the obvious? Think like a bird, and keep ahead of the game. If you are right and you feel there is something wrong (and remember, it's all to do with feel...) concentrate on the clues you have and then piece them together like a jigsaw. You've got to identify it before you can rectify it – and don't leave it until the situation becomes out of hand. It must not be allowed to snowball...'

The 'oily swell' movement of the airstream has changed and conditions are now becoming quite turbulent. As the pass narrows, the wind must increase – like it would in a venturi. I glance at the airspeed and RPM, and they are already set to the configuration for rough air. I remember doing it now; some instinct made me reduce the RPM to 1750 a while back. Pilots rarely do anything without a reason, what reflex prompted this action?

Eleven minutes have passed since I set the stopwatch, and by time, we have reached the point where I should reduce power for the final descent.

'Habilayn, Habilayn, this is Army Five-Zero-One, do you read?'

Still nothing. The snowball is gaining momentum and I cannot afford to delay any longer.

I decide to compromise; recognise my hunch that we are low – and therefore maintain my present indicated altitude, but drop half-flap and reduce airspeed to sixty-five knots to be ready for the end of the strip when it shows up. I should have done this before. Now, peer ahead and let's see if I can recognise any features? The grey haze has turned blue and looks solid; and at the same time my brain screams the answer.

Venturi! Although out of context, it is the clue. What happens when you force a fluid through the restrictions of a venturi? There'll be an increase in speed, an increase in temperature, and an increase in *pressure*. The altimeter is a *pressure* instrument; oily swell, static, increase of wind – the jigsaw is complete and can only mean one thing: at something under 500 feet above ground level, hemmed in by mountains on three sides, we are about to enter a thunderstorm.

Abandon any thought of making Habilayn, there is only one answer in this situation: get out now while you can. This is a classic example of being up the creek without a paddle; and I should never have let it progress this far...

The quickest way out is a one-eighty turn, and sitting on the left I instinctively pull the Beaver into a tight left-hand turn in order to see the ground. With half flap lowered the turning radius is not very great. I glance downwards out of my side window and my mouth turns dry. Directly below is the Arab fort. We are way off the centre line, for the fort is situated at the very foot of the mountains – and this turn can only end in disaster.

GO RIGHT! Instant reaction. Propeller pitch fully *FINE*. The engine howls and the airspeed is way back, bordering on the stall. *Just hold it there* – the DI is beginning to turn the other way. *Please don't topple.* I can physically feel the proximity of the mountain and dare not look out.

It is raining. A solid wall of grey water. How can one fly through solid water? There is a river pouring in from somewhere and my legs are soaked. The cloud is black and solid, and there is no point in looking out. I hold the bank and watch incredulously as the DI pass through three-five-zero degrees and then onto North. We have scraped by. I hold the turn until we have a safe zero-two-zero degrees showing and then roll out to recover my wits. We should be overhead Habilayn now and I continue tracking up the remainder of the wadi towards the dead-end at Dhala. Which doesn't give many minutes before we hit the mountain face at the end of the wadi, so altitude is the first priority. God I am soaked, and I seem to be sitting in a pool of water. Allow the speed to build up and slowly raise the flaps to ten degrees. Now, with 2200 RPM selected, trim to climb at sixty-five knots – still heading on zero-two-zero towards the dead-end; and directly into the storm, which is the only avenue open.

Up she goes! This is unbelievable! We are being sucked up into the heavens. The rain stops as abruptly as it started and we are in a black funnel between two flashing walls of cumulonimbus. The Vertical Speed Indicator registers 'off the clock' and the Altimeter winds up before my eyes – 4000, 5500, 6000 feet. I must soon think about a one-eighty turn, but this is too good to miss and we ride the thermal.

The altimeter passes through 9500 feet, which means we are clear of the highest peak – and it is time to leave.

Easy does it; I have been dreading this moment. We cannot be far into the storm and there will be worse ahead, so round we go – and forget what is outside. Also it's time I cleaned the aircraft up and put a respectable speed back onto the ASI.

I select flaps up, and give the hydraulic lever a pump with my right hand. At this instant the aircraft strikes something and the control column is torn from my left hand.

It is the mountain. I brace myself and for some reason start to count. Tut, tut, tut... CLANG! It comes from above.

Papers, there are papers everywhere swirling crazily round the cabin. The control column bangs back into my stomach and I grab it. I can smell burning. Yet, I am fighting with the wheel; the aeroplane is still alive. The instruments are haywire, with the exception of the RPM, which shows a steady 2200. Sanity at last in a Constant Speed Propeller and a steady dial. There is something banging and a gale blowing through the cabin. Are we flying? This is crazy! Or is it? The instruments are still haywire, but there is a pattern...

'*Here, stick these blanks over the instruments...*' *Mr Avery, booming over the storm...*

Okay! We are in a spin – but which way? The altimeter is unwinding through 11,000 feet. Eleven? Check. The thermal must have taken us up another 2000 feet during the turn. Left or right..? Quick! I can't think straight. Try right rudder...

It bites instantly. I can feel it. I hope we have enough room...

There is another flash of lightening which sears my eyes, and then it becomes continuous, one flash superseding and meshing into another. Everything stands out in amazing clarity. The Beaver's nose and wings are etched in sharp unnatural lines. Every rivet shows on the cowling; the catch on the wing-strut that holds the passenger door open; the three static wires trailing from the outer section of the wing; even a cut-off piece of parachute cord, still attached to the outer port bomb-rack. I can smell the hot fusing of the lightening.

That first clang must have been a direct strike. God knows what it has done, but at least we are still in one piece and it wasn't the mountain. We are being tossed about like a leaf in a whirlwind. The Artificial Horizon is sulking in the top right hand corner of the dial, but the good old Turn and Slip Indicator determines that we are flying again. More or less – except the Vertical Speed Indicator is once more off the clock and we are going up again.

Something is banging my shoulder and I look behind. It is one of the subalterns. The cabin looks a frightful mess with luggage and papers strewn all over the place.

'I said the back doors have come open' he is shouting. This explains the banging and the gale. The whole fuselage must have twisted to spring both doors open.

'The doors...'

'Well try and SHUT them...' How stupid! I wonder how wide they opened during the spin and whether we lost anything?

The banging ceases and with it the gale.

I push the control column fully forward and apply maximum boost and revs, but it makes not the slightest difference to our ascent. This is disturbing, for I love and trust the Beaver as an aeroplane and now it is as if she has a mind of her own. One thing is for certain; I am no longer in control...

The altimeter passes through 14,000 feet, and it starts to hail. The noise is incredible. Thank God this aeroplane is made of metal, for hail like this would soon strip canvas or wood from their frames and leave just a skeleton. I pray the windshield does not break and the engine keeps on running. I am weakening through lack of oxygen. *Why carry on fighting?* This is too big. I remember reading a paper about these fantastic vertical movements of air within a thunderhead. They are like contrary waterfalls, and mighty enough to lift tons of water in one section of the cloud to fantastic heights, where the water then freezes and falls as hail. Then the hail droplets are seized again and taken up to become enlarged, and so the process goes on. The paper had said that vertical air velocities of 116 miles per hour are required to sustain a hailstone three inches in diameter, and this size is by no means uncommon within a thunderhead.

How high does the anvil of this one reach – 20,000, perhaps 25,000 feet? We are supposed to use oxygen above 10,000. The same paper had listed the number of aircraft that had been broken into little pieces by the unleashed fury of tropical thunderstorms. The Beaver is pretty rugged, but won't stand this for long.

Keep fighting. I think this must be one of the occasions that warrant my extra flying pay. But I am helpless and I can't think what else to do...

Keep fighting. The noise of the hail wants to make my head burst. Or is it my blood roaring? I can't focus on the instrument, but I think we are at 21,000 feet, and everything is purple... The controls are heavy – shouldn't they be sloppy at this altitude? Perhaps they are icing up. Or perhaps I am very weak. It doesn't really matter. Try and relax a bit. St Elmo's fire. There was no St Elmo's fire. Doesn't that happen in thunderstorms? People say it's very pretty and quite harmless. I should have liked to see that...

* * *

There is a red light that shouldn't be there.

I come to, and focus my eyes on it. It is the Fuel Warning Light. I reach forward and change to the centre tank. The red light goes out and I am awake.

The air is calm and the visibility excellent. We are at 15,700 feet. I gingerly press the left rudder pedal and the aircraft responds instantly. This is flying! I check through all the other flying controls and everything is normal. We have collected some ice, but nothing too bad. No longer is the Beaver a mad fighting thing, but the docile friend I know.

There is a book lying under the rudder pedals. I retrieve it and turn round. The major has a cut across his forehead. With only lap belts and no shoulder straps, the passengers must have had a rough ride. I rouse the subaltern next to him.

'Here's your book...' He looks about him, then grins.

'Christ!' Then, 'you've lost the place!'

I wonder whether to mention the door-shutting episode? In the heat of the moment had I been a bit short with him? Perhaps it's best to say nothing. I show him where the First Aid kit is and ask him to sort the cabin out.

I re-set the DI and scan the surrounding mountains to see if I can recognize any feature. We are flying east and the terrain is totally unfamiliar. This is hardly surprising, for in the interests of search and rescue we normally try to stay on set-routes whenever possible, and we must be miles off our course. If I turn south we will at least be pointing in the right direction for the coast – and we still have plenty of fuel.

Gently I bank the Beaver in a lazy turn to the left. This is the long way round for south, but a two-seventy degree

222

turn will enable me to see as much country as possible.

The sky is black to the northwest, where the remains of the storm is still flashing. I have not had time to think about it, but can only assume we eventually met a downdraught and somehow got thrown out of the side of the thunderhead. I shudder and blank it out for later.

Just carry on scanning...

There! Surely that is the Jebel Jihaf, which dominates the Dhala airstrip? Bearing about two-five-zero. Habilayn will be due south of there, so if I head two-two-five, we shouldn't be far out. I look at my map and span the distance with my hand. We are flying over Yahar territory, which is marked on my map in red. Reputably no white man has ever been there – or at least walked out to tell anyone.

I look behind again and the luggage and equipment has been re-stowed and the subaltern has bandaged the major's head using a leg-bandage, which looks very dramatic. They all seem in good heart now that the aircraft is straight and level again. I tell them that we will arrive in about ten minutes and decrease boost and RPM for the descent. Just in time I remember to switch the radio back from the Brigade net to Air Traffic, and then casually try a call.

'Habilayn, Habilayn, this is Army Five-Zero-One, do you read?'

'Five-Zero-One, this is Habilayn, reading you fives.' That's a nice surprise – at least the lightening hasn't fused everything.

'Habilayn, Zero-One is inbound to your field, estimating nine minutes.'

'Zero-One, Roger. The wind is from the south at fifteen knots and the QFE is 984. Caution, we have just had the mother and father of thunderstorms, and the southern half of the strip is flooded. The storm should be well out of your way to the northwest by the time you arrive...'

I overfly the field still loosing altitude, and note the carnage below. The strip is half under water, and numerous tents have been washed away. What had been dried up tracks are now cascading with brown water and there is mud and debris everywhere. As I turn onto finals I look for Roger's Scout, and see it on its pad with the rotors turning; so at least he survived the deluge, and we are both still in business...

* * *

We got the whisky bottle out that evening. I told Roger about the thunderstorm and how foolish I'd been to be lured into the trap. All the signs had been there and yet I had ignored them and still pressed on, flying up a blind alley at zero feet with no visibility, entirely trusting luck. By the grace of God I was still here to tell the tale, but I didn't deserve to be.

'Partner' he said, 'I too have a confession to make, and shouldn't be here to tell the tale. I took some stores to the troops on the top of tabletop this afternoon.'

Tabletop is our newly conquered position. It is the highest mountain to the east of Habilayn, and with a flat plateau for a summit, looks like the top of a table – much like the strip at Ajra where Paul had crashed, only higher and more prominent.

'What happened?'

'Well I struggled up there – you need all the power a Scout can produce, especially in the heat of the afternoon. I just made it to the pad, which is on the very edge of the mountain and then had to shut down, because there was a load to take back that wasn't ready yet. They had a crew of Arabs up there doing labouring work, so I had a glass of jungle juice and chatted to the company commander whilst the sergeant got the Arabs to load the machine. Sacks and sacks of stuff – I didn't think of checking, because they are an air-minded lot and know what they're doing. A couple of soldiers wanted a lift back, so they got in as well, and then I wound it up.

'I was in a hurry, because I could see your thunderstorm coming up the wadi, and knew I'd have to hurry to make it in time. In fact it was just starting to rain, big menacing drops. I pulled up on the collective, and the helicopter just

'...and once out of ground effect, we went down like a brick shit house...'

didn't budge. "Christ, the air's thin up here" I thought, then gunned it again and really yanked up hard. It lifted a foot, and sort of swivelled round so that the right skid went over the edge, and I had no option but to follow it with the rest of the helicopter. So, in effect I just threw the whole lot over the edge... It's a sheer face, as you know, and once out of ground effect, we went down like a brick shit-house. I still had the collective lever fully up, but it made no difference, and we continued down in a semi-controlled crash. I managed to steer it with my feet, and just aimed for the pad at Habilayn, some 4500 feet below. I'd nearly got to the bottom by the time the rotors began to bite, and just managed to slow it up a bit before we hit the pad. Christ! Everyone thought I'd done it on purpose, and it was a brilliant bit of flying, but if only they knew! Thank God it didn't bend anything. I think my crew chief knew what was going on because he gave me an old-fashioned look, and checked the skids all over, but he couldn't find anything. When they unloaded it, they found it had been loaded with twice the weight there should have been! My fault, I should have checked it, but those Arabs had just been slinging it on as though it was one of their rug-covered lorries. Christ!'

We had another whisky, and then burst out laughing in nervous release. It was either that or crying, and both of us knew we would re-live what happened – as well as what could have happened, for a very long time. Then I remembered Tristan's letter, which was still in my pocket, and we read the news from Wallop.

Chapter 7

By my reckoning, twelve minutes have now past since they withdrew. If it wasn't for the wreck of the Beaver and the still form of the Arab lying in the sand, it's as though it never happened. Nothing has moved in the twelve minutes and there has been no noise from either side. Nor have there been any further signs of the rescue party. Perhaps the Arabs have just melted away...? I've arranged the remaining Very cartridges in a neat line at the base of the rock, so they are readily at hand – and I cannot think of anything else to do to prepare myself.

Other than wait and watch my front.

I suppose this is normal for the infantry. Periods of intense physical exertion, followed by long periods of inactivity – and you wait. Someone once told me that only actors and soldiers know how to remain absolutely still; but for me, other than standing to attention on parade, this is the first time it has been seriously put to the test. Also I'm fast coming to the conclusion that I'm not very good at it! Perhaps it's because I'm impatient by nature, but I just can't stand this waiting. I don't mind what it is, but I wish something would happen!

Now old Roger, he'd be quite content to lie behind this rock behind a levelled gun and wait for an enemy that may or may not be there. His temperament is suited to being a trapper rather than a hunter and he would relish this situation. But by the same measure he wasn't cut out to sit in a Chipmunk on instruments in cloud. Horses for courses – which is probably why, having totally opposite personalities, we make such a good team.

After that first time in the Radfan – the time when we gave our first impromptu air-display, the Brigadier asked whether we would be able to come up together again? He said that he liked our teamwork, and also the fact that we obviously knew each other so well. He was all for teamwork and this extended to the air support he expected. Thereafter we always tried to arrange our ten or twelve-day 'duty pilot' stints together and soon found our contributions were actually listened to during the evening 'O' Group! In the end the G staff left the 'Air' side for us to manage between us, and we soon found we could save many flying hours by rearranging sorties to suit the capabilities of the aircraft as well as merging many together. This suited everybody and also saved a lot of servicing and maintenance time.

After the thunderstorm had wrecked the camp, we had both been very busy fetching and carrying. Many of the positions had been badly sited in the first place and what initially had had the appearance of being a sheltered gully, turned out to be a dried-up watercourse, which quickly turned into a yellow torrent of water during 'flash' storm conditions. In some instances the suddenness and ferocity of the storm had actually washed vehicles away as well as many tents. It was also a good opportunity to revise the overall security of the camp and thereafter there had been no further infiltration's at night and placing of booby traps.

Once the aircraft had been seen to and made ready for the morning, there was not a lot to do in the evenings, so I was able to devote time to reply to Tristan's letter. In his letter he had said that he had passed his Final Handling on the AOP IX and was now halfway through Exercise Flight. Interestingly enough, he also said that he had applied to join the Army Air Corps permanent cadre, along with three others from his course. Having got the flying bug, he could see no other future and had no qualms about leaving his Regiment. This pleased me enormously and quelled some of the earlier doubts I'd had about changing badges. He went

'...in the early morning the air was calm and cool...'

on to say that the Army Air Corps had just published a policy defining their expansion, with a view to making the future promotion and career prospects on a par with every other regiment and corps. Which was all very encouraging.

I told him all about Aden and the flying conditions I had experienced so far; and how flying in the mountains varied hour-by-hour with the passage of the sun. In the early mornings the air was calm and cool, but by midday the heat reflected off the rocks causing up-draughts which, when you knew about them, could be used to gain altitude; but as the sun moved round, so they would disappear and then turn into down-draughts by evening time.

Then there was the business of the rubbish tip, which someone had sited right in line with the end of the runway. During the day the air was black with wheeling kites, scavenging for food. The soldiers called them shitehawks but their behaviour reminded me of seagulls following fishing boats when they were gutting. Either way they were a serious hazard when taking off – and a damn sight more solid than any seagull, should you be unfortunate enough to hit one.

I told him about the enormous difference there was between regiments and especially their 'air-mindedness'. Some units would mark out a dropping-zone and then automatically put down smoke for the wind direction every time you flew near, whilst others would just ignore you, and were only intent upon their concealment. I told him about the time I had landed at an up-country strip serving the company position occupied by a Guards Regiment. Two white flagpoles had been erected, one flying the Union flag and the other their Regimental Colours; and how the sentry had snapped to attention and slapped his rifle-butt in salute. Then, how a few weeks later I had landed at the same strip and there were no flagpoles and the place looked deserted. When I walked to the entrance the only sign of life had been the 'snick-snick' of a rifle being cocked from behind a sangar and the blackened face of a Royal Marine challenging 'Who goes there?'

Finally I told him about the time I met the Commanding Officer of RAF 1 Squadron, which operate the ground-attack Hunters. He was visiting Habilayn and wanted to see the battle area, so he accompanied me for the morning, sitting in the right-hand seat. We had to drop someone off at Monks Field, which is another narrow strip made up from an embankment jutting out at right angles from a mountain. So you can only land one way in, and have to take off in the other direction, regardless of the wind. From the air it looks a bit like an ironing board, with a drop on either side as well as one at the end. On leaving, I lined the aircraft up and then asked him if he would like to do the takeoff from the right-hand seat? He accepted gladly, especially as he said he had never flown an aeroplane with a propeller before. That came as a surprise, but by then it was too late. He opened up the boost to where I pointed on the dial, and promptly veered off the edge of the strip, for he had no idea about countering the propeller torque with rudder. I managed to grab it just in time and gave it a boot-full of rudder as we crabbed off the edge and somehow staggered into the air.

Before rejoining at Habilayn, I suggested we should fly up to see the head of the wadi, and the strip at Dhala on the plateau above. He was still flying, and by this time was beginning to enjoy the Beaver and especially the low flying, which at this speed was something quite novel for him. We flew up the wadi at about 100 feet and then went round the final blind corner and were confronted by the sheer mountain wall directly ahead.

'Christ' he said, 'I think you'd better have control...'

'Ummm?' I said, pretending to look at something out of my side window.

'For Christssake! You have control...'

'You had enough? Oh, all right, I have control then...' I said wearily, then left it until the rock face filled the windscreen, before hauled the aircraft into a vertical bank, slotting the starboard wing nicely into a little ravine I knew was there. Round we went, with the wheels just a few feet from the face of the escarpment until we were heading safely back the other way.

'You bastard!' he breathed, 'I'll get my own back on you for that. Give me a ring and come over to the Squadron one day, and I'll give you a ride in our two-seat training Hunter...'

I actually took him up on that, and some weeks later we flew the same course, screaming up the valley at about 500 knots until we came to the dead end. Then, back with the stick, he stood it on its tail and we powered straight up, until all the shapes and individual contours of the mountains were lost and merged into one; an insignificant brown mat seen from 20,000 feet.

* * *

A homecoming is always to be revered, wherever home may be. If I looked and smelt anything like Corporal Frazer who was sitting beside me, we were both in need of a good wash, a haircut and a change of clothes. Also the Beaver was tired and filthy and long overdue a service. Although it was mid-afternoon, Falaise was a hive of activity. There was another Beaver in the circuit doing circuits and bumps, which in itself was strange, as well as the sky being full of Scouts and the chatter on the radio filled with voices I did not recognize. All was revealed after we landed: 8 Flight had arrived from Kenya and were busily trying out their new Scouts.

'But who's flying the Beaver?' I asked Arthur as I slumped into one of the battered armchairs in the crew room. Glad for the excuse, he slumped into the one opposite and regarded me balefully from his immobile face.

'Biggles' he said, 'and it's a knuff, long story.'

'Biggles?'

'Mmm. I don't know how old he is, but he only looks about sixteen. His name's Adam Bartlett, he's a Gunner subaltern and he's one of 8 Flight's fixed wing pilots. They had a farewell party before they left and knuff, Colonel Mike went over for it and decided he'd better come back to Aden, so he could keep an eye on him...'

'Why, what did he do?'

'Well, the party was knuff, held in the grounds of a cricket club – typical colonial clubhouse with an immaculate pitch, and surrounded by tall trees. Everyone was there, all dressed in their best whites. At the start of the party it was raining, but then it cleared up and they all went outside onto the green. Then Biggles turned up and did a beat-up in a Beaver. He, knuff-knuff, came over so low that he flattened all the guests, and everyone got drenched and covered in mud, and then knuff, he left it too late to pull-up over the trees, so he had to tip it on its side and go between two of them – the only trouble was, there wasn't really a gap. Don't know how he did it – brilliant bit of flying by all accounts, but obviously the Colonel got a lot of stick, and decided he'd be a liability if he was left there virtually unsupervised, knuff, and so now he's part of my Flight...

'Anyway, Roger Wilson, Biggles and you are all going on your desert survival course tomorrow, so I'd be grateful if you'd keep an eye on him. Knuff.'

'Arthur! Roger and I have been *surviving* in the Radfan for the past two weeks, do we have to...?'

'Afraid so, we all have to do it, best to get it over with...'

Roger was waiting in our new Mini, and we drove back to the camp together. There was a party in full swing in the mess. The 16/5th Lancers were entertaining the advance party of the 10th Hussars who had just arrived and the party had been going on since well before lunch. They all looked a bit worse for wear and glasses of champagne were thrust into our hands as we entered. I decided to go and clean up first and went to the hut and dumped my kit on my bed before going off to find the shower. Then when I came back, I just thought I'd have a little lie down before joining the party and...

Perhaps it was because I was overtired, but the thing I had been dreading to face and pushing to the back of my mind at last surfaced and demanded attention. I lay there and thought about the thunderstorm. I started with the hurried takeoff from Khormaksar and then relived every moment of the flight and the events leading up to the final nightmare. How could I have been so complacent? To be lured into that trap, which in retrospect was now so obvious; and worst of all the fact that I had ignored and put to one side the alarm that had been ringing in my mind. It was sheer arrogance, and I resolved never to allow it to happen again. The CFI at Wallop had warned me about over confidence, and that flying was always a serious business...

Eventually I must have fallen asleep, but it was a shallow sleep and full of semiconscious dreams. I didn't dream about the thunderstorm, but all sorts of other unrelated fragments from the past ten days, which churned, over and over in my mind. And amongst them there was a face I hardly knew. He was a 16/5th Lancer officer – Peter something? He was wearing uniform, which was unusual, for the cavalry rarely wear uniform unless they have to, and then never in the mess unless they are Orderly Officer. Peter *Wearing*, that was it! And I can hear his voice saying 'Casevac. Mukerius!' and he gives me another shake.

'Casualty Evacuation...Come on...'

It is real, and still half asleep I focus on his face. 'Not me, old lad, I've just got back – go and find the duty pilot.'

Road to Mukeiras. '...a white scar that zigzags up the face of the escarpment...'

'You are the duty pilot, I've just checked the list – and anyway, the others are all pissed...'

'Christ!' This must be another of Arthur's little jokes. 'Mukerius? What time is it?'

'Four-fifty – how far is Mukerius anyway..?'

'Just over an hour – and who's the casualty, we haven't got any troops up there have we?'

'The request came from the Political Service. Don't know who it is, but it must be important if it came from them. They tried the RAF but there isn't a Twin Pin serviceable, so they passed it onto us...'

A Twin Pioneer is about the only other aircraft that could get into that strip...Mukerius is the town – if it can be called as such – that is just over the escarpment and about the place where we usually lose VHF contact when en route to Beihan and the Empty Quarter. From what I can remember, it is about 7000 feet high and you find it by looking for a white track that zigzags up the face of the escarpment from the plain below. But it's an unattended strip and there's no fire truck or ground party to organize lights of any sort. Which means if I am to get there before dark, every minute will count.

Why is it always so hard to get your brain back into gear when you've had a sleep in the afternoon?

'Umm. Would you mind ringing the Flight and ask them to prepare an aircraft? Fuel in the belly tanks only – and to take the rear seats out? No time to rig up a stretcher; the casualty will have to lie on the floor. Oh, and better throw in some blankets if they've got some...?

'Okay, I'll leave you to get ready. Good luck...'

My watch says 1704hrs as I leave the hut and jump into the Mini. Thankfully Roger left the keys in the dashboard, so at least I don't have to spend time hunting for them.

Come on! You can work the Flight Plan out as you drive. It's now 1704 – allow ten minutes drive to the strip, and if the aircraft is ready, say another fifteen minutes to get airborne, which will make it 1729. Mukerius is fifty-one minutes flying time, allowing for the climb to 9000 feet if I push her. There will be a bit of a head wind – say another three minutes, which will make it 1823. When is last light – 1825, or thereabouts? Christ, it's going to be a near thing! I wonder how long the RAF was sitting on it before they passed it on? Still, it's got to be worth a shot, and maybe last light will be a fraction later at that altitude...

I drive past the car park and into the dispersal area and park next to the Beaver that they have pushed out. It is XP 819 and the same aircraft I have been flying for the past two weeks.

'Sorry about the state of it sir, we haven't had time to clean it up yet.'

'What about the service that's due?'

'She'll go another couple of hours – anyway, it's the best aircraft available at the moment, and at least you know her... I've put your helmet and gloves inside, if you'd just sign the authorization here, sir...'

I swing myself up, and it feels as though I'd never left. They've taken all the seats out, including the co-pilot's seat next to mine and it feels a bit like sitting on an orange box in the middle of an empty warehouse. But already my fingers are flicking through the familiar drill and soon the engine coughs into life. I set the revs to a fast tick-over and watch the cylinder head temperature start its climb into the green sector. The outside air temperature shows ninety-seven degrees centigrade but it's the humidity that is the real killer and sweat is running into my eyes, blurring the instruments. Habilayn, at 3000 feet above sea level, is a far more comfortable climate to live in.

Whilst waiting for the engine temperatures, I complete my Flight Plan, basing the calculations on a takeoff time of 1730hrs and the 10,000 foot wind at 20 knots. There shouldn't be any cloud, so I can file VFR (Visual Flight Rules) and thus take a few short cuts, rather than IFR (Instrument Flight Rules), which is far more exacting for routing and the timing of reporting points and estimates – entirely necessary when flying the congested Airways of Europe, but somewhat ponderous for seat-of-the-pants bush flying in an empty sky! As part of the reporting procedure, it is normal to include your actual in-flight weather conditions, so if you are in clear sky you report Visual Met Conditions (VMC) or if you are in cloud you report Instrument Met Conditions (IMC); the saving factor being, should the weather conditions change, you can always amend your Flight Plan either way.

The cylinder head is nearly in the green, and I hit the T handle parking-brake and we start to roll. Pre-takeoff vital actions on the move, and set the clock on the facia to Zulu time, which is Greenwich Mean Time and three hours back. Always that feeling of apprehension before every flight.

Temperatures and pressures now all in the green and I swing onto the active runway and increase the boost.

The strip fades behind and with it all feelings of apprehension as brain and being fill with flight. I clear to the left and carry on turning until 041degrees on the moving card of the Direction Indicator, approaches 041 degrees on the outer ring, and to which I have set the cursor for our course. Four seconds before they meet I reverse the wheel, which time allows for the final momentum of the turn, and then with the two needles together, climb on track.

'Khormaksar Approach, good evening, Army Five-Zero-One...'

'Zero-One, Khormaksar reading you fives, and the QNH is One-Zero-One-Four'. I twiddle the knob on the altimeter until 1014 millibars, which is the Regional setting, shows in the window at the base of the instrument.

'Khormaksar, Zero-One was off Falaise at fourteen-thirty Zulu, and is outbound to Mukerius initially on a VFR Plan. Request climb on track to Flight Level Nine-Zero and we estimate the Zone Boundary at five-seven and Mukerius at fifteen twenty-three. We are a Casevac mission and may need an ambulance on return. QNH, ten-fourteen, go ahead.'

'Zero-One, you are cleared to climb on track. Call again level at Nine-Zero and again at the Boundary. Ambulance will be alerted.'

That's that done, now let's see how fast I can get this aeroplane to fly... It's good to fly in the evening when the desert has settled down. The lower altitude is still thick with dust and sand thrown up by the afternoon heat, but the air is no longer vicious with turbulence. The setting sun over my port main-plane is ablaze with red and gold, the rays magnified and distorted by the dust particles in the air. I wonder, as always, what is happening within the engine as it digests the dust? I can feel it gritty on my lips and caking to the drying sweat on my face, so surely it must be scoring the cylinder walls and pistons just the same? Ingestion of sand and grit has caused no end of problems with the engines in the Scouts, but the Beaver's old Pratt and Whitney's just keep thumping away...

We pass through 3000 feet and as a matter of course I check the engine instruments again. They all continue to smile happily from their green sectors and tell me to stop worrying. I then change the altimeter setting so that 1013 millibars shows in the window, for this is the standard setting that all aircraft use when they climb above 3000 feet. Thereafter, altitude is expressed as a Flight Level; thus 3000 feet becomes Flight Level 30 and 3500 feet becomes Flight Level 35 and so on.

In Controlled Airspace, you are normally assigned a height to fly by the Controller, but otherwise all aircraft above 3000 feet will now fly to the quadrantal rule. The quadrants are to do with the circle of the compass rose, which you divide into four segments by drawing a line from North to South and then bisecting it with another line from East to West. Working round in a clockwise direction and reading in degrees, the first quadrant will be from North to East or, 0 to 090, the second from East to South or 090 to 180, the third from South to West or 180 to 270 and the last from West back up to North, or 270 to 360 degrees.

Having established this, you now assign Flight Levels to each quadrant, starting with the lowest Flight Level (FL 30) in the first quadrant (0 to 090) and working round clockwise to each quadrant and adding 500 feet each time. So the first quadrant is assigned FL 30, the second FL 35, the third FL 40 and the fourth FL 45. Then back into the first quadrant with FL 50, the second FL 55, the third FL 60 and so on. Thus, if you wish to fly on any course between 0 and 090 degrees, you will fly either at FL 30, 50, 70, 90 – and so on upwards, depending on the height of the terrain below, or the weather conditions. All the Flight Levels in this quadrant will be round 'odd' numbers and there will be a 2000-foot separation between Flight Levels assigned in the same quadrant.

So, taking our course of 041 degrees this evening: this falls within the first quadrant, and I have therefore requested a climb on track to FL 90, being the lowest level within that quadrant offering a safety height to clear the escarpment. Should there be an aircraft inbound on a collision course of say, 200 degrees, you know he will be flying in the third quadrant (round 'even' numbers) and that the nearest Flight Level to ours will either be below at FL80, or above at FL100, thereby offering a thousand-foot clearance between us.

It is a good system and works so long as everybody plays by the same rules. The first rule is that all aircraft set their altimeters to a common setting, which is why the standard setting of 1013 millibars is used. Next, it is imperative that you fly at exactly the level you are meant to be on. It is very easy to be a couple of hundred feet or so higher than you should be... and then the other guy could only be a couple of hundred feet or so lower... and when you consider there is only 500 feet clearance between two adjoining quadrants...?

The final rule is always to broadcast your intentions if you are going to change your Flight Level for any reason. This is normally done through Air Traffic, who should know and be able to advise on all other aircraft movements. But your transmission will also be heard by every other aircraft flying, and they will be able to plot your route and know whether you are climbing or descending through their airspace. This is why I requested permission to climb on track to FL 90, fully aware that whilst doing so I would be transgressing through the separation layers imposed by the system.

As we as we pass through Flight Level 60, we break through the upper reaches of the dust layer. The stickiness and humidity is left below and the air is like wine. The ground is now veiled in darkness, with the haze merging into the desert, and only my world aloft has reality. Far ahead I can see what looks like a line of clouds, which is unusual at this time of the evening. In the early mornings you can sometimes expect clouds, especially forming over the mountains, but it doesn't take long for them to burn off in the heat. The line ahead looks as though it is hanging over where the escarpment starts – and where Mukerius is.

Time to worry about that later.

The time is 1455hrs and the altimeter shows Flight Level 90. I climb another fifty feet and then dive back to the Flight Level thus putting the aircraft on the step and gaining another knot or two. If you dive down onto an altitude, you can achieve a higher cruising speed than had you climbed up to the altitude and merely levelled off. Nobody can really explain why this should be, but it happens – and every pilot worth his salt does it this way.

Also, judging from the lie of the mountains on my port side, we are at the Zone Boundary, which means we have done well and have clipped two minutes off my estimated time.

'Khormaksar Approach, Army Five-Zero-One is at the Boundary this time, level at Nine-Zero, Victor Mike, and estimating Mukerius at Two-Three.'

They acknowledge and tell me to change frequency to Aden Centre on 118.9. RAF Khormaksar being a military airfield controls all aircraft movements within a fifty-mile radius of the base, whereas Aden Centre is the normal civilian Air Traffic Control Centre, whose vast brotherhood stretches from Africa to the Gulf.

I turn the navigation lights on and then dial the new frequency and give them my position, height and ETA and am accepted into the brotherhood.

The line of cloud ahead draws nearer, and even in the gathering dusk I can see that it is sitting right over the escarpment and where Mukerius should be. Also it looks as though there is a layer of stratus beginning to form beneath me. It is pointless to remain at this Flight Level, for if I continue I shall soon be right in it. Which leaves three alternatives. I could climb above and then fly inland to see how far it extends – and then maybe let down and weave my way in from the north? Or I could descend now, whilst there is still time, and see if the cloud actually envelops the ridge, or whether there is a gap?

Or, I could turn round and go home.

I leave the settings where they are and lower the nose to dive-off the excess 2000 feet, and tell Aden Centre I am

240

starting my descent into Mukerius. Having been caught out by the thunderstorm, I am tempted to play safe and reduce the speed to sixty-five knots with ten degrees of flap, for the last thing I want to do is to charge head-on into another blind alley. But against this is the time, for it is now 1517hrs Zulu and even at this altitude the light is fading fast. Even if I do find a gap, it's going to be a damn near thing...

The altimeter reads 7200 feet as I level with the base of the cloud and the speed has increased to 140 knots in the dive. I do not know the actual height of the escarpment, but it's about 7000 feet – and yes... there does seem to be a gap, with two peaks on either side disappearing into the cloud – and there's definitely another layer of cloud forming below, so we are about to be sandwiched in between. The face of the escarpment is rushing to meet me and now I think it would be prudent to slow her up... I reduce the boost and hold the aircraft steady just under the cloud base and watch the speed fall off; then ease up slightly so that my tail fin cuts the cloud. Can't get closer than that...

With the high ground disappearing on either side, the gap had seemed to be narrower than it actually is, and also there's a good 150 feet between the lip of the ridge and the base of the cloud. Which is a lot more room than I had when I flew up the firebreaks of that wood in the AOP IX. I am committed and we squeeze through the gap. Once over the lip I become aware of a few dim lights, which must be oil lamps from the town. The airstrip should be west – about there... In fact I can just see a white scar that is probably the loose gravel of the strip showing against the black background of the rocks. It's in the right place and is heading east-west, so it must be the strip. If that's the case, we are perfectly set up on base leg... and if I lower my side window and then cross the controls and slip the aircraft sideways... I can just about see enough to judge the height as the scar approaches... must try and remember what the altimeter reads on the ground, for it could be useful another time. As it is, and with no lights to give an outside reference, it's just a question of feeling our way down... No point in using the landing lights, for whilst slipping they would be pointing off to one side – and anyway, would probably destroy my night vision. We're almost there... About now! Kick her straight with rudder and haul back... the landing wheels thump home and we rumble along the uneven surface. I can just see the stones on the edge of the strip flicking past, illuminated by the faint red glow from the port navigation light.

I swing round and backtrack towards the lights of a vehicle that is bumping its way to the strip, then swing round again to point down the strip ready for takeoff and shut down.

'Cutting it a bit fine aren't you? I sent a signal requesting an aircraft at six o'clock this morning...' the driver of the truck is saying, as I take my helmet off. He then introduces himself as the Area Political Officer.

'Sorry, I came as quickly as I could. Where and who's the casualty?'

'It's the youngest wife of the Sheikh. The Sheikh is away – he's actually in Aden at the moment, and this girl is very pregnant. She's a week past her time and the baby is in a breach position, and none of the women here can do anything about it. I think they would have just left her to die. But, well it's a bit complicated, but if we can get her to hospital and save the child... and if it's a boy... the Sheikh badly wants another heir you see, and... I can't go into it all now, but believe me, doing this could mean a lot for the treaty we're negotiating. Anyway, we've been waiting all day, what took you so long?'

The girl is lying on a stretcher in the back of the truck with another woman attending her. Her purdah has been cast aside and her face is uncovered. She looks about sixteen.

'Look, I've just got an empty aeroplane. There's nobody else with me and I haven't got any drips or anything. In fact I haven't even got any painkillers. Is there somebody who can accompany her, she'll need somebody to look after her?'

'I thought you chaps were equipped for this sort of thing? I did say in my signal that it was a casualty who needed urgent hospital attention... Do you mean to say you just flew up here on your own?'

'Yes, I'm afraid it's me or nothing. I didn't get the message until five o'clock. So is there somebody who can look after her?'

'What, go with her to Aden? Good heavens no! I'm afraid that's out of the question. There's nobody here who would do. Nobody at all. I'd come myself, but... Well, I suppose you'll just have to manage best you can.'

I unhinge the rear passenger door and we lift the stretcher into the aircraft. The girl looks terrified and whimpers with pain. I strap the handles of the stretcher to the floor and cover her with blankets and then replace the door.

'I'd better get along then...'

From force of habit, I walk once round the aircraft – not that I can see very much, but it's a necessary ritual and were I to omit it, I know I would have no peace of mind once aloft. I pull the propeller through one compression and feel the edges of the blades for stone damage. The engine smells nice and is still cracking as it cools in the night air. There is no humidity here, and the air is quite chilly.

'I'll send a signal now, and make sure the Sheikh knows she's on her way. I delayed signalling up until now, in case nobody came...'

I take my time in starting up and go through the full drill. There is a different atmosphere for night flying and it's as well not to rush. Or perhaps it is because I have been doing nothing but rushing so far, and at last there is time to do things properly.

Pre-takeoff vital actions complete and a last look behind at the girl. She doesn't look at all happy and her eyes plead with mine. I can't speak any Arabic to reassure her, so give her a smile instead, and then turn back to my work. If anything, the cloud base has lowered slightly, so we'll be on instruments straight away. I carefully check that the needle of the Direction Indicator is pointing down the runway and decide to do an instrument takeoff. There is nothing to see outside anyway, and I can keep her straight on the needle as well as any lamp on the end of the runway – even if there was one! I jot the figures on my pad for the return Flight

Plan based on 1620hrs takeoff, which is in three minutes time. I'll climb straight ahead and according to the map there are no nasty peaks in the way. I'll be flying to Khormaksar instead of Falaise so my course will be 221 degrees, so I'll climb to Flight Level 100. Which makes my estimate for the Boundary 1647hrs and Khormaksar at 1708hrs Zulu.

Time to go. I push the boost lever all the way, which at this altitude gives me nineteen inches and release the brakes. Eyes glued to the DI and control column in the neutral position, which will give me tail wheel steering. No point in dragging her off at this altitude... At sixty-two knots the rumbling from the wheels ceases and we are airborne. Reduce RPM and establish the climb. I glance up from the instruments and we are already in cloud.

I didn't use the ADF on the way out, but see that it is already tuned to the Khormaksar beacon, so now flick it on. At this altitude it should home in, but the needle hunts aimlessly around the dial. I reach up to the selector box and press the button that connects the ADF to my headset, and listen for the signal. It should be transmitting 'KR' in Morse, which is Dah-di-dah, Di-dah-di; but there is only the hiss of static. Either the instrument is u/s or the Khormaksar beacon is not transmitting. Now what was that trick Arthur used? The ADF is basically a radio with a needle that points to the transmitting station. So if you tune it into the British Forces Broadcasting Service... what did he say the frequency was? Ah yes... suddenly the excited voice of the commentator reading the evening 'sports round-up' booms in my headset. I flick the switch up and the needle stops wandering and homes firmly onto their transmitter, which is situated quite near the Officers Club at Steamer Point, where Roger and I went on our first day. Well done Arthur, that'll do nicely!

If I can listen to the Sports Round Up means I'm also in range with Aden Centre, so I give them a call. Halfway through transmitting my Flight Plan, we break out of the cloud at 9200 feet so I amend my in-flight conditions from

IMC to Visual and report 'VMC on top and climbing on track to Flight Level One-Zero-Zero.'

They acknowledge and also advise that the Khormaksar Beacon is unserviceable, and give me the weather. In the short space of time, the cloud has built up and the whole of the coastal area is now covered. Maybe it will be cooler tomorrow? Which will be good for the desert survival course if nothing else...

The sky is full of stars, which at this latitude look huge, but there is no moon. I settle back lower into my seat and turn the instrument lights down. The cockpit is now bathed in a cosy red glow, and I am alone with the stars. Every two seconds the propeller disc reflects the amber light from the rotating collision beacon. It reminds me of Dunkirk harbour, and the cold wet night I spent counting the flashes from the lighthouse whilst waiting for the ferry to dock. I have a sudden yearning to feel rain on my face and to wear a thick winter coat again; and yet, were I in Europe now, I'd probably give anything for a holiday in the sun... And anyway I'm not alone, for I'd forgotten about the girl.

I can smell her musky Arab smell, and wonder about her. Being the youngest wife of the Sheikh, her lot would be better than many others, for females are never very highly thought of in the Arab world. As far as I can make out they spend most of their lives carting water from the well. Also it never ceases to astonish me how many blonde European women there are living in these remote Arab settlements. Inevitably they met their Arab 'Prince' when he was a student in their home town, and lured by the glitter of becoming an Arabian Princess, married – only to find that they were now one of a number of wives; and Princess or not, were still expected to carry water from the well. One of the Political Officers told me that many a message filtered through to them, all pleading for help and rescue. But once legally married, they were beyond political help, and there was nothing anybody could do.

I wait for the second-hand to finish its sweep and it is 1647hrs and time to report the Boundary. I call Aden

Centre and they tell me to change frequency back to Khormaksar and wish me a merry 'goodnight'. I dial 119.7 and pass my in-flight details. I then tell Khormaksar the nature of my casevac and the political significance and ask whether they have an ambulance standing by? They confirm and tell me that they'll also alert the Duty Doctor. They then give me their latest weather and inform me that the field is overcast with a cloud base of about 500 feet, and that Radar can offer a Ground Controlled Approach should I require one. From feeling my way down into Mukerius, this is the other extreme and luxury indeed, so I gladly accept, and ask permission to start my descent.

I focus the cockpit spotlight onto my circular slide-rule and compute the figures: 10,000 feet and 50 miles to run at say, 120 knots? No, I can do better than that! What height and distance will Radar want to pick me up? Say 3000 feet at a range of 20 miles? That leaves 7000 feet to lose in 30 miles...120 knots, which shows 466 feet per minute.

'Now, we are above a solid overcast and there is no question of luck. This is precision flying and it's for real...'

'Okay, Mr Summers, you are never far away, and I'm glad you are with me tonight...'

I set the levers where he would have put them.

The engine quietens as I reduce the boost and above it I am conscious of a high-pitched wailing. Is it the ADF playing up again? I switch it off, but the wail persists and I flick it on again. I glance behind. It is the girl. In the dimness of the cabin I see she has crawled off the stretcher and is crouched in a huddled ball in the rear corner of the cabin.

'Come on, Mr Summers, now what do I do?' But he has gone.

'Khormaksar Approach, Five-Zero-One, I need some medical advice, is it possible to talk to the doctor?'

'Zero-One, wait – we'll try and get him...'

I continue descending and watch the second-hand sweep round three complete revolutions.

'Army Five-Zero-One, this is Khormaksar. We've got the doctor here, pass your message.'

I explain about the condition of the girl, who is still crying out and obviously in great pain and also that she is no longer lying flat on the stretcher.

'Zero-One, what medication do you have on board?'

'Khormaksar, only what I've got in my emergency crash-pack. Probably some morphine?'

'Zero-One. No, better not give her that. What altitude are you at?'

'Khormaksar, we're passing through Flight Level Eight-Zero, this time – why?'

'Zero-One. Um. Living at Mukerius, it's possible this girl has never been below an altitude of seven thousand feet in her life. So as you descend – maybe the pressure...? I don't know, but her condition could get worse. She'd be far better off lying flat on her back on the stretcher. Is there any way you can get her back?'

'Khormaksar. I'm on my own and I've got an aeroplane to fly! Wait, I'll see what I can do... I'll be off the air for a few minutes.'

I wind the elevator trim slightly forward to compensate for my weight going back, then unclip my harness and unplug my headset. With no co-pilot's seat in the way, it is easy to slide out and make my way aft. The floor is slippery with blood. She is huddled in a ball and indifferent to my approach and looks very young and frightened. I squat down beside her, then try to lift her as gently as possible. She is quite rigid and resists, all the time keening in the same high-pitched wail. I can't leave the aeroplane to fly itself for much longer, so take a firm grip and then drag her to the stretcher and lie her down. I hold her there for a moment and she gradually relaxes. I place the fingers of each of her hands around the frame of the stretcher and then cover her with the sodden blanket. She understands and grips the frame with both hands so I point to my watch and hold up five fingers and give her a reassuring smile.

The aircraft has veered off course ten degrees to port, but maintained the correct rate of descent. I turn starboard twenty degrees, and watch the needle of the ADF as it starts to centre again, then strap in and plug my helmet back into the radio socket. Khormaksar are calling me.

'...One, this is Khormaksar, do you read?'

I reply affirmative and they tell me to change frequency to Khormaksar Radar. They do not ask about the girl – and there's nothing I can do anyway, so try to put her to the back of my mind and concentrate on the business of flying. But still I cannot help feeling guilty – I wish there were something else I could do for her.

'Army Five-Zero-One, this is Khormaksar Radar, we have a Gulf Air commercial flight climbing outbound to the east on a conflicting course. Turn right twenty degrees for identification.'

I change course as directed and at the same time we brush through the tops of the cloud and then become wholly immersed.

'Army Five-Zero-One, we have you established on radar and you are now thirty-six miles out. Turn left seven degrees, which is your new course for Khormaksar. In two minutes time the other traffic will pass to the south of you – Gulf Air 863, acknowledge.' The voice of Gulf Air 863 acknowledges and I follow suit and also tell them I am now IFR and entered cloud at 5600 feet.

I watch the second-hand. Two minutes pass; then three and I know somewhere in the cloud Gulf Air 863 has gone by.

The needle of the ADF is slowly moving to the left, which means the wind has freshened and I am being blown north off course. Just as I turn left three degrees to compensate for this, Radar calls and tells me to do the same. This pleases me; the man below is good and now has all my faith.

As we pass through 3000 feet Radar tell me to set the Regional QNH of 1014 millibars onto my altimeter and advise my range is now ten miles. They then tell me to turn right onto a new heading of 240 degrees and descend to 2000 feet.

I descend again and call 'steady at two thousand'.

'Zero-One, Roger, maintain for two minutes.'

I maintain and set the stopwatch, luxuriant in the knowledge that the responsibility for finding and landing at Khormaksar has been taken from me. All I have to do is to fly as directed.

'Zero-One, turn right again onto two-six-zero degrees, and you are now downwind for runway Zero-Eight. Set the airfield QFE of One-Zero-Zero-Six millibars and do your downwind checks. Then descend to One thousand feet on the QFE. What is your break-off height?'

The break-off height is a polite way of asking what level of Instrument Rating I hold, for the Controller can only talk a pilot down to the level determined by his Rating, after which the responsibility transfers back to the pilot. I set the levers to give me ninety knots, re-set the altimeter and complete the downwind checks. It's an eyrie feeling knowing that you are about to land, but still flying totally blind in cloud.

'Radar, Zero-One is at one thousand on One-Zero-Zero-Six, downwind checks complete, and you can take me all the way...'

'Zero-One, Roger that, do a rate-one turn to the left now, to bring you back onto the runway heading of Zero-Eight, and do not acknowledge any further instructions...'

I settle down for the final talk-down.

At 450 feet I am conscious of the lights of Aden below and know we are now below the overcast, but I keep my eyes firmly on the instruments as the talk-down continues. At this point I could break-off from the GCA, but am loath to do so, for somehow it would be an anticlimax for both the controller and myself, having got this far.

At 100 feet I am told to switch my landing lights on and report if the runway is in sight. Now I can look up! The runway stretches ahead, all 8500 metres of it brilliantly lit, and it looks a welcoming sight. We are dead on the centre line and I can see the headlights of the cars as they cross the causeway just prior to the threshold. The world of instruments has evaporated.

I report 'Runway in sight' and reduce the boost and push the propeller control to fully fine and then let the aircraft land itself in a fast flapless landing. The tyres screech in protest and we are down.

The ambulance and doctor are waiting at dispersal and whisk the girl away whilst I am still shutting the engine down. When the propeller finally stops, I find I am on my own and the dispersal is empty.

I sit for a minute, savouring the quietness. Being a pilot is a strange occupation; one minute you are the key figure and an essential part of the action... and then suddenly your part is over – and like tonight, you are left sitting alone in an empty aeroplane in a deserted airport. Or maybe we have an over inflated opinion of our profession, and to the uninitiated we are just another bus driver. *Ah well, may as well get home...*

* * *

By morning the cloud had gone, and it was as hot as ever. Arthur called the three of us into his office and explained the scenario for our desert survival course. 'We're going to drop you off in a Scout some forty or so miles to the northwest. It's as though you've crashed and all you've got to do is to make your way back. You'll have the normal aircraft survival pack; you'll wear what you've got on now – oh, and you'll carry your normal side arms. If you're not back in three days, knuff, we'll come and look for you...'

An hour later we watched the Scout disappear into the heat haze and were alone in the sand dunes.

Biggles was already cracking open the large canvas bag, which had 'survival' stencilled on it and laying the contents out in the sand. When spread out, there was an awful lot of it; including a tent, a portable stove with blocks of fuel, a whole range of First Aid accoutrements designed to cover every eventuality, sealed containers of water, some interesting packs of food, some spare clothing and a compass.

Of the three of us, only Roger had had the forethought to talk to one of the other pilots about it, so as he was the expert, promptly he was elected leader.

'Or maybe we are just another bus driver. Ah well, may as well get home...'

The first thing we realized was that we would never be able to pack it all back into the canvass bag again, which left two options. We could either divide the whole of the pack between us, and thus loaded make our way slowly but surely home. Or, we could ditch most of it and travel fast and light. Also, our expert assured us, it was best to conserve energy and rest during the heat of the day, and travel at night.

We thought about this, and decided unanimously that marching at night would be the sensible thing to do.

Which then left the rest of the afternoon to debate whether to be safe and carry all the gear, or just to take the ninimum and travel light. In the end Biggles and I outvoted Roger (who by now had passed on his full knowledge of desert survival, and thus his leadership status was deemed to have been temporary) and we decided to travel fast and light.

We set off at dusk, having put on woolly socks and divided the rations that could be eaten straight from the pack without cooking and all the sealed packs of water. At the last minute we also decided to bring the flysheet from the tent, which would enable us to erect a shelter from the sun. Fortunately the canvass bag had had numerous webbing straps, which we managed to adapt so that most of the equipment could be hung from our belts, leaving our hands free. But even then, it was enough to carry and we made slow progress climbing the soft dunes of sand, which seemingly stretched forever.

Just before dawn we came across a track. It was so narrow we nearly missed it, but it was definitely a hard beaten track, weaving between the dunes and leading in roughly the direction our compass said we ought to go.

'Ah yes,' our survival expert said, taking the lead again, 'I'd forgotten about these... it's a camel track; one of the main routes used by the Bedouin for, well, for camel trains and things... anyway it seems to be going roughly our way, so we may as well use it...'

We made better progress on the track, although it led us slightly east of our course, and would probably end up in Aden rather than Falaise. But after to the dunes it was a Godsend and would do fine for now. We kept going until about 1000hrs and then it became too hot, so we decided to lie up for the day. Some military instinct made us move away from the track and we erected the flysheet some way back behind the dunes. Having carried it all night we were dismayed to find how little shade it gave, and even then we had to keep moving it as the sun climbed up; but it was better than nothing.

Biggles – or Adam Bartlett turned out to be an entertaining companion. He had a thin wiry frame and during the night march had been tireless, bounding ahead, leaving Roger and I floundering behind in the soft sand. All the time he had chattered away without pause for breath so that by now we knew most of his life story. From a youth his burning ambition had been to fly, but coming from a long line of distinguished soldiers, his father had insisted he joined the army rather than the Royal Air Force. His natural choice of regiment had been the Royal Artillery, for they flew spotter aircraft and offered the only path to becoming an aviator. He had been appalled to learn that even as a Gunner he would first have to serve five years before he would be allowed near an aeroplane, but this did not deter him and he took it upon himself as a personal challenge to beat the system. By persistent badgering, somehow he managed to persuade his colonel to recommend him for the flying course and then once he got to Wallop he was virtually home and dry. He passed out as an Auster pilot and had been posted to 8 Flight in Kenya some eighteen months previously.

Once there he started to eye the Beaver. The AOP IX was good fun to fly game wardens around counting heads of elephants, but Beavers were the aeroplanes that did all the serious flying, and the obvious choice for a serious aviator. The Flight was too small to have a Qualified Flying Instructor on its establishment, and relied upon a visiting QFI to check the flying standards. So he decided to teach himself how to fly the Beaver. This coincided with a change of Flight Commander, who was pleasantly surprised to find he had another Beaver pilot on strength, which was very useful... And so Biggles continued to fly the Beaver and only reverted back to the AOP IX for his periodic checks.

In spite of his youthful appearance, he was a born pilot and extremely able, and as the personnel of his Flight changed, he soon became invaluable in this role. He had an irrepressible enthusiasm together with a certain disdain for authority, which together with his frank and open manner endeared him as a personality – and he was accepted as such. To beat up the wedding reception was entirely within character, for it would have represented an irresistible target, and to cause the whole assembly to dive into the mud would have tickled his sense of humour no end.

But it was a puzzled Neville Bamford who as QFI gave him a customary check when he arrived in Aden. Here was a Beaver pilot with over 1000 hours captain time on type, who didn't know the correct sequence for any of the cockpit drills! Sure he could fly the aeroplane, and all the right levers and knobs were pressed in order to make it do so, but everything was out of sequence and the speeds and power settings all rather haphazard...

Which was why I had found it unusual to find a Beaver doing circuits and bumps in the circuit at Falaise when I had arrived that time after my spell of duty pilot at Habilayn.

Moreover, it wasn't only in the air that Biggles' enthusiasm had been found to be irrepressible and unorthodox. At a Mess party when the Navy had been invited for drinks, he had decided to liven things up by taking a tray of empty beer cans from one of the Mess Stewards, and throwing the whole lot up into one of the fast revolving fans in the roof. The sight of senior Naval officers diving for cover from the ensuing missiles was too good to be missed! Then he'd had a better idea, and organized a competition whereby the ceiling fan was stopped and the participant had to hang on the fan, which was then turned on. It was rather like throwing the hammer only using the human form. When the revolutions became unbearable... and the winner was the person who was flung the furthest!

In the Flight lines, he decided the crew room next deserved his attention. The crew room was a comfortable place with a few battered armchairs, where pilots could do their flight planning, or bring their logbooks up to date, or just sit and read in between sorties. Also it was the only place that visiting passengers could use as a waiting room. By the nature of things, these visiting passengers were often fairly high-ranking officers, who would bury their heads into mountains of important looking documents and try to ignore everything else going on around them.

So Biggles invented the game of Drax.

It was most effective when there were lots of waiting passengers, and the more senior the better. The rules were simple. There had to be a quorum of three resident members and any one could say to another 'You're on!' whereby the person thus nominated was obliged to do something. Once 'On' you could not refuse and would remain at this status until the duty was honourably discharged to the satisfaction of the others. We had a number of Sergeant Pilots who couldn't believe their luck, and taking Biggles' lead would gleefully await the opportunity to put someone 'On' and then watch the fun.

It started innocently enough and the first victim was a large major of Ordnance who was occupying the best armchair and reading a newspaper from behind which billowed clouds of pipe smoke.

'You're on!' one of the sergeants tentatively said to Biggles who had been deliberately hanging back. He acknowledged with the merest nod of his head and carried on reading his magazine. He then got up and casually walked past the major's chair to the table and selected another magazine. On the way back, without altering his stride, he clicked his lighter and applied the flame to the bottom of the major's paper, and then sat down.

Nothing happened for a moment or two and the rest of the crew room studiously ignored the flaming outer pages, which were still hidden from the reader's view. Suddenly the major gave a roar and made a dash for the door with the flaming paper in his hands. He eventually came back looking very sheepish muttering apologies about his pipe and was more than ready to escape when his flight was called.

All this we heard about whilst lying in the patch of shade, for it had happened when Roger and I were away at Habilayn. Even Roger thought that Drax could offer a certain amount of light-hearted diversion and we spent the remainder of the afternoon exploring the possibilities. No doubt Arthur would find a way to channel the natural enthusiasm emitted from his latest protégé, but I couldn't help wondering how Biggles would fit in with the operational team at Habilayn once he got there...

The day wore on and although we didn't sleep much, at least our bodies rested. At 1700hrs we ate some of the dried food and finished one of the sealed containers of water, which made one less to carry. By 1740hrs we were back on the camel path walking line-ahead with Roger in the lead. It was not wide enough for two to walk abreast, but at least the going was easy and he set a good pace. We stopped at midnight and had a drink and stretched out for ten minutes, and then set off again, this time with Biggles in the lead. Suddenly he halted and held up his hand. We peered ahead and then silently left the path.

Approaching was a camel train.

There were about a dozen of them, tied to each other from tail to head and plodding forward in absolute silence. Each had an Arab perched on its hump, draped under a black sheet or blanket and obviously asleep, leaving the lead camel to pick its own way along the path. It made an eerie sight and one as ancient as the desert itself.

We crouched low as they approached, then Biggles rose up and walked to the lead camel. Incredulously Roger and I looked at each other as he walked alongside it matching its pace, then taking the reins dangling from its head, steered it off the path. Silently the whole train followed behind as he wheeled them round in a one-eighty turn, each stepping in the footsteps of the one before, like a well-executed manoeuvre from marching bandsmen. As the rear camel passed, he guided the leader back onto the path and then let it go. The whole train plodded silently off into the night, back from whence they had come.

Biggles was beside himself with laughter, tears streaming down his face and rolling on the ground. It was infectious and soon Roger and I were doing the same, each imagining the scene when the Bedouin cast aside their covers at sunrise and found themselves re-entering Aden...

Suddenly I stopped as another thought hit me. 'It may be funny now, but at any time, those Bedouin could come thundering back along the path looking for the joker...'

'Shit, you're right!' Roger said. 'We'd best get off the track and head off into the desert. What are those curved daggers they carry in the front of their belts – khanjars? And were they carrying rifles? Bound to have been, they all do – and they're no mean shots... Jesus, Biggles! What have you got us into now? We've only got pistols and we don't want to start another war...'

We left the track, with Biggles walking backwards trying to obliterate our tracks and then headed due south on a compass course. God knows how much distance we covered but by sunrise it couldn't have been that far. By this time our imaginations were running riot and prompted by tales of how the Bedouin knew about every blade of grass that grew within 100 miles, we decided to camp and lie low straight away. We took it in turns to keep watch during the day, which made for more room for the other two in the patch of shade, and waited the day away.

We set off again at dusk and the sea of dunes continued endlessly and by midnight we were exhausted.

'Well, either we carry on' Roger said, 'or we backtrack; a full night's march north again and find the track, and hope they've gone...?'

It was a difficult decision, for by going south, at least we were heading in the right direction, albeit the going was slow and exhausting. But the energy spent struggling through the dunes increased our water consumption and this was the critical factor. By restricting water to just a mouthful during the day whilst lying up, would leave just about enough to last for another night and a half on the march.

It was hard to judge what distance we had travelled over the dunes so far, but from our floundering progress, it couldn't be very far - and we thought it unlikely that we would be able to reach Falaise in a night and a half. If we were going to backtrack, water dictated that now was the time to do it. It would take a full night to reach the track again, by which time we would only have half a day's ration left. But once on the track again, at least we would make better progress, and as Roger said, this would be the logical place to look for us from the air if they were going to send a search party. Bedouin on the warpath no longer figured as a critical factor in the equation.

We put it to the vote.

Roger and Biggles were for going north back to the track, whilst I voted to carry on through the dunes on a course for home.

'Look' I said, 'I happen to know these dunes don't last forever, for the desert by the coast is flat and hard. Once we're on the flat, we'll make good progress. It's got to be worth a shot, rather than going all the way back...?'

Biggles was still adamant about going back, but Roger was now undecided.

'Your decision, partner' I said. 'Tell you what, why don't you flip a coin? Heads we go back north, and tails we carry on? One flip and we'll all abide by the decision...?'

Roger agreed to that and the idea appealed to Biggles, so Roger produced a coin and flipped. It span up and disappeared into the night, and then we heard it plop into the sand.

'Here, let me!' Biggles said, 'heads north, right?' He flipped and deftly caught it with a slap of his hand. We peered in the gloom.

It was tails.

We struggled on and dawn found little change. Having made the decision, we were now very conscious of time and distance and our dwindling supply of water, and nobody voiced any thought of stopping. Biggles, untiring as ever was in the lead and then waited for us on the top of another dune.

'Look!' he said.

The flat coastal plain stretched ahead, with the sand as hard as rock.

'Well done, partner' Roger said, 'it will be almost like a rest to walk on this, let's keep going until the heat gets impossible...'

We walked on until the drone of a slow-flying aircraft

stopped us and we all looked up. It was a Beverley flying slowly into wind and even as we watched it disgorged a stream of dots from the rear of its bulbous fuselage. The dots fell earthwards and then blossomed out into parachutes. They landed about 300 paces away some dragging along the ground and obviously in difficulties. Another Beverley followed with another load and then half a dozen three-ton trucks appeared out of nowhere. What a moment before had been an inhospitable and empty desert was fast turning into a military playground. One of the parachutists landed quite near and lay prone on the ground. We walked over to him.

'Hello, you all right?' Roger asked.

'Think I've bust my bleeding leg... Christ, this ground is hard!'

He told us that they were a Territorial Army detachment of SAS from the UK on a fortnight's exercise. The highlight of the exercise was a freefall parachute jump, which is what we had just walked into. Possibly they had not jumped for a long time, and certainly had not expected the rock-hard sand of the Dropping Zone, which had wreaked havoc throughout their ranks. There were many injuries, mostly broken legs and arms and it took some time to load the wounded into the rear of the trucks. We had nearly finished when a Land Rover drew up with a half-colonel sitting in the passenger seat.

'Thanks for your help – but where have you sprung from?' he said, eyeing our light-blue berets and unkempt and sunburnt appearance.

'We're about to ask you for a lift back to our airfield at Falaise, if you wouldn't mind swinging by that way...?' I said, giving him a salute, 'we've been on the go for a couple of days and we're almost out of water...'

He sent the trucks off with his second in command, and we climbed into the Land Rover and resumed our compass course for Falaise.

* * *

The next day Roger and I looked over the nearly finished Officers Mess building. It was very grand with open purdah walling to let in the breeze and the whole complex designed around a courtyard, the centrepiece of which featured a pond and a fountain. Inside, the rooms were white and spacious, each with their own air conditioner and altogether very different from the squalid complex of huts we now occupied. Although, our present mess hut had a certain Colonial charm about it and in a way we'd be sorry to leave. The 16/5th Lancer Quartermaster had been a gardener, his pride and joy being the lawn, which had flourished at the expense of vast amounts of water. It was virtually the only patch of green in the whole of South Arabia, and in the air you could spot it from miles away. There was a rickety veranda running around the Mess, which was a comfortable place to sit with a long drink in the evenings and listen to the crickets chirping. Vines of some sort grew up the walls and covered the whole of the roof, which added to its charm, until you encountered the numerous species of wildlife that had also adopted this unexpected abundance of lush vegetation as home.

But all in all, we decided the new building would be a much better place to live in, and we were looking forward to moving, in about a fortnight's time.

'Did you see that entry in the 16/5th Line Book?' Roger enquired.

The 16/5th Lancers ran what they called a 'Line Book', which dated back to the time the Regiment was first formed. It was almost a Regimental history in its own right and made fascinating reading with such entries as 'Lieutenant Lord Worcester wagers 100 guineas that Captain William Weatherby attends the forthcoming Mess Dinner night mounted on his charger...' and this dated 22nd June 1813 – the day after the Battle of Vitória during the Peninsular War, but disdaining to make any mention about the battle itself.

The latest entry, Roger told me, read to the effect that someone had bet a crate of champagne that Biggles ran the wheels of a Beaver along the roof of the mess to sever the growth of vines that covered it.

'Oh no!' I groaned, 'he's in enough trouble as it is...'

Biggles was already up to his neck in trouble. On returning from our desert survival trek, he had continued with his 'conversion course' learning to fly the Beaver correctly. The circuit at Falaise was becoming extremely crowded, for by now two regiments had been equipped with Sioux helicopters for their Air Troops and pilot training was at its maximum. Also the REME workshops were being expanded to cope with all the extra servicing, which meant some of the perimeter track had been taken for storing building materials. So Biggles had been told to fly to one of the up-country strips to practice strip landings, where he would be well out of everybody's way.

He flew to one of the strips in the Radfan, and then without bothering to clock-in with the Brigade, decided to sniff around the battle area. Flying around the side of a mountain, he found more than he bargained for, and got hit by small arms fire. He wasn't having any of that! Jettisoning his door, he grabbed the SMG he just happened to have with him, and flying with one hand and his knees, decided to take them on. What he didn't know was that a patrol was just positioning itself to winkle them out, and his unexpected appearance made the enemy scatter and ruined the attack. He landed back at Falaise minus a door, but very pleased with himself – only to find the wrath of God, in the shape of Colonel Mike waiting for him. The interview had ended by his being grounded and put on permanent Orderly Officer until a suitable fate could be found for him.

Then there had been the business over Drax.

The Area Commander of the Federal Regular Army together with some members of his staff were waiting for a flight when Biggles, on his Orderly Officer's rounds, stuck his head around the door and was promptly put 'On' by one of the sergeant-pilots.

He thought for a moment and then went to the phone and dialled HQ Middle East Command in Aden.

'Ah, can you put me through to the Commander in Chief, please? Sorry? No, no – the Commander in Chief's office. Who? Oh, Security here, telephones... Is that the Commander in Chief – oh, it isn't? Well, could you put me through to his office please? Security here, yes it's quite urgent...

'Is that the Commander in Chief? Ah! Sorry to disturb you, sir, but it's about the new security order you signed... Yes, I'm sorry if you are busy, sir, but this won't take a moment. No, it's about the telephones, sir... The order you signed about being able to use the telephone from the window, sir. What? Well you did, sir... In case of emergency the telephone cord has to be long enough... Well it's got to be able to reach so that someone can use the telephone from outside the window, sir... Well I can't help that, sir; I'm just doing my job... Well, as I explained, sir, if you could just measure... Well, pick up the phone, and see if the cord is long enough to reach the window... Yes, that's it, sir.

'It's not! Well how short is it..? About a metre..? Well, tell you what, sir, I seem to have plenty of slack my end, if you pull, I'll just let some off...'

He carefully replaced the receiver and looked triumphantly around the crew room and then exploded into laughter. The others, who hadn't believed their ears sat stunned for a moment and then took it up and soon the whole crew room was engulfed in peals of laughter, so much that Arthur wandered in to see what was happening. On seeing a full-colonel doubled up with mirth, he assumed everything was all right; but then he noticed Biggles revelling in the midst of it, which made him frown and leave with a worried look.

All would have been well had the colonel not told the story when he got back to his office. It went round Middle East Command like wildfire, and eventually reached the ears of the Commander in Chief, who then telephoned Colonel Mike...

Biggles never did move into the new mess. Early next morning I was woken by the distinctive whine of an approaching Pratt and Whitney, followed by a roar and a prolonged crashing noise and then the echo of a 'thrub-thrub-thrub' as the Beaver climbed away. We stumbled out of our huts to find the roof of the mess a mass of tangled vines and foliage where his wheels had sliced through, leaving two parallel lines. It was an exacting piece of flying and he must have locked the brakes to rip it apart so effectively.

He won his case of champagne and we drank every bottle at his farewell party, for he left the following day.

Nearly a quarter of a century would pass before I again became aware of his distinctive voice. I was waiting in the queue to take off from London Heathrow, looking very out of place in a small twin engined aircraft, little bigger than a Beaver. A large QANTAS jet had followed me around the ring, and I heard the pilot acknowledge to the Tower to draw up behind the light twin. I searched my memory for I knew that voice from somewhere... and suddenly the vision of Biggles bounding over the sand dunes flashed through my mind.

I pressed the transmitter button. 'You're ON!' I broadcasted at random.

There was a long pause, then, 'Don't tell me you are still following camel tracks in that little thing..?' the captain of the QANTAS jet replied.

263

Chapter 8

The only thing moving is a beetle. It has crawled from the Very light cartridges at the base of the rock, and is now heading out across the wadi towards the Beaver – a journey that will take it some weeks to accomplish. It is unlike any beetle I have ever seen before, for it is camouflaged sand-yellow and seems to have an armoured skin set in overlapping segments, and its legs have little spades on them to help propel it across the soft sand. It seems to be quite at home in its environment, and maybe it even knows where it is going. Up and down the ripples of sand like a tiny ship ploughing through the waves, and leaving a diminutive track behind it, which will presumably disappear after a matter of moments like the wake of a ship. It reminds me of the first time I saw HMS Albion from the air, and the bend in her wake when she turned into wind that time I first landed on her...

※ ※ ※

'The best thing to do, is to treat it, knuff, like a strip that moves...' Arthur was saying.

'A strip that moves? Surely you can do better than that? There must be other factors...?'

'Well to my knowledge nobody from the Army Air Corps has ever done it before so, knuff, you'll just have to be careful. Anyway, I've arranged for you to stay the night on board and then you can fly on to Perim in the morning and pick up General Cobham plus two, and take them back to Khormaksar. It's time you put your new rating to work.' Although he was a frequent passenger and well known to the Flight, I had not flown General Cobham before, for to

264

'..the best thing to do is to treat it as a strip that moves...'

fly a full general you have to have a VIP rating, which is only attained after a minimum of 1200 hours captain time, which milestone I had just passed.

'How far out is this ship? I'm thinking about fuel – it's a hell of a business refuelling at Perim.'

'Don't know. Knuff. She left last night and the longer you leave it, the further she'll be. You'll be able to home into her on the ADF – I'll give you all her frequencies before you leave. But I know what you mean about fuel... I don't know if *Albion* carries Avgas, I imagine all her helicopters are turbine, so maybe not. To be on the safe side you'd better fill the tip-tanks. Just remember you'll be landing heavy...'

'I'd best go and pack a bag then.'

HMS *Albion* was an aircraft carrier. Or correctly speaking she was a Commando Carrier, for she did not have a long flight deck that was set at an angle to keep aircraft well away from the superstructure, nor did she have a ski-jump arrangement at the end of the flight deck to throw jet aircraft into the air. Instead she had a straight deck and no arrester wires, for she had been designed exclusively for assault helicopters, which didn't need such arrangements. She had called in at Aden on her way back from the Far East, and was now on her way to South Africa; only she had had to sail without her new 'Commander Air'. The intention had been for him to join the ship at Aden, but his flight out from the UK had been delayed and he was now stranded at Khormaksar.

The obvious solution would have been for the ship to send a helicopter back for him, but for various reasons this had been discounted, so someone had come up with the bright idea that a Beaver was just the aeroplane to unite him with his ship. Furthermore, if he was that desperate to join his command, he was in no position to refuse – even if it did mean risking a deck landing with a pilot and an aircraft neither of which had ever attempted it before. Also it would be extremely useful – and possibly of future tactical significance, to see whether army fixed wing aircraft could operate from a Commando Carrier...

As 'Commander Air' was an aviator, I had been going to suggest that he might find it interesting to sit in the right hand seat; but as it turned out this was the only place he could go. I found him at Khormaksar surrounded by a mountain of luggage and assorted crates, which he passed off as 'just a few spares', which he had brought out from the UK with him. In the end we had to collapse the rear bench and then take out and re-stow the two central passenger seats stacked one on top of the other in the rear of the cabin, before everything would fit in. Even then it was a tight fit and it took some time to lash it all down.

With this weight as well as carrying full wing-tip tanks, we used a lot of runway taking off and I climbed straight ahead to 2000 feet on the runway heading of 260, before clearing to the left in a gentle turn to bring us round onto 195, which points straight out to sea and hopefully was an intercept for *Albion*. I'd requested Flight Level Eight-Zero and we bore on upwards burning fuel from the front tank, so that the weight could be transferred inboard from the tip-tanks as soon as possible. Over the sea the visibility reduced to about a mile and by the time we attained Eight-Zero we were virtually IMC in thick haze. This was made worse by the reflection of the bright sun, and once again it was as though we were in our own isolated bubble of reality, totally detached from the rest of the world.

I had been looking forward to sharing the cockpit with a fellow pilot, for apart from instructors, the last time I had shared a cockpit had been with Major Anderson on our trips to Germany during the Beaver conversion course. But so far, the Commander Air had shown little interest in the aeroplane or the proceedings, and had remained completely lost in his own thoughts. I put the Beaver on the step at Eight-Zero and then spent some time adjusting the trims before taking my hands and feet off the controls. Although designed as a workhorse, the Beaver was the most beautifully balanced aircraft to fly, and once trimmed properly would hold course and height as effortlessly as any autopilot. This broke his reverie and he watched the instruments with interest as the aircraft flew itself. I fished in my bag for the flask of coffee I had brought along, then waved a hand at the co-pilot's wheel.

'Do you want to have a go?'

He put his hands and feet on and tried a few gentle movements and then turned to me and grinned, and with it the atmosphere lightened.

'She's very light...' Once again the intimacy of flight was working its magic. 'You got a map?' he said after about fifteen minutes, 'I'll try and work out where *Albion* is... oh, and my name's Frank.'

I passed him the map on which I had drawn a pencil line that petered out with a question mark.

'Mmm. May I?' He nodded at the ADF, which was still tuned into Khormaksar and showed a back bearing of 180 degrees, then flicked the switch to the tuning mode and re-tuned the frequency dial. Finally he flicked the switch back and the needle hesitated and then swung round to hunt around the zero mark.

'We're a bit far out...' He leant across and looked at the Air Speed. 'What wind are you working on?'

'Thirty knots, more or less on the nose – ground speed, about hundred and ten at this altitude...'

'Mmm. I'm strictly a chopper pilot and we don't normally fly as high as this. Smooth, isn't it? You landed on a carrier before?'

'No. Ah, no! I was told to treat it like a "strip-wot-moves..." in fact, if you've got any tips, they'd be very welcome?'

'Christ! Well... for flying on, the Captain will turn the ship into wind, but he hates doing this, especially if it's far off his course. Shouldn't be too bad today though, with the wind virtually dead ahead. Then they'll ask you how many knots of wind you want over the deck, and they'll try and adjust the speed of the ship to give you what you ask for. It's a bit different in a helicopter and we can normally bang them on whatever the wind conditions. I've never flown fixed wing in earnest, but I gather from our guys the idea is to be positive with plenty of speed and drive it in and rely on the arrester hook to stop... shit, you haven't got one of those, I suppose?'

'No... I'd been thinking about that. The only trick I've got is to dump full flap when I know we're down. Fully down they're all drag with negative lift, and usually makes the aircraft sit down...'

'Well, it's going to be interesting if nothing else... The main thing to remember is not to land too far over to the left. If your wing goes over the side of the deck, it'll pick up the additional slipstream from the side of the hull. Even in a chopper we are wary of this and try to keep clear of the edge. It's vicious and enough to pick your wing up and put you into a turn just as you land. Then, you'll find this will be exaggerated by the vortex that occurs behind the island, which will also tend to suck you in... oh, and do a nice steep approach so to avoid the back draft and turbulence from the stern of the ship. I think that's about all...'

We droned on and gradually the ADF needle stopped its hunting and settled on 350. Like a compass, the ADF is calibrated into 360 degrees, but this must not be confused with a magnetic heading. It is strictly a radio compass and the needle always points to the source of the transmission. Pointing at 350 means the beacon is ten degrees to the left of our present heading. To home in, you turn the aircraft ten degrees to the left, which will bring the ADF needle straight up onto 360, with the aircraft now pointing directly at the beacon. It is tempting to then follow the needle home, but this must be resisted, for if you have a crosswind you will for ever be chasing the needle by turning into it and your track over the ground will become an arc instead of a straight line. Instead, having turned the aircraft to point at the beacon, you set the cursor on the Direction Indicator to point straight up, and fly on this compass heading, and should the ADF needle wander away from 360, will indicate from which direction any crosswind is blowing. You can then fine-tune the aircraft heading by quartering the drift until both needles remain central, and this will then give you a straight track over the ground.

Without a fixed destination and with no landmarks to gauge distance travelled, it is difficult to assess the strength of the wind, and my gut feeling is that it is in excess of the thirty-knots forecast. I transfer the last of the fuel from the tip-tanks, and then thankfully turn the selector to draw from the rear tank. We are still heavy, but at least now the wings won't snap off as a result of a heavy landing.

Frank has been doing some calculations and shows me the revised cross he has pencilled onto the chart. 'Give it another twenty-minutes, then you could try calling them..?'

It is good to fly with another pilot.

He is obviously used to flying over the sea, but it always makes me uncomfortable; for some reason engines never sound so sweet as they do over land.

'Should I call them *Albion*, or by their daily code number?'

'Oh, *Albion* will do, I'm sure the whole world knows we are here... give them a try now, if you like...'

I give them a call and they say that they have had us on radar for the past ten minutes and our range is forty-three miles. Frank puts the ruler on the map, and marks our position. It is further back from the estimates I had marked, which confirms my suspicions about the wind.

'I reckon we're pushing nearer forty knots headwind' he remarks, following my thoughts.

'Mmm. Anyway, time to slide down the line...' I call Aden Centre and tell them we are starting our descent and then change back to *Albion* and tell them the same. From habit I put the equation into my circular computer and read off the figures, then juggle the levers to give a rate of descent of 400 feet per minute and re-trim the aircraft to fly hands off. Frank watches this with interest and smiles when he sees the needle of the Vertical Speed Indicator settle on 'Down 400'.

'Nice way to fly' he remarks, then 'you staying on board tonight? Won't that just make it further for you to get back tomorrow?'

'No, I'm going on to Perim Island to pick up a General and a couple of his staff. Perim's down at the bottom of the Red Sea, so if I leave first thing, the three legs will make a nice equilateral triangle. That's why I had to bring the passenger seats with me, else I'd have left them at Khormaksar...'

'Army Five-Zero-One, this is *Albion*, do you read?'

'*Albion*, Zero-One, Go.' I glance at the altimeter and we are at 2000 feet. That will make it about ten miles to run. I increase the boost and RPM for I think it will be prudent to hang onto this height until the ship is in sight.

'Zero-One, you are now range ten miles, set your altimeter to Nine-Eight-Seven and what wind speed will you require over the deck?'

'*Albion*, Zero-One. Roger to ten miles. Ah! Twenty-knots over the deck? QFE of Nine-Eight-Seven is set.'

'Zero-One will have twenty knots – slightly over the port quarter? Call again, ship in sight.'

I click the button twice and set the altimeter. This really is a strip-wot-moves...

'There she is!' Bill says.

'Christ! Have I got to land on that? It looks no bigger than a matchbox...'

'You'll find it's large enough when you get down. But I don't like the way they've stored all that equipment – assault boats and things, on the deck near the threshold. I'll have to do something about that...'

I descend to 1000 feet and overfly the ship. I can see where she turned from the wake she is leaving. Then I see the equipment – an assortment of assault boats and vehicles in a block on the starboard side at the very aft end of the deck, just where I want to put down.

'See that round patch on the deck just to the left of the equipment? That's the aft lift down to the hangar. Try and put down on that, and you'll be about right.' Frank was saying.

'You sure there'll be enough room? That stuff's encroaching onto the flight deck. We've got a long plank of a wing you know...'

'...although it's tempting, the main thing to remember is not to land too far over to the left...you see that round patch on the deck, that's the aft lift down to the hangar. Put down on that and you'll be about right...'

'You should have enough room, it's deceptive... you'll see.'

I turn left and prepare to do a conventional square circuit. By the time the downwind checks are complete, the ship has flipped past. There is some wind out here... I hold a thousand feet on base leg and turn onto finals. The ship seems to have steamed miles ahead. I set up for landing and reduce the speed to sixty knots still holding 1000 feet. Very slowly we start to overhaul her. There's got to be more than twenty knots of wind over the deck! More like thirty plus, by the time it's taking to overhaul her. I can now see the hatch – which is a damn sight larger than the handkerchief Sergeant Barker used to put down for our spot landing competitions in the AOP IX's... but I do not like the closeness of the vehicles and equipment stored on deck and instinctively edge away to the left. I reduce the power and immediately the ship draws ahead again. This is ridiculous! We seem to be hanging like a kite on the end of a piece of string. The temptation is to put the nose down to lose height, but this is against every rule for a short landing; speed must always be the critical factor. By playing the throttle I manage to creep over the threshold, slightly left of the hatch, but still I do not like the closeness of the assault boats together with what has now materialised into a small landing craft. Now that we are virtually on top of them, there is obviously not enough clearance. Should I over-shoot... or ease over a bit more to the left? There is a line of white hats watching from the outside wing of the bridge. I veer away from the assault boats, then reduce the power and hold her steady...

The port wing suddenly flicks up and swings us in towards the superstructure, and the white hats disappear behind the parapet. It is exactly like the time the AOP IX pulled the same trick on me, so long ago. Only this time there is no wide expanse of grass field, but only a narrow steel deck confined on one side by the wall of the super-structure. There is insufficient airflow over the wings for the ailerons to be effective, which only leaves a boot-full of left rudder and maximum revs to get us out of this. The engine howls and the forced slipstream punches us back into the air and makes the rudder bite. It slews us round and we corkscrew up... and flip straight over the side of the deck. The slipstream around the hull now hits us – but at least it can be used to advantage, so again with rudder I kick into it... and we are flying again.

I climb away. '*Albion*, Zero-One is executing a missed approach' I announce, doing my best to imitate Arthur at his casual best. Then sneak a look at Frank beside me. He is sweating profusely. 'Sorry about that – it'll be okay next time, I've got it sussed now...'

'Zero-One, *Albion*. Roger to your missed approach, you are cleared to overshoot. Do you want us to move the assault boats?'

'Negative, I'll land over them next time and put down halfway along the deck. What wind do you have over the deck?'

'Zero-One, wait... Zero-One, wind speed indicating forty knots. Sorry, I know you asked for twenty... will this be a problem?'

'*Albion*, not now that I know... I'll call again short-finals.'

We went round again and this time it went like clockwork. I held altitude until almost over the stern, and then using the gradient of the wind, powered in against three-quarter flap to land with a thump halfway along the deck, dumping the remainder of the flap the instant we made contact, which held us down.

'*I told you Lindbergh; think like a bird. Once you understand the wind, it will always be your friend. If you do not understand it, it will be your enemy...*'

At first light there were not nearly so many white hats peering down from the bridge, but I was very conscious of the Captain's presence as he turned the ship into wind and then stood staring down whilst the temperatures took forever to climb into the green. This time they had given me a genuine twenty knots of wind over the deck – and being light, I thought the Beaver would just leap into the air. But I couldn't have been more wrong. The Air Speed Indicator said we should fly, but some skin friction kept us pinned firmly to the deck and I couldn't haul her off. We ran for the whole length of the deck until I thought we were going to plop off the end, then just as disaster was inevitable, we met a wall of rising air that the ship was pushing up in front of it, which literally threw us into the air... but it was a nasty moment.

I didn't know it then, but it was a moment that would repeat itself – and one that I would never come to terms with, on all the subsequent takeoff's we did from *Albion* later in the year.

I did a low pass over the ship and gave a wave to Frank who was standing next to the Captain and then set course for Perim Island. The wind was now on our tail quarter and I didn't bother to climb above 2000 feet. I picked up the coast of Africa and then angled north and after an hour the coast of Arabia appeared and closed in from the starboard, and then there was Perim Island surrounded by a turquoise

'...this time it went like clockwork and we landed with a thump on the aft lift...'

274

'...and then there was Penim Island, surrounded by a turquoise sea...'

sea. With the tail wind, we arrived some twenty minutes ahead of schedule, but General Cobham and his two staff officers were already waiting at the strip.

Arthur had told me that he was a 'grand old boy', but could be an 'exacting' passenger and was a stickler for accurate time keeping, so I was pleased we were early. Arthur had also told me to fly him with consideration, for he was a great supporter of Army Aviation, and did an enormous amount to promote our cause in the corridors of power that mattered.

'Look here, young man' the General buttonholed me before he climbed in – and he always insisted in sitting in the co-pilot's seat. 'I've done a lot of flying in my time – I was flying before you were born, so you don't have to tell me anything about it. So I'll tell you now: I don't want any hanky-panky – and none of that banking business. You understand? No damned banking!'

'Right, General – I'll do my best.' I kept the flight as gentle as possible using the minimum amount of bank in the turns, which meant using blatant amounts of rudder in

275

order to steer. Some of the turns were grossly out of balance, resulting in wild skids that would have made Mr Summers shudder, but so long as we didn't bank the General didn't seem to notice.

But my good intentions all came to nothing when we landed at Khormaksar. With the southerly gale blowing, meant the main Two-Six runway was eighty degrees out of wind. (Runways are numbered by their true bearings, thus the bearing of runway Two-Six is 260 degrees, or if you use it the other way it becomes the reciprocal Zero-Eight). With the wind from the south, I asked the tower if I could use One-Four, being the little-used dirt runway, but at least would only be forty degrees out of wind. But this was being worked upon and I was told to use Two-Six or nothing.

There are two ways of landing in a crosswind. Either you bank into it, so that you counter the sideways drift by constantly turning into it, thereby achieving a straight track over the ground. Once established, this track should be the same as an extended line from the runway. Just before touchdown you level the wings and literally fly the aeroplane onto the ground, landing on the main wheels only. This landing is known as a 'wheeler' and uses a lot of runway before you can start to apply the brakes and bring the aircraft to a halt. The other way is to bisect the wind angle and then aim-off and head into it, which means the aircraft – although now pointing away from the runway, is still tracking in a straight line over the ground and on the same extended line from it. The advantage of the latter method is that it is executed at the normal landing speeds, always bearing in mind that the slower you go, the more you have to head-off to counter the crosswind. Just before touchdown, you choose your moment and then kick the aircraft straight with rudder to land firmly on all three points – and once on the ground, are travelling at a speed whereby the brakes can immediately be applied as well as being able to steer in the normal way.

It was a difficult decision. If you've got the room, banking into the wind and using a lot of runway with a fast wheeler is generally the accepted method. But the General had already demonstrated his fear by going rigid in his seat at even the slightest suggestion of a bank. Besides, most of my training had evolved from the techniques used for short strips, where, if there happens to be a howling crosswind, a wheeler cannot even be considered.

Either way this crosswind exceeded the aircraft's recommended limits, but there was no ready alternative. And at least I knew my aeroplane.

I slowed to seventy knots and selected fifteen degrees of flap and turned left onto finals and then crabbed on round to bisect the wind angle. And on... and some more... and then some more yet..! So much that I had to look through the General's side window in order to see the runway. But we tracked down beautifully, and I managed to kick her straight just at the right second – and all in all, it was one of my better landings.

When I eventually got back to Falaise, Arthur was waiting for me as I shut down. He had just received a message from the General's Aide at HQ Middle East Command, who relayed that the General didn't want to fly with that pilot again, because he landed sideways!

But fate (or maybe it was Arthur) dictated that I would fly General Cobham many times again. So much, that in the end I think he used to ask for me – presumably on the basis that I was the Devil he knew. Or maybe the other pilots were not so condescending when it came to executing flat turns and skidding all over the sky. I think the reason he always insisted in sitting in the co-pilot's seat, was so that he could keep an eye on things – and which is probably why he made General. By sitting there, you automatically become involved with what is going on, and after a while I decided I knew him well enough to enlarge upon this and began to explain what I was doing and why. He took great interest in this, and even ventured to hold the wheel on occasions, which helped alleviate his fear of flying. I then explained why we had to bank an aeroplane in order to turn, and once he understood the reason and that it wasn't the pilot being deliberately obtuse, I was able to carry out balanced turns again. I even landed him on HMS *Albion* once, which was highly illegal, but true to his word, he smoothed over any trouble that could have ensued.

Throughout this time, HMS *Albion* was much in demand. As a Commando Carrier she could offer instant support to the two operational theatres in Borneo and Aden, and by sailing between the two, she always managed to be there when she was needed. Nine months after my first landing on her with the Commander Air, she appeared again and it was decided that it would be useful if the whole Flight could learn how to operate from her deck.

Arthur was in the process of handing over the Flight to his successor and with a straight face, calmly told him that I was the local expert (blatantly omitting to mention that my 'expertise' had been gained solely as a result of a single landing) and that since Neville Bamford the QFI was away, I would be the obvious choice to conduct this training. Arthur declined to come, and his successor, Major Brian Young said he was too busy taking over the Flight and would leave it for another time.

I found a matchbox and put it on the crew room table, and said this amply represented the size of the ship as seen from the air and then went on to explain about the wind effects and the speeds and settings I had found best for the approach and landing. Then over the next few days lead three or four Beavers, each with two pilots, so that all could have a turn. We did this whilst she was at sea and within range and in the end became quite proficient at it. In the event, we never had to live on board or fly off her tactically, but it was all good practice, and everyone enjoyed it. *Albion* then went off again and life returned to normal.

We dined Arthur out in the mess, and next morning I flew him to Khormaksar to catch his UK flight, prior to picking up General Cobham and two of his staff and flying them to Addis Ababa for a meeting.

We had time to spare, so I helped him with his baggage to the waiting lounge. He was in uniform, but not the customary shirt, corduroy trousers and desert boots, but now almost unrecognisable in well-pressed Khaki-drill, a new Regimental hat and shiny brown shoes. Also he had unpinned his wings, and only the three poppers remained, leaving an empty space above his left breast pocket. This was unnecessary, for once you have won your wings you are always entitled to wear them, but mentally, he had already left us.

Which made me unspeakably sad.

He was one of the best pilots in the business; but he would never fly again. He had applied for the Army Air Corps permanent cadre, but had been rejected on the grounds of being too old in his rank, and another flying tour was now out of the question. The only job his Regiment had come up with was some obscure post in their training battalion, which he confessed he was not looking forward to.

'Well, I've enjoyed knowing you and especially your help in the Flight' he said with only an eyelid twitching in his immobile face. 'I'm sure you'll, knuff, look after things until Brian Young finds his feet.'

'...and it was decided that it would be useful if the whole flight could learn to operate from her deck...'

279

We sat down opposite each other on the facing bench seats and I couldn't think of anything to say. He looked up, embarrassed and then went on, picking his words with care.

'You have the *makings* of becoming an able pilot and one of the few who understand the poetry of flight... it's difficult to explain to people who don't understand, but I think you know what I mean. I watched you land just now, and... Knuff. Only you can't afford to be a dreamer – army flying is all cut and thrust and there's no room for poetry. Take my advice; don't stay with fixed wing for too long. Helicopters are the way forward with the Army Air Corps. There's no poetry of flight with them, but they're the future if you want to stay on as an army flyer. We all know they are expensive to run and take three times more servicing than something like a Beaver, but the army has no regard for expense and, knuff, all that counts is that helicopters are becoming more versatile and suitable for the job. The new generation helicopters will have all the range and speed the army will *ever* need, as well as an attack capability...

'So the sooner you get onto a chopper conversion course, the better it will be for your career. I expect they'll end up by putting all the old lags onto Beavers – but it would appear... well I'm even past that now. What was it Bob Summers called you... Lindbergh? Knuff, very apt – now *there* was a man who lived for flight... Dear old Bob, I even applied for his job when I heard, but there were about a hundred others before me...

'Well, so long, you'd better go and find General Cobham – and, and take care...'

I walked back to the Beaver and gave her a long look. Are you soon to be relegated into a second-line liaison aircraft and flown by an old lag? With your pedigree, surely you deserve better than that? Anyway, I still enjoy the 'niceties' of flying you. I climbed up the landing strut and started up.

I'm really going to miss you, Arthur... Then I taxied around the airfield to the military sector where I found General Cobham looking at his watch.

The flight to Addis was interesting in that in spite of overflying Somalia and halfway across Ethiopia, it was much nearer than I had thought. I had even checked the Flight Plan twice the previous evening, but the distances were right, and we could do it in one hop without refuelling. We climbed up to FL 100 and the weather was glorious and as clear as crystal, and from that height we could see for miles. We crossed the Gulf and I could see where Perim lay, away up to the north, where the sky finally merged with the sea. I cut the corner and left Djibouti to starboard and tracked straight for Dire Dawa before turning west for Addis. From Dire Dawa the ground began to climb up to meet us and although still at FL100, twenty miles before touchdown at Addis, we seemed to be almost brushing the trees! The airport was just over nine thousand feet high, and there was high ground all around. Biggles had told me he had once flown here in an AOP IX from Nairobi, which was about the same distance, but I imagine the performance must have been extremely marginal and I don't think I would have fancied it.

The General's meeting lasted for a couple of days, which was all too short a time to explore the city. After Aden, the climate was wonderful and I loved the Italian influence and the happy disposition of the people. It would be a good place to come for a holiday. But the General had his timetable and had to get back.

At that altitude we used a lot of runway for the takeoff, and then turned east and set course for Aden, which at least was now all downhill. The weather wasn't so good as on the way out and I had to climb to FL 150 to get above the cloud so we crossed Ethiopia and then Somalia using the beacons and then headed out to sea, where the cloud ceased but once again became virtually IFR in haze. The beacon at Djibouti had very limited range, so I decided to tune the ADF to Khormaksar well in advance, so that it would start homing the minute we came into range. Whilst tuning the knob, it suddenly squawked into life on an active frequency, which I recognized as being the same as used by HMS *Albion*. But the last I'd heard, she was still in the Far East, so what other beacon was using that frequency? There was only one way to find out and I dialled *Albion*'s VHF radio frequency.

'*Albion*, this is Army Five-Zero-One, do you read...?'

There was no reply.

Oh well, perhaps it was the ADF picking up some freak interference...

I was about to resume tuning when a voice came on the air.

'Aircraft calling on frequency One-One-Seven-decimal-nine, state your intentions.'

'Ah, this is Army Five-Zero-One on One-One-Seven-Nine, I regret I do not have your code for the day...'

'Five-Zero-One, wait. Out.'

There was a long pause, then 'Army Five-Zero-One, do you read?' That voice I did recognize, for it was my old friend Frank, the Commander Air.

'Zero-One, reads you fives...' They were obviously being cagey, so I was wary in calling the ship by its name again, in case it infringed their security. But this was then dispelled by Frank's next transmission.

'Zero-One, *Albion*, where the devil are you?'

'*Albion*, Zero-One... haven't a clue!' I gave the time-honoured reply all aviators use when asked if they know where they are. 'I think we're somewhere over the sea enroute from Addis to Aden – I've got a general and his staff on board.'

'Zero-One, *Albion*, we've got you on Radar now, range fifteen miles to the southwest. Wait, wait-out.' There was another pause, then: 'Zero-One, do you want to land on? I've got the skipper with me and he says we'll give your general a cup of tea...?'

This was too good an opportunity to miss! The General beside me had missed what had been going on, for he wasn't wearing his earphones and was half-asleep. 'Fancy a cup of tea, General?' I said as I did a flat turn and pointed towards *Albion*.

'That would be very nice, my boy, got a flask have you?'

I put the nose down and told *Albion* to expect us. 'We can do better than that, General, just hang on a minute...'

Albion swam into view out of the haze, and with by now practised ease, we thumped down onto her deck.

The General's face was a picture; but after the initial shock he took it in his stride, and was soon ushered down to the wardroom with all the ceremony that the Navy are so good at. But with the exhilaration of the moment, I had completely forgotten to cancel our Flight Plan, and realized it wouldn't be long before Air Traffic at Aden would wonder where we had disappeared. I made my way up to the Flight Control, and met Frank coming down. I explained my predicament and asked if he would contact Aden for me?

'Not on your life! You can risk your career if you like, but I'm having no part of it. This visit has got to be strictly unofficial, and I'm sure the Captain will make that very clear to your General.'

I went down to the wardroom and found the General. 'Come on, sir, we'd better be going else we'll be posted as missing...'

'Not now, my boy, we're having a lovely party!'

Eventually I got them out and strapped back into the aircraft. After the usual hairy take off, we climbed away and back up to altitude. We were an hour and ten minutes overdue. I started to explain to the General, but he cut me short and said he wouldn't have missed it for anything! So we agreed upon a story whereby he had ordered a diversion for a reconnaissance, and if anybody didn't like it, they could report to him!

There was a hue and a cry when I casually clocked in with the next position report, but secure in the knowledge that I had the General's backing, said we were unable to divulge any further details about the reconnaissance – and that was the end of the matter.

Had Arthur still been there, he would have hugely appreciated the General's unexpected cup of tea on *Albion*, and would have regarded it as another feather for the cavalier attitude of army aviation. But I didn't say anything about it to Major Brian Young, for our new Flight Commander had very different ideas on how the Flight should be run and I don't think he would have appreciated it at all.

He started with the aircraft, which were painted and smartened up, and then to the pilots who although not painted, were also smartened up. New armchairs arrived in the crew room and the game of Drax, which had survived in memory of its creator and by now had diversified to even more sophisticated levels, was henceforth forbidden. In his quiet way, Arthur had asked me to help the new Flight Commander to find his feet, but it soon became very clear that he knew exactly were his feet were going and my services would be uncalled for.

Unlike Arthur, Brian Young was full of energy and had a habit of popping up where you least expected him, and soon made his presence felt at all levels. He addressed us on his first morning, a small wiry man with a small moustache and a clipped voice, and looking every inch the professional gunner that he was. He had obviously learned to fly back in the AOP days, for he wore the old gunner wings with a bomb as their centrepiece, the same as Major Ball used to wear, and probably was of the same vintage. We were told that we were on a war footing, and as such, flying would be conducted in a professional and soldierly manner. Moreover, we were there not just to fly and would be given additional responsibilities on the ground. For a start, all pilots would be expected to give lectures on subjects relating to the military and political situation every week, and all Flight personnel not otherwise on duty would attend.

We looked at each other with wary eyes. The team was the same, a happy loose-knit community created by Arthur's trusting and laid-back leadership – albeit unconventional and lackadaisical at times. Could that all blow away overnight? We made our way back to the crew room, and then I remembered I needed some new flying gloves, so broke off and went to see Corporal Clarke who ran the stores. I put my sweat-encrusted gloves on the counter and asked for an exchange pair.

'Sorry, sir' Corporal Clarke said, looking in his ledger, 'I can't exchange these, for you've only had them a month. Major Young's orders, sir.'

'Since when did the length of time come into it? These gloves have had it, and I need a new pair.'

'Can't help that, sir, Major Young says this Flight uses more gloves than any other Army Air Corps unit world-wide, and I'm to ration them to one pair every two months, sir.'

'That's because we are probably flying more hours than any other Army Air Corps unit at the moment. I flew ninety-six hours last month...'

'Sorry, sir. Can't break the rules, even for you.'

I walked back to the crew room. The rest were there sitting in the uncomfortable new armchairs. WO2 Charley Robinson, who was the oldest pilot amongst us and by far the most experienced, both as a flyer and long-serving soldier, had taken it upon himself to voice his opinion.

'I've seen all this before' he was saying in his gravelly voice, 'and believe me, a new broom never does any harm, however stiff it appears to be at first sight. And just remember, compared with any other unit in the army we're lucky, for not only is our job highly individual, but to do it properly, we actually have to fly away from the broom cupboard as much as possible! The only bad thing about the job is that we have to carry passengers...'

WO2 Charley Robinson had a thing about passengers. The story went that he parked his aeroplane at Khormaksar dispersal and then deigned to ignore the party that was waiting for him. Eventually a young captain was dispatched by his CO to find out what was happening. Seeing Charley sitting in his seat, he shouted up 'I say, is this our aero-plane?' whereupon Charley lowered his window and growled 'No, it's mine!'

But upon the issue in question, Charley Robinson was absolutely right. Undoubtedly the Flight could do with a certain amount of smartening up – but when it came to the team, there were not many improvements that could be made. Sure, we could all salute each other some more, and our affected attitude could become less offhand; but when it came to the job – we were all seasoned pilots, we knew the theatre and everyone pulled their weight. Moreover, what Arthur had taught us, was to get on with the job with as little fuss or dramatisation as possible.

The idea of weekly lectures on the other hand, posed some head scratching – for nobody really knew what the political situation was any more. What we did know was that the war had taken a new turn. No longer was it confined to the mountains of the Radfan, for it had now spread to the town of Aden itself and was fast becoming an Internal Security operation as well. Bombs were being placed in the outside vents of air conditioners, exploding into offices and married quarters; vehicles were being booby-trapped and the beaches were no longer safe for families and had to be protected by armed guards. It was inadvisable to wander the streets of Aden alone, and predominantly Arab areas like Crater, were placed out of bounds to civilians.

Helicopters were much in demand for this new role, especially the small Sioux from the Regimental Air Troops, which were ideal for this purpose, but also drawing upon the resources of the Scouts from the two Army Air Corps Flights. Which left the Beavers of 15 Flight supporting all the other activities that were still going on up-country.

Three weeks after he arrived, Brian Young asked me to show him around all the airstrips. Up to now, apart from having them repainted, he hadn't been near the aircraft, for he had been busy reorganizing the Flight administration, as well as marking his pitch with the REME Workshops. With the Beavers flying more and more hours, the servicing and spares could no longer keep pace, so much that aircraft were on the point of becoming grounded. The best ally the work-shop commander could have was an irate flight commander who was unable to fulfil his operational role due to lack of spares, and much of Brian's time had been spent supporting and lending his weight to this cause.

On returning from leave, Neville Bamford had tried on several occasions to pin Brian down so that he could give him the customary theatre flight check; but Brian had always had to cancel at the last moment on the grounds of being too busy. Today was his first opportunity to go flying, and of course Neville now was busy, which was why it fell to me. Neville's flight check would have to wait.

To save time, I pre-flighted the aircraft and then waited for him, sitting on the wheel in the shade of the wing. It was the hottest time of the day, and as Brian marched briskly out carrying his helmet and a bulging flight bag, I couldn't help comparing him with Arthur, who would have sidled out crabwise and then dodged from patch to patch of shade in a circuitous route, leaving the minimum unshaded distance for the final spurt to the aircraft.

Dear old Arthur, I wonder how you are coping with the stores in your training battalion?

Brian arrived and climbed up into the left-hand seat.

'Do you think it right that pilot's are allowed to authorize their own... why is their no Decca in this aircraft?'

'I'm afraid the Decca chain doesn't extend as far as Arabia.' I said with a smile.

'What, none of the aircraft... how do you navigate then?'

'The old-fashioned way; time and distance. It's a bit daunting at first, but once you get to know the main routes it all seems to fall into place. Anyway, it'll take about three full days to visit all the strips, so where would you like to start?'

'Three days?'

'Well, more than three days if we do them all and actually land on them as well, but I thought we could overfly some of the more obvious ones. But some are a bit tricky... yes, three days should about cover it.'

'I see. Well, where do you suggest?'

'Well, the easiest thing to do is to split the country into three and go north one day, then east and west. There're quite a few strips grouped together around the Radfan, and I expect you'd also like to meet the people at Brigade, so that will take care of the rest of today. Then the most frequented long distance route is up to the northeast, Mukerius, Lodar, Meifa, Ataq and about half a dozen others ending at Beihan on the edge of the Empty Quarter, where there are another lot of satellite strips. We ought to start early for that – before first light if possible and even then we won't get back until well after dark. Unless you want to split the northeast sector into two days? Then, that will leave the third day to cover all the stations west.'

'I had no idea – I thought we could do the lot this afternoon? Well, we'd better go and have a look at the Radfan, I suppose. I haven't got that much time...'

He rummaged in his flight bag and produced a flip-card, and then called every item for the pre-start checks, following with his fingers as though querying the position of each knob. Then, with the engine finally running, he turned the card over and methodically started on the after-start checks. I could see the puzzled look on the face of the crewman waiting to pull the chocks away, knowing all the other pilots would have been well on the way to Habilayn by now. Thinking back to my own time, I had no longer needed the flip chart by the time I was halfway through the Beaver conversion course at Wallop. So long as you started at the correct end of the cockpit and followed the sequence through, there was little you could miss and it wasn't as though the Beaver was an airliner. Brian was obviously a meticulous pilot.

'Now then, have you planned the route and if so, may I see your map? I haven't marked anything on mine yet – and why aren't you wearing gloves?'

'I – ah – they're no longer any good and I can't get my hands into them any more. I tried the stores, but had to come away in the end without any.' He looked at me but said nothing. 'Anyway, we won't need a map – it's only forty-five minutes and you just go due north.'

'No map? You should always fly with a map; it's the first rule for an army pilot. How can you fly without a map?'

I felt in the pocket of the co-pilot's door and found a map. There was only one map that was any good and it covered the whole country, and we generally left them in the side pockets for the passengers to puzzle over. I passed it to him.

'Now let me see... where d'you say Habilayn is, due north? Ah yes... is this the best map you've got, its not very clear? Now I'd better mark in the wind...'

I couldn't believe it! This man was behaving like a novice. It was as though this was his first cross-country in a Chipmunk. Yet, he was a second-tour pilot, and supposedly had just completed his Beaver conversion course. He must be putting on an act, for there is no way he could have got through Wallop, fumbling through his checks and still marking wind angles on his map as though he was a twenty-hour pilot still in Elementary Flight.

'Where did you fly on your first tour?' I enquired, as we taxied out.

'Oh, Germany mostly... on Auster V's. Long time ago now, things have changed quite a bit.' He parked by the side of the active runway, and reached for his flipchart again. He saw my puzzled expression. 'I – er – I was ill for a lot of the conversion course... so I didn't do the whole course, which is why I'm still a bit rusty. They were going to put me back a course, but I told them this was an operational Squadron, and it was absolutely imperative to take over the Flight as soon as possible... so as I was an old pilot, they let me through.'

'Germany must have been fun – lots of CATO's and low flying under wires. Did you clock many hours on Austers?' I asked as casually as I could.

If there is one thing that is a breach of etiquette, it is to ask how many hours a fellow pilot has, especially if he is your new Flight Commander. If you know the person, or have similar experience of course it's different – it's much like asking someone his or her age. But, since the opportunity presented itself I was loathe to let it go. We hadn't even left the ground yet, but something wasn't ringing true.

'Yes, we had our moments.' He looked at me, then added, 'well, at least most of the others did, I seemed to spend most of my time rewriting the Standard Operational

Procedures for Aircraft in the Field. I see that our Operational Procedures here are extremely skimpy and out of date, so that's one of my first priorities to put right. Fortunately I kept most of my notes...'

We took off and flew towards Habilayn. My misgivings were not unfounded, for it soon became very obvious that although on his second flying tour, he was a low-time pilot. This showed in just about everything he did, to the extent that he still managed to make the simplest things hard work, and his flying was strictly by numbers and the book. Everything became a major 'problem' to be tackled head on, rather than absorbed and taken in stride, which only experience can teach you. Flying is rather like riding a bicycle; however rusty you are, some things are impossible to forget. Brian Young was strictly a paper pilot, and way out of his depth.

By the time we reached the Jebel Maniff at the entrance to the pass, I had quietly assumed the instructor role, gently reminding him of the correct settings to use and then extended this to include the more elementary functions of conforming to course, speed and height. Far from taking offence, he seemed grateful for this and made copious notes about the few features of the route. Habilayn was busy so we overflew and I showed him the main battle area and then the wadi where the three strips served the company positions. I decided to overfly Blair's and Monk's Field, both of which jut out from a mountain and were strictly 'one way in and the other way out', and flew on to Paddies Field, which of the three was by far the easiest.

'Care to try a landing here?' I asked as cheerily as I could. 'Set it up just like the strip at Wallop, only do a right-hand circuit to keep well away from those foot hills. You often get sniped at if you fly low over those...'

'Right-hand circuit? Is there any Air Traffic Control on the strip, and what's the QFE?' he asked, looking at the altimeter reading 4000 feet.

'There are only Royal Marines down there, and you just have to judge the height... so, nice tight circuit and do your downwind checks sooner rather than later.'

'Downwind Vital Actions' he read from the chart. 'Let me see, Brakes – OFF, Mixture – RICH...'

'You're not looking out! It's no good looking down at the flipchart. Swing her right round in a one-eighty onto finals now, and chop the power, we're much too high!'

I was tempted to take over and sideslip her in, but that wouldn't have achieved anything. And Paddies Field was the easiest strip of the three! Must remember to keep my voice calm and casual, there was nothing to gain by flustering him.

'I don't think we're going to...?'

'No, I don't think we are. So, overshoot... that's it, revs to two thousand and boost to twenty-three. Leave the flaps at fifteen degrees and settle for seventy knots. Now, round we go and let's try again.'

We tried three times, by which time the Royal Marines were all out of their tents, wondering what all the noise was about, and my Flight Commander had gone to bits and was just a state of nerves.

'I have control' I said after the third attempt. 'Look, Brian, I think it's best if we head for home. This is not really the place to practice this sort of thing...'

'No, I agree, you'd better fly... I've had enough. I thought it would be all right and it would all come back to me, but I'm very rusty and I'm not used to the Beaver... and as for these strips! I'm sorry, you've been very patient... perhaps I should have allowed them to back-course me at Wallop...'

It was an uncomfortable flight back. And it put me in a difficult predicament, which I wasn't sure how to handle. Several times he made to say something, but then never came out with it. As we shut down, he looked at me and said 'Look, I think it would be best if...'

'It's okay, Brian – I understand...' and we left it at that.

But as I drove back to the mess I realized that it couldn't be just left. It was a question of divided loyalties – between the man and the job. For better or worse, Brian was my new Flight Commander, and as such demanded my... but there was more to it than that, and it had to be faced. He just wasn't up to the job as a pilot. Perhaps he intended to run the Flight from the ground? But that wasn't right and wouldn't work either. He wore a pair of wings and drew flying pay, and at sometime he would have to set the standards for the pilots under him. The easiest thing for me to do would be to forget about it and do nothing; but that would be irresponsible, for if I did nothing – and worse, if he did nothing about it himself, he would end up by killing himself – and maybe some others.

I went up to my room and lay on the bed. In the end I decided to compromise and say nothing to the other pilots, but to have a quiet word with the QFI.

I gave Neville Bamford a ring that evening from the mess, and he invited me around for a drink at his married quarter. I explained the afternoon's events and the reason I was there. He stopped me half way through. 'Okay, say no more, I get the drift. Just leave it to me, it's all part of my job...'

That evening a signal came through from the Federal Regular Army. They were involved in a skirmish at Beihan, and urgently needed air support. I'd just got back and was about to turn in when Brian came to the mess and found me.

'I'd like you to go' he said. 'You'll be taking Corporal Frazer and enough spares to last for about a month, so get your head down and leave as early as you can.'

I felt like a traitor, and nearly blurted out that I'd just been to see Neville Bamford, but then decided to say nothing. Nonetheless it made me feel wretched, for in every other respect he would make a good flight commander and inspired confidence. I think he knew, for he thanked me again for the afternoon's trip, and then added that he would arrange to see Neville in the morning. With that he smiled, and left.

Chapter 9

Overhead Ad Daymah I reset the cursor of the DI to 292
degrees and nod at Corporal Frazer who is flying the
machine from the right-hand seat. He looks down briefly
and then turns the aircraft away from north and centres the
DI onto our new course, which is the last leg for Beihan.
During the flight we have swung anticlockwise through 106
degrees to skirt the Yemen border and are now only thirty-
five minutes from our destination.

Corporal Frazer who has been a valued mechanic with us
for the past eighteen months, has applied to go to Wallop
for the flying course, and takes every opportunity to get his
hands on the controls – and this isn't the first time I have
given him an unofficial flying lesson. He will make a good
pilot, for he has the right attitude as well as that instinctive
feel for an aeroplane, and I hope he makes it. Also it will
mean a step up for him, for upon gaining his wings he will
become a sergeant pilot and then maybe able to transfer
from the REME to the Army Air Corps, should he decide
this is where his future lies.

I am glad it was he who volunteered to look after the
aeroplane for our period in Beihan, for we have worked
together many times and know each other's ways. It was
Corporal Frazer who had been in charge of the ground
party at Habilayn when Roger and I were first asked to act
together as a team, and whether by chance or design, thereafter he had always been there whenever we were, and so
became very much part of the same team. Only this time,
there are just the two of us to manage the Beaver – although
there will be extra hands available from the small detach-

ment of RAF who look after the airfield at Beihan and man the crash truck.

On the way out, and as part of his flying lesson, I had explained the quadrantal rule for selecting Flight Levels, and with our change of heading to 291, he decreases altitude by 500 feet to FL 85. He is learning fast. At this height we can see for forty miles. On our left to the southwest are the brown barren mountains of the Yemen interior, their shapes blurred and distorted from the heat waves coming off them. Behind and to the right I can just make out the vast sandstone cliffs of the Wadi Habban, which is not unlike the Grand Canyon in America, only on a slightly smaller scale. At he head of the Habban, fringing the sands of the Empty Quarter lies the ancient town of Ataq, which was one of the staging points on the old trade route. To our right stretches the desert of the Rub'al Khali, where I first ventured with Paul Aston to drop supplies to the sappers on their survey - and the occasion when he left the fuel selected to the front tank until the engine ran itself dry.

Away out in the desert, something catches my eye and I reach for the binoculars. It is a series of dots, which with the binoculars focus into a Bedouin camel train heading west towards Beihan. I am not sure what's going on in Beihan, but it would seem the nomadic tribes are gathering from far and wide.

Corporal Frazer touches my arm and points ahead. We are heading for what looks like a thin, twisting column of smoke, which is in fact a dust devil – or a whirlwind, sucking up a column of sand and a frequent occurrence in this part of the country. This one looks as though it has attained the height of our Flight Level, and is still building. I tell him to give it a wide berth, for they can be like hitting a brick wall if you fly through them. Looking beyond it, I can now see the five mountain ranges, which resemble the spread-out fingers of a large left hand, each finger protruding from the back of the hand and running north for twenty or so miles, before petering out into the desert. We cannot reduce altitude until we have crossed over the first two ridges - or the

'...at the head of the Habban ... lies the ancient town of Ataq on the edge of the Rub'al Khali...'

thumb and forefinger of the hand, and then Beihan lies in the valley between the fore and middle finger.

Beihan is the last civilization on the fringe of the Empty Quarter and is as old as history itself with legends too numerous to tell. Was it here the Queen of Sheba buried her jewels? And what civilization built the ruined city of Timna some eighteen miles to the north, the ruins of which have remained untouched over the centuries and where you can still pick up carved alabaster heads lying in the sand? Beihan has always been a trading centre and now has a thriving industry for locally made rugs and jewellery, both much in demand in markets throughout the whole of Arabia. Only a day's camel ride from Ataq, the town originally prospered by being the next link on the old spice route from the East to the Roman Empire, and has continued to thrive thereafter.

'Spices of Arabia' in fact came from India. They were shipped by Dhow across the Indian Ocean to the south coast of Arabia and thence by camel train across the deserts to the Red Sea. Then across North Africa to the Mediterranean coast and finally by sea to Rome. As the demand for spices grew, so the transportation costs rose as each country and state along the route increased their levy to allow the caravans through. In the end a Roman Legion was dispatched to investigate the inflating costs and with armour and all their other accoutrements marched from Rome, back down the route. Ill equipped for the desert, the Rub'al Khali finally finished them and only a handful emerged, cut-off and 3000 miles from home. To this day, one can come across a blue-eyed Arab living in Beihan; living evidence of the long arm of the Roman Empire.

Survival of the fittest has always been the law of the desert, and like many other Border States, Beihan has always had to be at combat readiness. The State is ruled by the Emir, whose right-hand man and commander-in-chief is also his uncle. Like a monarch of old, the Emir and his family live in a four-storey palace, adorned with white battlements and golden balls on the roof. And also as a monarch of old, the Emir's rule is absolute and his word final. Be it settling family feuds, repelling nomadic raiders, or the intricacies and demands arising from the town's strategic location on the Yemen border, Beihan has always been a turbulent place – which is why a Battalion of the Federal Regular Army is also permanently stationed there.

I motion to Corporal Frazer to reduce the power and we skim over the final ridge, and there, five thousand feet below, lies Beihan asleep in the sun. The only change in the last thousand years has been the construction of a long metalled runway. After Khormaksar, it is probably the best runway in the whole of the country and runs north-south in the centre of the wadi just south of the town. Originally funded by the Emir, it is now maintained by the RAF and also used on a regular basis by Aden Airways who run a weekly schedule, thus ensuring that Beihan is now part of the modern world.

Once overhead the town, the noise of your engine is usually enough to alert the RAF crash crew – or FRA guard of honour should you have a VIP on board, for there has never been enough traffic to warrant the permanent installation of a radio facility or any form of Air Traffic Control. Having blipped your engine, you turn north towards the desert and descend into the wadi until about 1500 feet above ground level, and then turn within the confines of the mountains to backtrack and overfly the town, prior to landing straight in on a southerly heading, the runway being long enough to accommodate any downwind component. Should the wind be above twenty knots and from the north, you can always overfly the runway and the wadi is still wide enough for a fairly large aircraft to turn and then land back into wind.

But today we have no passengers and, I reason, as good a time as any to enlarge upon Corporal Frazer's flying lesson. I motion for him to keep his hands and on the controls, and then push the column forward and we fall on the town like a descending hawk.

We level off just above the mud houses and then steer for the tent at the edge of the runway, where I know the RAF fire crew will be lying asleep.

One pass is enough and we flick past the windsock, which is lying limp against its post.

'Keep your hands and lightly on, and follow me through. I'll show you the fancy landing we used to end our air displays with at Habilayn. Wait until you are about halfway down the runway... about now, and haul back into a steep climb. Vital Actions for landing: Brakes – OFF; Mixture – RICH; Carb-air – HOT; Propeller – FINE; Fuel – FRONT and pump – ON. Watch your speed... apex of the climb now, so hard left rudder and at the same time drop seventy-five percent flap. Harness – LOCKED and round we go – speed is just right at fifty knots... and maintain with a trickle of power, and trim...'

The runway swings into view, looking right for short finals. I sneak a look at Corporal Frazer and his eyes are alight, which tells me all I want to know. The runway is alive and distorted with heat waves, which make it difficult to judge our exact height – but our speed and attitude are right, and the Beaver lands herself nicely on all three points.

I leave him to taxi the aircraft off the runway and across the soft sand to the edge of the camp, where the FRA sentry can keep an eye on it, and then he swings it into what little wind there is and shuts down. I take my helmet off and savour that end of flight feeling. The silence, after the continuous roar of the engine; the whine of the gyros unwinding; the hum ceasing from each radio in turn as my fingers travel around the cockpit; the unfamiliar obstruction of the stationary propeller through the windshield; the hot engine smell, mixed with leather and sweat – and which, for some reason, you can never smell when aloft; and finally fatigue, as the tensions of flight evaporate.

Corporal Frazer has already jumped down and put the pitôt head cover on as I drop to the ground. The fire truck screeches to a stop and covers us in a cloud of dust and the RAF corporal in charge and Corporal Frazer exchange the usual inter-service pleasantries.

'Do you know what the flap's all about?' I ask the RAF corporal. He tells me that the whole FRA battalion is out, and that there's a war going on in the hills to the west, and also that the FRA Commander Area West is in the British Officers' Mess.

'Shall I refuel her now, sir?' Corporal Frazer intervenes.

'Yes, may as well be ready for everything. It takes a bit of organizing to get the drums out of the compound.' I nearly remind him to check the date on the drums and to filter the fuel through chamois leather if it looks at all dubious, but he knows all this.

'I'll check the dates on the drums and also see to the engine and airframe logbooks,' he replies, reading my thoughts and again confirming my good luck in having him as a crewman.

'Okay, I'll wander up and find Colonel Ward and find out what's going on.'

I fish out my beret and pistol belt from amongst the luggage and walk towards the camp gates. The green flag of the Federal Regular Army is hanging limply from its flag-pole, and the sentry shoulders arms and slaps his rifle in salute. There's nothing sloppy about the FRA and they delight in maintaining a Brigade of Guards standard even at a desert outpost. I return his salute and make my way to the British Officers Mess. Apart for the occasional visitor, the mess is hardly used now, for the only British officers left on strength are the Brigadier at FRA HQ in Aden, his two Area Commanders – who are both full-colonels and a hand-ful of specialist officers who are there for advisory purposes. Other than those, the FRA is now entirely officered by Arabs; the majority of whom are Sandhurst trained.

The FRA Area Commander West is Colonel Ward – and the same officer who was in the crew room and witnessed Biggles' final game of Drax when he telephoned the Commander in Chief. He has never forgotten it and seem-ingly the outrageousness of the incident has endeared him to the Flight, for he is now an enthusiastic and frequent user of the Beaver, this being the only practical way to visit his far flung command. During the last eighteen months I have flown him on many occasions and from the intimacy of the cockpit have got to know him quite well. His flights are

'...I fish out my beret and pistol belt from amongst the luggage and thus transferred from airman to soldier, walk towards the camp gates...'

299

always interesting and his destinations invariably ambitious, usually terminating at 'temporary' landing grounds far out into the desert.

I find him sitting on the floor of the mess, surrounded by maps and papers.

'Aha! Good, I asked for you – noisy devil' he booms as I enter. 'Nearly flattened the damn tent, arriving out of the blue like that. There's some jungle juice in that jug, help yourself, then come over here and have a look at these maps...'

I help myself to some juice and then join him on the floor.

'I want you to re-supply the battalion by parachute' he continues. 'I've got all the gear – been indenting for the damn stuff for months now, in case this should happen. The battalion is in the hills out the back there, and it takes two or three days for a mule train to get through to them. Even then only half of them make it for there's only one track and they keep on getting sniped at and the Emir is getting fed up with loosing all his guides...' He hands me a marked map and an Operational Order.

'...and it takes two or three days for a mule train to get through...'

300

'You'll find all the frequencies, timings and so forth on the Order and I've ringed the company positions on the map – but it looks easier than it is, for it's virtually impossible to map read up there. At the moment our chaps are holding these four peaks, which are roughly in a line, and 'No-man's-land' is that valley running along their front. You'll find them; they've put red panels out for you. Oh, and I've got an Irish Guards officer who is something to do with the Political boys and he's up with the battalion HQ. Useful chap; he speaks fluent Arabic and I wouldn't mind hanging on to him. He also seems to know a bit about aeroplanes so he'll be able to talk you in on the radio.

'Anyway, I'm going to make my way up there with the next patrol, and I'll stay with them for a couple of days. It's a damn hard climb, still, should do me good! Give me until

'... there's only one track ... Federal Army Patrol carrying lunch'

'...it's a damn hard climb...'

lunchtime tomorrow, and I'll give you a wave from the top! I think I've thought of everything that you'll need, so you can start as soon as you like and then run to your own timetable. They're getting a bit low on everything so you'll be hard at it for the next few days. Try to stock them up, for there'll be a lot more for you to do when I get back, but we'll talk about that later.'

There is plenty to digest and I take out and note separately all the parts of the order that are relevant to my task. I then study the map and decide upon the best way to approach each position, and then rule in and mark the compass headings and the timings for each run-in. By planning the flying side now will free my mind for any tactical divergence that could arise later, for once aloft it's all too easy to set a wrong heading or forget something equally basic when you're under pressure – and then there's never enough time to think it out properly. I refold the map to my liking and walk back to the aircraft.

Corporal Frazer has finished refuelling and is looking dubiously at a three-ton truck, which is full of stores.

'The RAF corporal says he helped make them up into parachute packs, sir. Jerrycans in bundles of four for the wing racks and the food and ammo to jettison from the cabin. I've taken all the seats out....'

'Right, get the driver to back the truck under the wing and we'll lift the jerrycans into the racks and then see how much we can get in the cabin. There's hardly any wind – at least down here, so we may as well give it a go straightaway. We'll drop one wing bundle on each position, so if we take both rear doors off, you'll be able to shove the other bundles out from both sides.'

I show him the four positions I have marked on the map, and then simplify it by using the back of my left hand again – the positions all being about the knuckle of the hand and before the middle finger stretches out into the desert. Then, I run through the sequence I have decided upon and tell him the amount of time he'll have to pull the bundles forward and attach their static lines for each run. Finally we go over the commands and hand signals used for the dropping drill. I start up and with the engine ticking over, patch into the army radio on the selector panel and then tune it to the FRA frequency shown on the operation order.

We are ready to go.

We climb to the north and after twenty minutes the mountains on either side of the wadi sink into the encroaching desert to become lost amongst the dunes. At 6000 feet I ease the aircraft round in a gentle 180 degree climbing turn, conscious of the four swinging bundles under the wings and head back on the reciprocal. Overhead Beihan again, I zero the stopwatch and then change to the heading for the first dropping zone.

The Colonel was right, and the map bears no resemblance to the ground whatsoever. It looks just like a flat, brown plateau and with the sun overhead there are no shadows to show any contours or relief. Of the four company positions, each supposedly occupying their own separate peak, there is no sign. I glance again at the map and it just shows the mountain ridge as the Jebel Rakhamah and then in red letters below 'Relief Data Unreliable'.

'Keep your eyes peeled, Corporal Frazer, we're supposed to be there in four minutes...' I hold the course and hope for the best.

The Guardsman should be in range by now, so I give a call, remembering to use the army procedure. In spite of

'...and after twenty minutes the mountains on either side of the wadi sink into the encroaching desert...'

having been brought up with the army method, I find it unnaturally cumbersome when compared with the International Air Traffic procedure, and nowadays have to think twice and double check what I'm going to say, before each transmission.

He comes back straightaway, a practised drawling voice, reversing the call signs back into the Air Traffic mode, and omitting all the unnecessary 'Hello's and 'Overs'. Well done the Guards! This man knows his business. I glance at the stopwatch – ninety seconds to go and time to slow up. I reduce the settings and then drop twenty degrees of flap and allow the airspeed to settle at sixty-five knots.

'Ah, Zero-One is now range two miles – can you see or hear me? And can you send a long transmission, please?'

'Rog, Zero-One... I can just hear you to the northeast. Commencing long transmission. One-ah, two-ah, three-ah... Mary had a little lamb...' The homing needle on the Green Salad flicks over to the right, and I turn after it until it centres. '...And the last time I talked to Mary on the radio, she was covered in ice and fell out of the sky and hit Wallop like a frozen packet of peas..!'

What the..? 'Guy, you bastard! Is that you?' All radio procedure now forgotten.

'Hey-Ho, old lad – how're you doing? Just thought I'd pop out and see what's going on. Better than sitting on the beach! We'll catch up later... Now, you're homing in nicely – can you see the positions yet?'

Of all the people... good old Guy! I can imagine him sitting on the hill... his dark Guard's SD cap tilted slightly forward on his head, as Guardsmen always seem to wear them and his ebony stick on the ground nearby. I also wonder whether he is feeling at all wistful, never having had the chance to flap the wings he had worked so hard to get – but now is not the time to dwell, for we're almost there and the ground still bears no resemblance to the features shown on the map, let alone to the Colonel's verbal description. Where are the four peaks and the valley between the company positions and the enemy? Perhaps if

I descend a little... I take off some boost and hold the airspeed steady.

'Still homing in nicely. The targets are very small and the wind is all over the place – suggest you descend a bit, and go a touch to your right...'

This is ridiculous! Hold it – what's that? Yes, that must be the valley, only it's more like a gully... now, follow it up... it's getting quite turbulent now from the heat bouncing back off the rocks. Now, the first position should be about...

'I think I've got them, sir' from Corporal Frazer. He is leaning out through the open door and the rest of his transmission is drowned by wind roar.

But I'm damned if I can see them! I pull the aircraft round in a left-hand bank in order to see out of my side. Got it! A pink patch, which is the panel - and there is the peak, and there's even a white-taped cross for the DZ.

'Don't fly over there, they're shooting at you!'

I tighten the turn, ever conscious of the wing stores. We're not supposed to go above rate three turns with external loads.

'They're still shooting at you...'

The aircraft is flying like a pig and with the ungainly load the ailerons need maximum movement to counteract the vicious turbulence. We complete the circle and I climb away to take stock of the situation.

'Sorry Guy, made a bollocks of that! Just give me a minute to work it out...'

I can see all four positions now and also the valley, which runs northeast to southwest. The wind at ground level will obviously channel through the valley – say from 045 degrees, whilst the upper air wind is roughly from the north. So if I bisect that angle and use 020 degrees for my flyline... only that will mean setting up and starting right over enemy held territory. Damn! So what alternative? Fly parallel to the valley on the home side, which will be crosswind to the wind aloft? Parachutes will probably drift away south... and the DZ an impossibly small pimple to hit? And how about wave effects or other wind distortions around the peaks?

'Can you put down smoke, please?'

'Rog. Wait, out.'

Out of small arms range I set up a circuit and the second time around see the smoke. A red smear at first, thickening every second at the source, but disintegrating instantly in turmoil at the edge of the peak. No pattern there whatsoever – and certainly no predictable flight path for a parachute.

Still, nothing ventured...

I have never attempted a crosswind drop before. In gusty conditions it can be difficult enough to hit the target when running directly into wind... if only there was some feature on the ground that I could use to establish a flyline. And that unpredictable wind at ground level..? I smile as the thought prompts a forgotten memory from the past. A child's picture of a passenger liner with three funnels, smoke issuing forth from each of them and going in three different directions. Then trying to explain to the teacher that in freak conditions, surely it could happen? And here it is now, and the teacher will never be the wiser...

I bank away and fly out on the reciprocal of the intended flyline. Allow fifteen degrees for drift and set the pointer of the DI to the intended course. Three minutes out, far enough, and gently round again. DI steady and reduce speed to sixty knots.

'Stand by to drop, Corporal Frazer.'

'Stand by, sir,'

Altitude steady, on course – more or less; take off another three degrees drift. Ailerons are very sloppy now and we are really wallowing at this speed. Select Number One rack on the bomb-panel, and check: Light – ON. Target crabbing into view – God, this is impossible! It will be pure luck if we get anywhere near.

'Five, four, three, two, one – Drop!' I press the red button.

'...away, sir, both chutes open.'

'Watch and see how they're running, we'll go straight on to the next position.'

'No good, sir. Too high and we dropped too late. In fact it looks like they're going to go miles... no, it's all right, they're curving back. Wow, beauty, sir! They're just down from the target.'

'Nice one, Zero-One' from Guy. 'Was that a fluke, or was that a fluke?'

'Corporal Frazer, stand by with the next. Right-hand door, this time.'

'Stand by, sir.'

I turn another five degrees into wind. The next peak looks even smaller than the last. Select Number Four: Light – ON. DZ coming up – we are definitely further upwind.

'Four, three, two, one – Drop!' And correct the swing as the bundle leaves the wing. That's the outer two gone...

'Chutes away, sir. Both running... looks better than last time.'

Where's the next position? Help! We are almost on top of it.

'Hit, sir. Both chutes have landed just on the upwind slope. They should be able to scramble up and get them.'

'Stand by!' Select Three: Light – ON. 'Two, one – Drop!' Press the button.

Too late. Miles too late!

'Hold it, Corporal Frazer...'

'Away, sir. Sorry about that – I didn't have time...'

'Never mind, my fault – I shouldn't have tried it... the positions were too near.'

'Strewth! They've gone miles away, sir. Down the valley...'

I could kick myself. What a waste.

'You bollixed again, Zero-One! I thought you'd got the hang of it after last time...'

'Sorry, I know you're thirsty...'

Now, how about this last one? I bank away, as already we are on top of it. Ought I to take this load back, rather than risk loosing another one? Round onto track again. The valley looks wider here – I wonder..?

'Stand by, Corporal Frazer, I'm going to run in low, and we'll do a free fall.'

'Stand by, sir.'

I push the column forward and aim for the hill. Select Two: and light is – ON. The controls stiffen with the increase of speed. Now, steer so the port wing will just pass over their position. Down... lower yet... damn this turbulence... slip into the valley, and the hill fills the windshield.

'Four, three, two, one – Drop!'

Button, and haul back. Christ, their radio aerial – hard rudder and lift the wing. Missed it! Up over the edge, and away at nought.

'Beautiful, sir, they both rolled right onto the cross.'

'Did they burst?'

'No, I don't think they had time for that!'

'Hey! Hey!' From Guy, 'I told you not to fly over there, the whole front was shooting at you...'

'Well, I don't think we got any hits. Look, it's too rough at this time of the day. We'll come back later this evening and have another go when the turbulence has died down.'

'Okay, old mate – see you later...'

We re-supplied the Battalion twice a day, as near to first light and last light as possible. After three days the hitherto featureless ground began to take shape and become recog-

'...and Nequb, which was a tented camp...'

nisable. After ten days, re-supplying the battalion became a matter of routine. We would takeoff in the dark and climb up into the morning, and in the calm air sneak along low and slow on the home side of the valley and just pop up into view for a few seconds to roll the goods onto the target. In the mornings the enemy had the low sun in their eyes, which made us almost impossible to see; and in the evenings we waited until the last glimmer of light, and then did the same, concealed by the gathering darkness. It meant landing back at Beihan in the dark, but the crash crew soon became adept at positioning two vehicles with their headlights on, and placing a single hurricane lamp at the end of the runway – and to this day I would still choose this lighting arrangement rather than the bright floodlights of a fully lit runway. Floodlights are fine, until the occasion when you may have to overshoot – and then is not the time to find that you've lost your night vision.

The next day two more companies of FRA arrived in a couple of Beverley's, followed by another Beverley with a mountain of stores, and Colonel Ward came back from the

'...in reality were just hard stretches of deset, picked clean of stones and marked with four whitre-painted rocks at each corner...' Beaver and Saladin of the 10th Royal Hussars at Ayn. (*Courtesy Capt. O.N.P Mylne. 10th Royal Hussars*)

hills to greet the reinforcements.

Things were hotting up.

The majority of the new troops went to reinforce the other FRA outposts in the area. There were five main outposts, Ayn and Naquub, which were tented camps and Negid Mergid, Manawa and Ahwar, which were ancient forts, strategically placed from battles of old. All had their own airstrips nearby, most of which had been hastily constructed – and in reality were just hard patches of desert, picked clean of stones and marked with four white-painted rocks at each corner. Manawa was the worst and was situated in the next wadi, right on the edge of the border. The two ends of the strip were hard enough, but the middle section was a hollow of soft sand, which you couldn't avoid and had to plough through both on landing and takeoff.

With the arrival of the reinforcements, the Beaver began to earn its keep, for after the morning parachute run Colonel Ward would be ready for his rounds, which usually took the remainder of the day – and then back to Beihan in time to load up again for the evening re-supply drop. In the end we took all the rear seats out and left them with the RAF crash crew, and the Beaver became an airborne truck. Every hour of daylight was precious; short takeoff, climb to 100 feet; fifteen or twenty minutes to the next strip, overfly and check there are no stray camels or goats on it; round again and land. Leave the engine running whilst the FRA soldiers unload and Colonel Ward gets out, more stores and soldiers on board, 'All ready?' Off to the next strip and the same happens again. Then back to collect the colonel and leapfrog on to the next strip. Up, down; up, down – seemingly an unending round from one strip to another and then back again, with soldiers squatting amongst rations and boxes of ammunition as best they could.

On the morning of the eleventh day we delivered the goods as usual at first light and then Guy asked us to reconnoitre the head of the next wadi to the west, where there had been reports of a large gathering of tribesmen. Colonel Ward had left at midnight and was on his way back up the

This page and opposite: '...Negid, Mergid, Manawa and Ahwar, which were ancient forts...' (*Courtesy Capt. O.N.P Mylne. 10th Royal Hussars*)

hill again and Guy wanted a full intelligence report for him. If we had a helicopter here, it would have saved the Colonel an awful lot of walking and I had to admit that Arthur's words were beginning to ring true.

We flew over to Manawa and then headed south, following the wadi along the border. After a few miles the valley began to fill with tribesmen all making their way south. Most were on foot but some were mounted on camels as well as a few horses. They brandished their long rifles at us as we flew over. At the head of the wadi two tented camps were in the process of forming about a mile apart, both on the Yemen side of the border. It was almost like watching a film-set of two medieval armies preparing for battle, and I was tempted to go lower for a closer look. But any aeroplane makes an irresistible target and is considered fair game to a tribesman, whichever side you happen to be on, so we kept well out of small arms range. I reported back to Guy and he relayed that it was nothing to do with us; there would be no FRA involvement and that we were there merely to observe and to keep well clear.

The diversion made us late for breakfast that morning, and as we landed back at Beihan, there was a visiting Twin Pioneer parked on my loading spot. I shut down alongside it and then walked up to the mess and hoped the Twin Pin pilots hadn't eaten all the breakfast.

By now I had established a routine whereby on landing after the early morning parachute run, I would then take time to have a shower and shave. There was only an oil lamp in my tent – and besides, if I left it until then, the sun had had a chance to heat the water up in the showers. After my shower I would then meet Colonel Ward in the mess and join him for a hasty breakfast, over which we would plan the remainder of the day. But now, with the Colonel on his way up the hill, curiosity got the better of me and I decided to look in at the mess first, and make my number with the pilots of the visiting Twin Pin, in case they left whilst I was still in the middle of my ablutions.

The mess tent was full of RAF officers sitting around the table drinking coffee. As well as the pilot and navigator, who were both Flight Lieutenants in flying suits, there was a Group Captain, two Wing Commanders and a Squadron Leader, and all looking as though they had just stepped straight off the parade ground, immaculate in their best khaki-drill uniforms.

There was an embarrassed pause in the conversation as I entered, and the FRA mess steward gave an expressive shrug of his shoulders and scuttled out. The pause persisted and I looked down and realized the state I was in. Faced with this bevy of senior officers, I was immediately conscious of the stubble on my face and my unkempt appearance. I was in my working shirt and trousers and eleven days of hard flying and living in a tent had taken its toll. Damn!

I saw the Group Captain's scrutiny leave my face and focus on my shirt.

Which was a disgrace – for this morning one of the parachute bundles had snagged up and I had had to unclip my harness in order to reach back and give Corporal Frazer a hand. In the haste of the moment, the loose shoulder straps had snagged behind the pair of wings clipped on the front of my shirt, tearing them off leaving a large rent, and then as I'd twisted, the harness had caught under both of my shirt epaulettes and ripped the buttons off! I'd found the wings - still with a large piece of shirt attached to them, as well as the two sleeves that show your rank and slip over the epaulettes, all on the floor of the Beaver just now, and had put them in my pocket. But to any outsider I was now rankless, with two flapping epaulettes, a torn shirt, unshaven and generally looking most unmilitary.

'Morning,' I said, deciding to brave it out, 'any breakfast left?'

'And who the Devil are you?' the Group Captain said icily, standing up.

'Ah, well, I live here – welcome to Beihan... may I?' I replied, pulling a chair up to the table. More to the point, I wondered what they were doing here? They were the visitors and Group Captain or not, his attitude and tone was far from endearing.

'No you may not! I don't know who or what you are, and frankly I don't much care. I happen to be in the middle of an Orders Group with my officers, and I will not tolerate people just bursting in!' The mess steward arrived with two pieces of toast and set them before me with a mumbled apology. 'So just get out and see to your duties, whatever they are – and you can take that toast with you', he snapped.

I poured a cup of coffee and tried to calm my rising temper. Why was this man being so belligerent and anyway what was this invasion from the RAF all about?

'Group Captain, if you want to have a meeting with your officers, I suggest you go along to the admin tent... there's plenty of room there. This happens to be the FRA Officers

Mess, and as such also happens to be my temporary home. It's not a Royal Air Force Mess and with the greatest respect, sir, you are out of order. I don't know what you are doing here and I have no wish to intrude – but there's a lot going on at the moment and – well, as I said, if you want to have some privacy, I'm sure Colonel Ward wouldn't mind if you used his admin tent. Now, I'd like to finish my toast, drink a cup of coffee, and then I'll see to my business – or "get out" as you so bluntly put it...'

Although shaking inside, I held his eye. The others shuffled their feet and didn't know where to look in the embarrassed silence that followed.

Oh my God, now you've done it! What's a Group Captain? The same as a full-Colonel? It doesn't matter, a junior Captain doesn't tell a senior officer that he's out of order – whatever his service and especially in front of his junior officers... even if he is bloody rude. Still, it's done now. I wish Colonel Ward were here...

The pause lengthened and eventually he dropped his gaze. 'I-er-beg your pardon' he said. 'I had no right... and I'm sorry...'

I stood up. 'That's all right, if I'd known you were here, I wouldn't have barged in – I've had a long morning...'

'You say you live here, are you seconded to the FRA?' he said moderating his tone slightly.

'Well not exactly, I'm just here to help out in the emergency. Probably be another month or so. I've got a Beaver outside and I'm doing the odd flying job for the FRA...'

'What odd flying job?'

'Well, my aircraft is the only one they've got, so it's being used for just about everything. The battalion is at battle stations up in the hills and they need re-supplying, as well as reconnaissance and liaison...'

He swung round to one of the Wing Commanders. 'I didn't know the army were involved. You told me that we were giving all the air support?'

'Ah, well not *all*, sir, the Army Air Corps have been giving a certain amount of *backup* as it were...'

I spluttered over my coffee. 'Backup?' I said as mildly as I could, 'what backup? Apart from a couple of Beverley's which arrived last week bringing the reinforcements, you're the first Air Force aeroplane that has been near the place... anyway, what are you all doing here? Does Colonel John, the Area Commander West, know you are here?'

'Where is Colonel Ward?' one of the wing commanders asked, 'we sent a signal yesterday via HQ FRA telling him about this visit. Did he get it?'

'Colonel Ward, Wing Commander, is up in the hills with his men – so I don't know whether he got your signal or not. But anyway, he's got enough on his plate at the moment, so what's this visit about...?'

The Group Captain swung back to me. 'We are here, to receive the AOC who will be arriving at any minute now with a Cabinet Minister, and then we are going to conduct them on a flying tour of the battle area... which I had been told we were giving close air support to.'

'Ah...well, I'm sorry there isn't much of a reception party for you – or for the AOC and the Cabinet Minister. Who on *earth* arranged it? The Emir's away and there's only a skeleton staff here...'

'The whole thing is a ghastly cock-up, if you ask me' the Group Captain snarled at the Wing Commander. Then turning to the pilots. 'Have you sorted out those maps yet? There's only one ridge west of Beihan, it can't be *that* difficult?'

The pilots were busy drawing lines and jotting headings onto a map, much as I had done a few days earlier. Only without an Operation Order, their task would be almost impossible. Ought I to offer some practical advice on how the ground lay? I hesitated, and then decided to say nothing. I think I'd already said too much.

The sound of a turbine-powered aircraft flew overhead. 'Look, I think I'll make myself scarce. Don't want to be in the way or anything, and I ought to catch up with some sleep whilst I've got the chance. Good luck with the battle tour...' I smiled and left them.

Actually I was feeling worn out, for the previous day

Colonel Ward had cancelled the morning airdrop, and I had flown him and the Emir's chief of staff – or right-hand man, or uncle – or whatever his capacity had been that morning, to Salalah in the Oman instead. It was a long flight over unfamiliar territory, for I hadn't been there before. We didn't leave Salalah until after dark, which made a difficult flight back, dead reckoning in the dark, and with no navigational aids. Thankfully the weather was clear, so I decided to follow the coast at low level down to Al Mukalla and then turned north and climbed up over more familiar territory to Ataq, before finally turning west, and back on our usual route to Beihan. We had eventually landed at 2240hrs to the lights of the vehicles, and then had had to refuel and load the aircraft in readiness for the morning parachute drop.

I had a shower and shaved and then lay down on the camp bed and pulled the mosquito netting down. I heard the whine of the turbo engines approaching in fine pitch and mentally followed through with the landing, and then heard them taxiing back, before the descending whine of the engines as they shut down. Then later, just as I was nodding off, I was conscious of the Twin Pin starting up. The 'bang' of the cartridge starter, followed by the 'chat-chat-chat' as the propeller turned through its revolutions.

'Bang-chat-chat-chat-chat-chat.'

I wonder how many cartridges they carry? Those Alvis Leonides engines are never very good at starting when they are warm. In fact, a Twin Pin that visited our strip at Falaise the other week used up every one of its cartridges when it tried to start again. In the end we had to wrap a rope around the propeller boss and then tie the other end to a Land Rover parked at right angles to it. On the word GO, the Land Rover drove off pulling the rope and spinning the engine up – much like starting a large lawnmower.

'Bang-chat-chat-chat-chat.'

They are strange looking aeroplanes; easily recognizable by their three tail fins and the rough clattering noise the engines make when they are flying. Charley Robinson always says they sound like a tractor with a broken camshaft! They're larger than a Beaver, but designed to do much the same job. I suppose they must be about ten feet longer with twenty-five feet more wingspan, and carry about three times the payload.

'Bang-chat-chat-chat-chat.'

In fact, for their size, their strip performance is remarkable – but it's at the expense of drag, making them much slower than a Beaver. Also they are very heavy to fly. I had a go in one once when I was at Habilayn, and was amazed at the amount of sheer brute strength it took to operate the controls. No wonder they need two pilots...

'Sahib, wake up! They want you at aeroplane...' The mess steward's shape is outlined in the door of the tent.

I roll out of bed and automatically dip my face into the bucket of water, which is kept in the corner for washing in, and then fully awake, find my beret and pistol belt.

Epaulettes still flapping. 'Damn, damn; where's my other shirt?'

'Other shirt in dhobi, sahib...'

'Shit! Okay, this will have to do.' At least I'd managed to shave.

'Sahib... wait!' He darted to my wash bag and found my nail scissors. 'I'll sow them on for you afterwards...' as deftly he snipped the offending epaulettes off. 'Hurry, sahib, Air Force officer very cross...'

I make my way out to the, now, three aircraft parked outside the gates.

'This your Beaver?' The Air Marshall is a big man with two rows of medals under his pilot's wings. He too is immaculate in khaki drill, presumably for the benefit of the portly civilian who is with him, and whom belatedly I recognise as a Cabinet Minister. I give them both a salute. 'Damn Twin Pin won't start, do you know where the battle area is, and can you take us in that?'

'Yes of course, Air Marshall... Minister...' I look round for Corporal Frazer, then see him by the Beaver and in the process of putting the seats back in and re-hanging the passenger doors. If anyone deserves a medal, it is that man.

'How many would like to come? I can take one in the co-pilot's seat and four, or at a pinch five, behind.'

'No point in pinching – I'll sit up next to you, and the Minister and – Harry! Do you want to come for a ride in this brown aeroplane?'

'Right, sir.' The Group Captain said, snapping to attention and at the same time managing to give me a filthy look. He then gestured to one of the Wing Commanders who handed him a map of the surrounding area pinned to a board.

'Just one thing, are you qualified to fly someone of Cabinet rank?'

'Well, I don't honestly know... I've got an ordinary VIP rating, but whether that's enough to fly a Cabinet Minister..?'

'Mmm. Bit late now, it'll just have to do. I've never flown in a Beaver before – what's the wingspan?'

Oh God, why does this always happen to me? It's daunting enough to have to fly a Cabinet Minister, a real live Air Marshall and a belligerent Group Captain, without being subjected to an examination as well. And why is it that RAF Officers always seem to be so obsessed by the wingspan? The CFI at Wallop was just the same...

And now my mind has gone completely blank. Try the cavalry approach...

'Wingspan, Air Marshall? Oh about fifty feet, I suppose...'

'Fifty... What, exactly fifty feet? Hmm. And what's the maximum all-up weight?'

'Ah! I seem to remember it's around five thousand and ninety pounds.' In fact, I knew perfectly well that that was the figure, for it's one we use a lot, but once started...

'Range, with maximum fuel?' There was no stopping him.

'Just short of eight hundred miles – but then we can carry extra fuel in the tip-tanks, which can make it go a bit further... are you ready to hop in?'

I leave him to climb up the strut and with Corporal

Frazer, settle the Cabinet Minister and the Group Captain into the centre seats. Corporal Frazer has found some passenger headsets from somewhere and shows them where to plug them in. I then look at the map the Group Captain is carrying. It is blank.

'Got a chinagraph pencil Corporal...? Ah, thanks!' I ring the four peaks and then mark in the relevant company positions, as well as the battalion HQ. Then I mark a cross on the known enemy positions, and hatch in the dead ground. I am conscious of the Air Marshall watching this from over his shoulder.

'The positions are a bit difficult to spot from the air unless you know where to look, sir, but the four peaks have all got a red panel on them, and once you spot those you'll see it will all make sense.' The Minister grunts and looks nervous.

I climb into my seat and start up, and then test the internal communications. Beside me, the Air Marshall watches every action; but there is only one captain of an aircraft and he sits in the left-hand seat, and his scrutiny no longer bothers me.

I takeoff and climb to the north as though we are on the parachute run.

'Do you want to fly, sir...?'

'Love to!'

'Okay, you have...'

'I have...' The Air Marshall and I are at home.

I explain the engine settings, speeds for the climb and cruise, height to fly and course to steer for the first position. His reactions are instantaneous and he is immediately in tune with the Beaver.

'Nice aeroplane...'

'Mmm. I find she's perfect for the job and dead reliable.'

'God, I wish I had your job – and was your age again. You've got the best job in the business, do you realize that? And I like your outfit – it's like the Air Force used to be, before we became rule-bound. What rank are you, by the way, you don't seem to be showing any...?'

'Yes, sorry about that, Air Marshall. I'm a captain; only my epaulettes got torn off by the seat harness when one of the parachutes hung up this morning. I'm not a very good advert for the Army Air Corps at the moment, but I only brought two shirts with me, and I've wrecked one in the first fortnight!'

'You been here two weeks – what you and the Twin Pioneer?'

'No, just me and a corporal. We haven't seen the Twin Pin before today.'

'Oh... I was led to believe? I see... at least, I'm beginning to. Oh well, you're doing a good job on your own. Just you and a corporal eh? We'd have had a whole team of people to back one aircraft... I didn't think you were a sergeant-pilot, for you'd have been stamping your feet and calling me "Sir" every minute. I find it amusing when certain army officers address me as Air Marshall... no Air Force Officer would dream of doing that...'

'I wouldn't count on that; you should meet some of our sergeant-pilots! Anyway, no disrespect intended, sir... it's just that in my regiment...'

'No, no – I quite like it, and after all, why not? I say, this is a nice aeroplane to fly – plenty of power and you can't beat a Pratt and Whitney.'

'Well at least they start on the button every time. I pity those Twin Pin pilots trying to start those Alvis Leonides with a cartridge. They always play up when they're hot... now, we're just coming up to the first position – see their red panel, at two o'clock? Don't go any further west, better not invite pot shots with a Minister on board.'

Guy calls on the radio and asks what we are doing. I avoid our usual banter and keep the transmission professional and to a minimum. He replies in like form and says that the Area Commander has just arrived on location, and has also just read the signal about the visit and sends his apologies. He then asks me to go and have another look at the two tribal armies in the next wadi.

'I have, Air Marshall.'

He smiles. 'You have...'

I alter course and explain on the intercom what we are doing, and descend into the next wadi. There is a pitched battle in progress. Skirmishers on each side firing at each other with their long old-fashioned rifles from positions behind rocks, and cavalry on horses and camels in the open space between the camps, hacking away at each other with long curved swords. It is as though we have been transported back in time and are observing a battle from the Crusades, looking down from what equally well could have been a spaceship. We fly up and down at a safe height, but nobody takes any notice, for they are all too busy killing each other.

The Minister will have quite a tale to tell at his next Cabinet meeting.

Having seen enough, I report back to Guy, who is obviously far more involved with the FRA and local intelligence than I had been led to believe, and then turn the aircraft north and follow the wadi out into the desert for a few miles. I let down to just above the dunes and from this height they are an awe-inspiring sight, rolling away for ever into the distance. In amongst them, it makes you appreciate the enormity and emptiness of the desert, and easy to imagine what it must be like to be down in it. I climb back up to 100 feet and then backtrack towards the entrance of the wadi – or the tip of the forefinger protruding into the sand, and then briefly make a detour to circle the strip at Nequub giving the FRA subaltern a wave as he comes running out, before heading back towards Beihan.

If we were on our own, I'd be tempted to show the Air Marshall the army version of tactical low flying – and then maybe he would appreciate one of my landings off a stall turn? He probably would too! But I doubt very much whether the Minister would, so decide to keep the flight as gentle and smooth as possible, with slow unhurried movements. We fly over the rooftops of the town, still at a hundred feet and then over the runway, and see the crash crew run to their vehicle. My fingers travel around the cockpit and complete the downwind checks, as I gauge the distance travelled over the runway. Then, in one flowing movement turn into a gentle one-eighty whilst pulling the speed back as the flaps go down, and power-in for a short landing. We kiss the runway, roll a few yards and reach the place to turn off to cross the sand to the parking area.

'Well done, Lindbergh, I'm pleased you resisted the temptation to show off – I nearly despaired for a moment! That landing was more than enough...'

I go through the shut down drill whilst still on the move, then pull the propeller lever back into fully coarse, and as the revs drop, follow it with the red mixture lever, and finally starved of fuel the engine dies. We continue rolling silently for the remaining few yards, and without having to use the brakes, stop in our place beside the Twin Pioneer.

'All right you bastard, you may pretend not to know the wingspan, but I know you can fly!' The Air Marshall says. 'Great stuff... great little aeroplane, and I really enjoyed every minute of it. I'd give my right arm to be able to join you for a week of hard flying – but unfortunately I've got to go back to being an Air Marshall again. But thank you for that breath of fresh air. Anyway, we've got a tight schedule to keep, so we'll get off straight away and get out of your hair.'

The Minister and the AOC departed, and we stood on the side of the runway and saluted as they swept past. Then we looked around for a rope and a Land Rover to start the Twin Pioneer...

That night there was an uncanny silence. All the semi-wild pye-dogs, whose dismal howls would rend the air whilst on their nightly rampage scavenging for food, left the town. The dogs had smelt blood from afar and were on their way to eat the dead and wounded on the battlefield over the border.

At some time during the early hours Colonel Ward arrived back at the camp and left a note saying that he wanted to come with us on the early morning run. More than anything he wanted to see the state of the battlefield in the wadi.

He looked utterly exhausted as he climbed into the Beaver, having spent the last two nights climbing up and down the hill. He asked briefly about the visit and I told him about the Minister and also the fact that he had witnessed the battle when it was at its gory height. This made him smile and he wryly commented that at least one member of the Government would understand what the letters FRA stood for when he saw them against the allocation for next year's funding.

Having re-supplied the positions we dropped into the next wadi and had a look at the battlefield. There were still bodies lying on the ground, though whether still alive we could not tell. Of the living and the two tented camps there was no sign. We landed at Manawa and he told the subaltern in charge to assemble a patrol and to go and find out, but to time the penetration for last light. On no account was he to be caught over the border. We then flew back to Beihan and on the way he explained that the battle, although strictly tribal, would possibly alter the situation up in the hills. Many of the erstwhile enemy had slipped away to become involved, and he wasn't sure whether they would return. In any event the situation in the hills wasn't achieving anything and had fast become stalemate, so any change would be no bad thing. For the time being he intended to leave his troops in position, but was aware that his flanking outposts could now become the major targets in which case they would need rapidly reinforcing.

Guy was in the mess when we returned.

At least I thought it was Guy, but had to look twice before I recognized him and obviously the shock registered on my face. I had last seen him when he was in hospital after his accident – and then there hadn't been a lot to see, for he had been covered in bandages. Nothing could have prepared me for such a change in a person. Gone was the debonair Guards Officer with a walking stick, who handled his AOP IX like a sports car and couldn't wait for the weekends so that he could drive to London and continue with the London scene. One side of his face was hideously scarred and his black hair had turned white. He got up awkwardly from his chair, and I could see that he was also permanently lame. He smiled a crooked smile and we stood and looked at each other.

'Hello, old mate, I'm a bit of a mess these days...'

I stepped forward and then embraced him. 'Guy, you old bastard, what have they done to you? But at least you are alive – and it's good to see you.'

'Hallo, you two know each other?' Colonel Ward intervened.

'We learnt to fly together...' I started to say.

'And that says it all,' Guy concluded. 'We shared a pretty intense time together... and one I wouldn't have missed for anything – so yes, you could certainly say we know each other...'

'Well, I'll leave you together for a bit – I'm sure you've got a lot to catch up on, then come and see me in my office, Guy – I shall want you to go into town and contact some of your Arab friends to see if you can find out what's going on?'

Guy told me that after his accident he had spent nearly a year recuperating, and then had limped in to see his colonel to find out what his prospects were. The colonel had been very good, and explained that there was no way he could ever serve with his Regiment again, but they were prepared to keep him on strength until he could find alternative employment. Then someone had come up with the idea of the Political Service, who took selected officers virtually on permanent secondment for field intelligence duties; so he had gone off and done the Arabic course and now here he was! Sometimes he wore uniform and sometimes he didn't which, he said, gave him the best of both worlds. By coincidence, the Irish Guards had also just arrived in Aden, so their mess was always open to him whenever he was there – which, from what I could gather, wasn't so very often.

Corporal Frazer needed to service the Beaver, so I spent the rest of the day giving him a hand, and we got it ready to fly again in time for the evening parachute run, which also served as a test flight. We landed back just after dark and then loaded up again for the morning run, after which I walked up to the mess for supper. I dined on my own, for Guy had disappeared into the town and Colonel Ward was out somewhere. The Colonel came into the mess later and said he had just heard from the subaltern at Manawa. They had found two Arabs on the battlefield who were still alive, and had managed to carry them both back to Manawa, but they were both in a bad way. Not only had they received horrific wounds but they then had to feign death in order not to be finished off by the enemy, during which time they had nearly been eaten alive by pye-dogs.

He concluded by saying that the Emir wanted to interrogate one of them at the earliest opportunity, so could I fly to Manawa and bring them both in on stretchers?

I explained that I would rather not attempt a night landing at Manawa, which was bad enough during the day, and that the earliest I could go would be at first light.

'Hmm, I thought you'd say that. Just hope they'll be still alive by then. Oh well, you'd better do that first thing, then after we've interrogated him, I shall want you to fly me back to Aden. I shall be staying there for a few days, so I'll come back on the Aden Air schedule, but the Emir has asked if you could meet his two boys off the UK flight and bring them back on Friday? They're both at Harrow, and it's school holidays. Don't worry about the authorization, you are still on charge to us, so I'll do all the necessary...'

'Well if I fly you down to Khormaksar later today, I'll spend the night at Falaise – which will give me a chance to pick up a new shirt and some more clothes! The Beaver's loaded up for the parachute drop now, so we'll do that first and then go on to Manawa?'

'Yes, only be as quick as you can. Which reminds me, I'd better see to jacking-up the mule train again whilst you've gone. Just as well I remembered it – I'll go and do that now; see you in the morning, as quick as you can make it!'

As we climbed up into the morning, I told Corporal Frazer the plan, and asked if he needed anything from Falaise? He told me that he had already sent a signal with a shopping list for new spark plugs and a few other items, as well as more clothes for himself, all of which he had arranged to be put on the next Aden Air schedule flight. In the end we decided it would only cause more confusion to undo this... but damn the man, I wish I'd thought to do that earlier!

We delivered the goods, then went on to Manawa to pick up the two casualties. One had died during the night, but the other – and the one the Emir needed to talk to, was still hanging on, but only just. We loaded him into the empty aeroplane and Corporal Frazer scrounged some more blankets to cover him, for it would be a draughty and cold ride with no rear doors at this time of the morning.

Before takeoff, I saw the subaltern and asked him whether he could do anything about the soft patch in the middle of the strip? With constant use it was becoming a lot worse, especially on takeoff. He said there was a hard strip of sand on the right hand edge, and walked out with me and pointed it out. The narrow strip was about two feet wide, but as he said, at least it was harder than the rest.

That takeoff was nearly to be my last. I found the narrow strip with my starboard wheel, which left the port wheel dragging in the soft, slewing the aircraft round at the critical moment, just under flying speed. Falling off the side of HMS *Albion* had been nothing in comparison to this! Corporal Frazer had to hang on to our stretcher-case as he nearly slid out of the door, and all in all, it got the adrenaline working overtime. Once airborne I circled the camp and shook my fist at the subaltern who had obviously witnessed it, for he grinned and bowed low and then gave me a thumbs-up – which I hoped meant he was going to do something about it.

We took off for Aden at noon, with Colonel Ward in the front, and the rear cabin piled high with Beihan rugs, which many of the 10th Hussars had ordered. The Arab at the shop had also offered me a roll of money if I would fly four young girls to Lodar, which he said would save him a twelve or fourteen-day round trip by road. Apparently there was a shortage of girls in Lodar and he was at the centre of a flourishing trade! Obviously jewellery and rugs were not the only things manufactured in Beihan... He was most insistent, for he said the rains were due and the roads would soon become impassable. Anyway, I declined as gracefully as I could, but mentally gave him full marks for initiative. I mentioned it to Colonel Ward as we strapped into the aircraft, but he merely shrugged and passed it off by saying that Arabs had been notorious slave-traders since the beginning of time and that this was just a modern version and perfectly legitimate. Anyway, it was nothing compared to some of their other activities!

We climbed out of the wadi and then I turned west and away from our course for a few miles and hunted for the thermal that could usually be found there. We were in luck and I dipped a wing into it and climbed up, spiralling round and round like a glider. There's nothing like knowing your home ground and I was beginning to know these mountains as well as the ones at Habilayn.

We left the thermal at 12,000 feet, having used only a fraction of the fuel that a climb to this altitude would normally have taken, and set course for Ataq and the first dogleg for Aden. After all the ten-minute hops of the past days, it was good to be on a proper flight again and I was looking forward to getting back – albeit only for a night, and to sleep in a proper bed again. The weather was heavy and sultry and long before the escarpment – and only some twenty minutes after Khora, scattered clouds began forming underneath, which soon turned into a solid carpet. It reminded me of the time I flew the pregnant girl down from Mukerius, which must have been at about the same time of the year. I had meant to ask the Colonel about the rainy season and how long it lasted in Beihan, for the Beihan rug-man had also mentioned it, but the Colonel was fast asleep.

Right on time the ADF swung into life, which confirmed our crossing the escarpment, and I gave Aden Centre a call. Again like the time with the pregnant girl, Khormaksar Radar offered a GCA, but on hearing that the ceiling at

Khormaksar was 2000 feet, I opted to let down through it under their surveillance, for there was only the flat sand of the coastal desert underneath, and no uncharted high dunes to worry about. From FL 120 it was downhill all the way and we made good time and the Colonel was still asleep as our wheels touched down at Khormaksar. I dropped him off and confirmed that 1100hrs was still the expected arrival time for the UK flight in the morning, and said that I would see him back at Beihan in three days time.

Falaise was still on the air, so I asked the tower if the fuel point was still manned, and being told that it was, taxied straight over after landing and filled the three belly tanks, ready for the morning.

Neville Bamford came out as I finally shut down outside our dispersal, and offered me a lift up to the mess. I showed him all the carpets in the back, so he brought his car onto the apron and we loaded it up. On the way to the mess, he told me that Brian Young had returned to Wallop for a full flying refresher course – so, as well as being QFI, he was now in command of the Flight on a temporary basis. Whether Brian would return to assume command would depend on how well he got on with his course. He also thanked me for the way I had handled the situation, and that he had made no mention of my involvement when he had had to take the matter to Colonel Mike.

There was the usual party going on in the mess, and my entry with the pile of Beihan rugs was greeted with enthusiasm. The 10th Hussars really were a splendid regiment to share a mess with, and the party went on well into the night...

It was just as well that I didn't have an early start, for I had a thick head in the morning and the UK flight had already landed by the time I reached Khormaksar. I found the two boys waiting in the reception area – sitting on the same bench where I had left Arthur on his last day. I drank black coffee whilst we waited for their luggage, and when this eventually arrived, the three of us made our way out to the Beaver. It looked very out of place parked amongst the airliners and sleek executive jets in the civilian compound, and I think the Emir's sons were expecting something rather more modern and stylish. But she was the only aeroplane in the park that could have got out of the strip at Manawa, and to my eyes this gave her a dignity of her own. We piled their luggage into the back and then the boys tossed a coin to see who would sit in the front.

* * *

The younger boy wins the toss, and I help him clamber up and show him how the shoulder harness fits. With good grace, his brother has already settled himself in the passenger cabin, so I check his lap belt and then climb into my seat. Both boys are not in the least tired after their long flight, and chatter excitedly as I start the engine and relay my Flight Plan over the radio. The tower informs me that the weather to the northeast has not changed since yesterday and the ceiling of the overcast is still at 2000 feet. Immediately airborne I turn onto course and just have time to establish the climb before entering the cloud, and then force my aching head to concentrate on the instruments. I have asked for the usual FL 90, but twenty-five minutes later as the altimeter approaches this we are still on instruments and there is no sign of the cloud lightening. We are still IMC when we reach my estimated time for the Zone Boundary, and I inform Khormaksar Approach of our inflight conditions before changing frequency to Aden Centre. Once established with Aden Centre I request a change of Flight Plan and ask for clearance to continue the climb until we break out on top. I hear the surprise in the controller's voice and he grants my request and then asks me to inform him at what level we break out and become VMC.

The clouds begin to lighten as we pass through FL 110 and then suddenly the sun filters through. I call Aden and tell them we are Visual Met Conditions on top, and request FL 130 for our cruising altitude. I have never known the cloud to be so thick in these skies and it makes me wonder whether it will break at the escarpment, or carry on into the interior for a few miles like it did yesterday. I lean the mixture right back and we carry on above the dazzling glare. Maybe it's due to the lack of oxygen, but my head is still suffering from last night, and a pain is beginning to throb behind my eyes. The bright glare thrown up from the clouds 2000 feet below doesn't help either.

'Lindbergh, you're not concentrating. Forget your damn head and fly...'

His voice breaks my reverie and I realize with a start that I am ten degrees off course and a hundred feet above my flight level. I check with the ADF, which is still holding Khormaksar on a back bearing, and it too is showing seven degrees off. I double the error and turn fifteen degrees towards the needle and at the same time sneak back down to altitude. After five minutes the ADF centres again, and I turn seven degrees right, and back onto course. At least this exercise proves that there is no adverse wind, and confirms the upper air forecast of twenty knots from the southwest. Also, I managed to correct the course error in time, for the stopwatch now reads that we should be overhead Lodar and time for our first course change. I turn left onto 029 degrees, which will now take us across the escarpment and on to Khora – the landmark Arthur pointed out to me, so long ago.

But as the minutes tick past, I realize there will be no Khora visible today, for the carpet of cloud continues and stretches as far as the eye can see.

We droned on, and I search for a sign of a break, which surely must come soon? I feel cheated, for this is against all the rules and the cloud cannot continue for much longer. Suddenly, it is very important to fly accurately, for one can only rely on dead reckoning for so long and any error automatically is compounded with each change of course. With no visual landmark, the only reference I have been able to use was the back bearing from the Khormaksar beacon before I turned north overhead Lodar. At least then, I was on the correct line – but I could kick myself, for in my fuddled state, I had turned on the estimated time shown on the original Flight Plan, which had only allowed time to climb to FL90 and not the additional four thousand feet to FL 130.

Which means I turned early, and will now be west of track.

Damn, damn! This really is back to basics, and the sort of elementary mistake made by a novice.

'And who, not so long ago, had seen fit to elevate himself to the seat of judgement when it came to Brian Young's flying? Moreover, since when has familiarity of a route been an excuse for sloppy flying?'

Lured by the familiarity of the route, I had just sat back, complacent in the knowledge that the cloud always burns off over the hot and high ground of the interior. Maybe it still will – but by then it could be too late, for through my own stupidity I am also off track and without navigational aids I am unable to correct this. What I really need is a definite fix.

The clouds stretch on unbroken and there are no landmarks... Today the goal posts have been moved – and I am no longer ahead of the game.

My headache is forgotten and I concentrate on the needles. We are now long past VHF range from Aden Centre, and the ADF needle hunts aimlessly about the dial. Also I am beginning to worry about fuel. I filled the belly tanks up at Falaise last night, but since then have had two takeoffs and a long climb to 13,000 feet, burning forty gallons per hour. Should I turn back now? We could still just about make Khormaksar and now is the time to decide, for this must be about our point of no return?

'Don't guess! Work it out...'

I put the figures into the computer... and then do it again. Reluctantly I accept the reading. We passed the point of no return twelve minutes ago...

Why the hell didn't I fill the tip-tanks up at Falaise last night?

I glance at my two young passengers and they are both

asleep. The flight out has at last caught up with them. It would be good to be able to talk to somebody, for suddenly I feel very alone.

I reach up and check the tuning on the Sunair HF radio, and then release the aerial so that its drogue drags it out behind. There is a meter that shows the optimum tuning length of the aerial for each selected frequency and the needle flicks up for a second and then back to zero as the length of the wire increases. I turn the switch that activates the motor to wind the aerial in again, and slower now, watch the needle until it flickers again, and then stop winding when it shows the maximum reading. It is a fiddling business to tune properly, and even when tuned, is a temperamental set to use, and really is an instrument best suited for a trained radio operator, who has the time and patience to fiddle with the fine-tuning and also take into account the 'skip' distances.

By comparison, UHF and VHF radios are simple and foolproof, for they both use a small vertical aerial, and their range is determined by 'line of sight'. Thus, the higher you are, the longer the range and also the less likelihood of encountering obstacles that can block the radio waves. Not so the Sunair, which works anything but 'line of sight'. Being a High Frequency radio it uses a horizontal aerial, the length of which has to be carefully tuned to each frequency. Trailing out behind, the radio waves leave the aerial at right-angles to it, and go down to the earth and then bounce up to the ionosphere and back again, thus 'skipping' around the globe. To add further complication, the 'skip distance' can alter dramatically with a change of heading, or with any inconsistency in the density of the humidity in the atmosphere, so it becomes very much a 'hit and miss' situation. It is very easy for your transmission to skip over its intended destination, to be received by somebody listening out many thousands of miles further on. In the past I have talked to operators in Nairobi and Delhi, who both received the same transmission! Arthur said that once he even worked an operator on the polar route to Los Angeles... but apart from the comfort of being able to talk to somebody, unless you can reach your intended destination, these 'chance operators' are rarely in a position to be able to offer practicable help.

'Aden Centre, Army Five-Zero-One..?'

I imagine the transmission skipping around the globe, but there is nobody there to catch it, for the set remains mute.

'*Mr Summers*..?' But he too has gone.

We are on our own.

We are due overhead Khora in two minutes. Or rather, we're about twenty miles west and to the south of Khora... come on; it's time to start thinking positively. In spite of being over cloud we are only a few miles off track and so not that desperately lost. But, if I keep to the Flight Plan and change course at Khora for Ad Daymah, this will compound the error and throw us even further off track.

So what are the alternatives?

I could turn back now and steer the reciprocal of 209 degrees, and once back over the escarpment will be able to intercept the ADF beam from Khormaksar. But I know I cannot make Khormaksar, so how will this help? The only place we could land would be Lodar, for there is nowhere else. Once over the coastal plain, I suppose I could let down through the cloud – but the ADF beam is at its extreme range there, and either way we'll lose it once we descend below about 5000 feet. Even then, I won't know if I am east or west of Lodar... for I have never had occasion to land there. In fact, I am not familiar with the strip, the surrounding country, or whether there are any obstacles. I have always passed overhead at 9000 feet and from this height it just looks like any other insignificant strip – and even should I be able to find it, I know for certain there is no fuel there. Also, what about the political situation? Are there any conflicting interests between Lodar and Beihan? I haven't heard of anything, but then I'm hardly in a position to... The truth is, I just don't know – and it would be just my luck to deliver the Emir's sons into the hands of someone who would then delight in taking political advantage from the situation... the whole thing just doesn't bear thinking about!

Two minutes are up, and I turn due north for Ad Daymah. When in doubt, stick to the Flight Plan. There are too many unknowns about Lodar. Besides, there's always a chance the clouds will start breaking up, once we are near the Empty Quarter...

But they don't.

During this last leg I have worked out that when the time comes for the final course alteration from Ad Daymah to Beihan, we will be nineteen-point-nine-nine miles west, and three-point-eight miles south, of the turning point. I have recalculated this many times, double checking the figures with the computer – and then drawing it as a three-dimensional sketch, also allowing for the wind. By plotting our actual route against the intended, and converting both the climbing and cruising speeds into distances and then further plotting our three changes of course, my drawing now shows as three interlinking parallelograms. Then by squaring off the corners, our progressive error becomes perfectly obvious in the shape of a right-angled triangle within the parallelogram. I am pleased with the result, for it looks simple on paper and as such, means it can also be solved geometrically. In effect, by turning early, we merely cut the corner, and according to my triangles, the error can be rectified if we continue north for a further ninety-five seconds past the turning point, and then shorten the last leg by nine and three-quarter minutes – and we should end up smack over Beihan!

I let the stopwatch run on for another ninety-five seconds and then turn left onto 292 degrees and the final leg. The clouds stretch on over the Rub'al Khali, and our fuel shows that we still have fifty minutes to continue to enjoy them.

Which still allows time to address a final alternative. If my geometry is correct and we are now back on track, albeit further along; and if I have plotted the wind correctly; and if since loosing the ADF beam at Lodar I have been flying as accurately as I believe I have – that makes three 'ifs'; we have enough fuel to reach Ataq. It's either Ataq or Beihan and now is the time to decide. The advantage of Ataq is that it is situated in the middle of a flat plain that stretches for some miles north into the Rub'al Khali, before the desert turns into its more familiar form of undulating and shifting sand dunes. From a flying point of view, these dunes are best likened to uncharted hills, and their heights can vary from anything between three and four hundred feet. The other advantage about Ataq is that there are no unfriendly borders nearby. But against this, to the south and east of Ataq there is the wadi Habban and its vast sandstone cliffs – and it would only need one of my 'ifs' to be a minute or two out of place..?

'Are we nearly home?' The youngest boy asks.

'Yes, nearly...' I give him a smile, and with it the decision has been made. I too, now regard Beihan as 'home', and if we have to feel out way down, there's nothing like doing it over your home ground.

I look at the fuel gauges and then turn the fuel selector back to the rear tank. Surely I can scavenge some more? It takes eight minutes to suck dry. I then turn the selector to the centre tank and do the same, eyes glued to the emergency light. This tank takes a further ten minutes before the light glares its ten-second warning, and I change back to the front tank. In forty-five minutes from now, whatever happens, it will all be over.

If, if, if..? If my calculations are right, we are over Beihan – and now it is time.

The clouds are still unbroken and our world has not changed. I select the army set, which is still on the FRA frequency, and try a call. Echoes from the past, for I did this long ago, when icing up over Salisbury Plain, and Guy was waiting and answered. I blip the engine and circle round. I could be miles away, but maybe they can hear, and if so, maybe they'll think to listen out on their tactical radio?

'*Come on Guy, where are you?*'

I try another call, but nobody answers. Maybe we are over Beihan, and maybe we are not, but aeroplanes cannot wait, and now it is time to go down.

I turn north and lock the harness of my young passenger

beside me, and then turn around and check the lap belt around his brother's waist. I fly due north for fifteen minutes, and then reduce the power and select twenty-five degrees of flap. Speed back to sixty-five knots and trim. We brush through the tops of the cloud, in and out, white wisps turning to grey, and then become fully immersed.

There is turbulence in the cloud, and at this slow speed the aircraft bucks about and is difficult to hold. The cylinder-head temperature is falling quickly and I reach down and pull the carb-air lever halfway up. In spite of desert temperatures, moisture in cloud can still cause icing, and I was caught out by this once before. Through the lurching and buffeting I hold the airspeed at sixty-five and the DI centred on north, and we continue down. It goes on forever. The grey turns to nearly black, and large drops form on the windshield and then run up and over the roof. Normally the drops are small... this cloud must be very dense and full of moisture. The minutes tick by, and it is tempting to push the column forward, which would plunge us out from the maelstrom and get it over with. Indeed, the reverse is the case, and our present descent of 400 feet per minute is now too fast. We've got to feel our way down, especially as we near the ground and by reducing the descent to 200 feet per minute will give us more time to recover. I hold the nose up and catch the speed with power as it begins to fall off, and maintain sixty-five knots.

Roger would hate this...I smile and this thought strengthens my resolve. *It's only a cloud for God's sake, you've done it hundreds of times before, so what's new?*

But all the other times, I have either been under radar surveillance, or at least I have known my position. That's the difference. We could be descending into anything, and then still be totally lost underneath when we do bottom out... and either way we'll only have about half an hour's fuel left. This whole trip has been wrong and I have flown blithely on, and was never once ahead of the situation. That's the truth of the matter. There's no way a pilot approaching 2000 hours should have ever placed himself in this position in the first place. I don't deserve to...

'Stop it, Lindbergh. Just keep the VSI steady, descending at 200 feet per minute, and use every sense you've got to be aware of any change outside. Sometimes even the best pilots are caught out, and apart from the first half of the flight when you were wandering all over the sky like a novice, I think you've done everything possible. There are times when every pilot is faced with a situation like this, and to see it through, you need courage, and a steady nerve. So use those 2000 hours, and fly... Lindbergh, look up, the wing, now!'

I look up and briefly see his face reflected in the windshield. And then notice the drops. They have turned yellow. Large yellow drops leaving a streak of sand as they slither up over the screen. If you look straight ahead into cloud, there is nothing solid for the eye to focus upon and so your eyes will remain at the focal length they were when last used – in this case being the distance to see objects within the confines of the cockpit. Mr Summers once told me never to look ahead, but always look at the wing, and then follow it out as far as possible, which distance is enough to refocus your eyes and you can sometimes see beyond. I do this now, and see that the grey-black cloud has turned a dirty yellow.

It is pouring with rain, and we are amongst the dunes.

Calmly now. I arrest the descent by raising the nose and gradually feed in power, still holding the speed at sixty-five. But this is too fast for the limits of my vision, so I pump down more flap and reduce the speed to sixty, countering the extra drag with still more power. We are in a valley between two sand dunes, still heading north into the vastness of the desert. So, the first thing to do is to see if we can somehow turn around. The rain is horrific – stair rods? Why stair rods, for God's sake? This rain is yellow, it's like following a truck on a dirty motorway, and the visibility is little better. Ah, this dune is ending, and shortly followed by another. If I can squeeze through that gap..?

We are through and now heading roughly west.

I wish I could see further... there! Another gap? No, it's a false entry, carry on... But there is a pattern to them, rather like waves in an ocean. Can I get over the top...? No, their tops are definitely in cloud; so don't even think about it. Sink back down again, wheels just off the sand. Thank God for all those hours spent at Wallop flying tactically, it comes as second nature.... How about there? No, another false entry, but there's a passage to the side... Good one! We are through and now heading 200 degrees. We are nearly round, and maybe it's my imagination, but the dunes seem to be getting smaller. There! Shit, it's a rock, not a dune. Can it be the start of one of the fingers? Jinx round a bit more – yes, it is, but which one? Left or right? Quick!

The Yemen is to the right, so I go left, and the sand immediately flattens down. Already there is brown water running and filling the long dry hollows. We are definitely in a wadi, but it could be any one of the four gaps between the fingers – if indeed it they are the right fingers. Still, there's only one way to find out... follow it and see where it goes. The boys are loving every minute of this now that we are out of the dunes. To them it is just an enormous adventure and they are cheering each time I miss a patch of scrub with our wheels, and for them the diminishing tunnel that the wadi resembles and the fact that we are flying almost blindly up it in a tropical downpour, is all part of the game. Or maybe they just have total confidence in their pilot... how little they know!

Thinking about it, it *must* be one of the wadis between the fingers, for there are no others that have the same north-south heading. So, if that's the case, and working from the little finger at the end – if it's the end wadi, we're in the Yemen; if it's the next one Manawa should show up; the next one is the one we want with Beihan, and the bottom one has the fort at Negid Mergid which has a pretty good strip.

Luck has been with us and I still hardly dare to believe that we have tempted fate and got this far. For one way and another the odds have been against us from the moment we climbed into the overcast at Khormaksar. And there's no getting away from it; it has all been my fault. If we'd had full tip tanks we could have turned back. We are not meant to land with them full, but had I been earlier, I could have taken off from Falaise and then filled them at Khormaksar, so that's no excuse. There are many lessons to be learned from this flight...

Fuel? We are still okay, and have about thirty-five minutes. We hardly used any in the descent... Shit! I have forgotten to wind in the Sunair aerial! *See? There's another thing...* I wonder if we have lost the drogue? I flick the motor on and it winds in. But it makes me smile, for one of the pilots on the previous Beaver course forgot to wind it in and actually landed with it trailing behind, narrowly missing a Chipmunk and slicing it in half. Ever since then it has been included in the downwind checks – which is excuse enough for now, for although at nought feet, we haven't found a runway to warrant any downwind checks yet!

Where was I? Ah yes, fuel. If this is the wrong wadi, do we have enough to turn about and fly round again into the next one? We should know in a minute...

The boys are pointing excitedly at a lone hut in the wadi. I steer around it, then suddenly we are upon a herd of goats in an enclosure. They are tethered and run round and round in panic, falling over each other as we roar amongst them. Next, there is the town with the streets running with water. People are out in it, laughing and splashing their bodies in the rain. The white battlements of the Emir's palace are obscured in cloud.

Now, it is time for the downwind checks!

The runway appears and all I have to do is to cut the power and hold her steady, and we splash into it in a welter of spray.

Corporal Frazer is the first to arrive in the crash truck. He opens the rear port door and holds it against the slipstream as I shut the engine down. He finds the pitôt-head cover and the stopper with its red streamer for the static vent, and puts them both in place. I take my helmet off and lower the window, and then help the Emir's young son who is having difficulty with the harness.

'We heard your engine, sir, but we thought you'd turned back. I told them you'd never be able to land in this... Jesus, I mean, sir!'

The Emir's chauffeur driven car is next to arrive. In it is the Emir's uncle whom I flew to Salalah. He formerly shakes hands with the boys, then relaxes and gives them both a hug.

I suppose I'd better climb out and get wet with the rest.

The uncle makes his way to my side, with a boy hanging on each arm.

'Hello Captain!' he says. 'Thank you for bringing the boys. And this lovely weather, make everything grow! It only happens like this once every five years. Today we are lucky..?

'Very lucky. Very, very lucky indeed' I reply.

Epilogue

I must have been miles away, for suddenly everything is happening.

A Land Rover lurches out from the rocks near the Beaver and a Royal Marine Sergeant runs ahead into the clearing and then doubles back and looks inside the Beaver. More troops appear and fan out into a circle, their weapons at the ready.

'Is anyone there?' the Sergeant shouts.

The Colonel comes out warily from behind his cover, and then the others follow. I make to get up and join them, and then stop and listen. A twin rotor Belvedere appears, nose high in the flare and then settles down into the clearing, covering everything in dust. Then I hear the noise I have been waiting for – the penetrating buzz made by the tail rotor of an approaching Scout. It too flares and hovers, and then settles down near the Beaver.

Of the enemy, there is no sign.

I collect the flares and the Very gun, and make my way over to the others. The RSM hands me my SMG and I tell him that I gave his pistol to the Political Officer. Two Royal Marines have picked up the dead Arab and are loading him into the Belvedere.

Roger joins me.

'Hello, partner' he says, then walks to the Beaver and with an aviator's eye follows the line of the approach we had made. 'What happened?'

I tell him the full story. Being hit taking off from Blairs, flying through the mortar explosion as we left the ground, the heaviness of the controls, the realization that we were losing fuel, and how the engine finally stopped at the apex of the climb. Then the glide down the face of the mountain followed by the dead-stick landing, having first missed the hillock of rock. I also tell him that I think I killed a man by burning him alive with a flare.

'Well, sounds as if you've had quite a day!' He says, relishing the understatement. 'Probably fragments from the mortar explosion that punctured your fuel line. Hmmm. XP 777 – wasn't that your rogue machine? The other's will be pleased it's written off... Go and get your helmet and I'll give you a lift back. We'll go straight back to Falaise, else we'll be late for dinner!'

I walk back to the Beaver. It is full of holes, but my helmet and flight bag have not been touched. I retrieve them and then walk over to the Colonel as he is climbing into the Belvedere, and tell him I am going straight to Falaise in the Scout but no doubt we'd meet again soon...

There is a shout and the sergeant appears from behind the rocks, dragging the lifeless body of the Arab I had burnt with the flare. Rather than leave him the Arabs had cut his throat. Or maybe, I tell myself, his companions had done it as an act of mercy, his body being too charred to survive. Either way, I don't want to look and turn away.

I feel sick – and it is as though a weight descends onto my shoulders. Is this what being a soldier is really all about? I try to remember every detail of what actually happened, but it is still a blur, for it all happened so fast. I tell myself that it was self defence... and had he got nearer he would have had no hesitation in killing me; but it is no good and the weight is still there – and I know it will remain.

'You okay, partner?' Roger says as he fires-up the turbine. 'You did well to get it down in one piece.'

I push the thought of the burned body to the back of my mind.

'Mmm, what? Yes. Yes she may have been our rogue aeroplane, but she flew like a good'un at the end...'

'Well, you still did well. Do you remember that time when we were at Wallop, and you told me about how you did a practice forced landing in an AOP IX? The time when you said it floated on and on, and in the end you had to do a ground loop to avoid hitting the trees?'

His hand closes around the twist-throttle on the collective lever. Then, in a co-ordinated and flowing sequence of hands and feet, he lifts the helicopter off the ground, simultaneously easing the stick forward with his other hand and his feet busy on the rudder pedals, which in place of a rudder control the pitch of the tail rotor behind, thus countering the torque from the main rotor above.

The Scout dips its nose and gains speed.

'...When you told me about it, I couldn't help feeling that you were being unnecessarily vigilant – following that landing through as you did to the bitter end. I didn't say so at the time, of course, but...'

'Yes, I do remember. I don't altogether agree that I was being over vigilant though. I seem to remember that I was committed and it was the only thing to do...'

We skim along the bed of the wadi and then still in a nose down attitude, he pulls more collective and we lift effortlessly up.

'Well, I was going to say, partner – I've changed my mind! If you hadn't tested yourself to the limit as you did then, I don't think you'd ever have managed to land that Beaver with a dead engine...'

We fly over Habilayn and then angle south for the Jebel Maniff at the end of the wadi.

'Do you know, partner, all the time we've known each other, this is the first time that we have ever actually flown together...?'

I smile and remember the first day we'd met at Wallop. How we'd both looked over the field from the Control Tower in the twilight of that long summer evening and made our pact to see it through together, neither of us knowing what the future held.

I expect I'll see Wallop through different eyes when I go back for my conversion course onto helicopters. Arthur was right and perhaps now is the time? I'd heard from Tristan *the other day, and he said that helicopters were gradually taking over from the Beavers in Borneo – and that he was now wondering whether it was time to change. I could write to him when we get back and perhaps we could arrange to go on the same course? That would make it worthwhile!*

Or would it? For now there this other thing.

Killing the Arab has brought it all home to me. In order to progress with my career I must convert onto helicopters. But is this the only way forward? Having blooded my sword, makes me realize I never want to be in that position again – and therefore the big issue that has to be faced is whether to continue flying for the army...? It's not only the killing, but as John Foster foresaw at Wallop – and the very reason he RTU'd himself: as an army flyer you are inevitably at the sharp-end, but unlike the rest of the army, you are always unprotected and exposed. David Bartlett got killed two weeks ago. It was all so unnecessary. The poor man took his Sioux up for an air-test one evening – just doing his job. And whilst doing it, and totally absorbed in putting the aircraft through the various tests on his check-sheet, he got shot in the butt from below. Nobody knew where the shot came from, and it wasn't as if he was even near enemy territory. He must have been killed instantly for the Sioux hit the ground under full power. All that was left were pieces of twisted metal, scattered over the side of a hill – and that included David, for by all accounts there wasn't much left of him to put into a coffin...

As if flying wasn't dangerous enough...? With sudden insight I realize that a soldier's real enemy is the fear of death – and this often strikes when you least expect it. If you can condition yourself to beat that fear, you will make a good soldier. A pilot, on the other hand will also sometimes face death, but rarely is it unexpected. If he is good, he will use every opportunity to steer away from it. Or, if he has to meet it head on – as sometimes can happen, at least he has a chance to use his skill and experience to fight it.

I just don't know. Perhaps I am just very tired and need a long rest. Best think about it later...

*Dear old Tristan... we'd kept in constant touch by letter –
and he too had had his thunderstorms and his icing-up and
been lost over the clouds. Every pilot has – or at least, those
who fly on a regular day-to-day basis have. Anybody can fly
on a sunny day; the real test comes in knowing what to do
when things start to go wrong. Only experience can teach
you that. Tristan, or any other member of the Flight could
have force-landed XP777 in that wadi this afternoon. It was
kind of Roger to say what he did, but in the end it was the
hours and hours of constant training that made it possible.
What was it Mr Summers said – 'It is no good going off to
"practice" engine failures, because in reality things never
happen that way...'? That man taught me so much... and I
know now that the only pilots who will live to be 'old pilots'
are the ones who have continued to test themselves – and
without cheating, have had the courage to cut the engine
before looking for a field.*

*We reach the Jebel Maniff and I search for my personal
landmark – the lone outcrop of rock half a mile further south
in the desert. When flying north to Habilayn I always look
for it, for I know it is on an extended centreline of the wadi.
Or when outbound, if you fly to it and then set 182 degrees,
it will take you straight to Falaise, whatever the weather.*

*Roger flies to the rock and then changes course. We have
never discussed it, but he too uses the rock – and it gives me
comfort. He is about to finish his flying tour and go back to
the gunners; but were he to continue, he would live to be an
old pilot.*

*I like the way he flies his Scout. It's not a bad helicopter,
but already dated compared to the new generation of helicopters currently under evaluation. Take the Lynx for
instance, now there's a helicopter I would like to get my
hands on...*

His thumb flicks the intercom switch again.

*'Oh by the way, partner, I bumped into the padre yester-
day – he wants you to fly him around the strips on Christmas
day...'*

List of abbreviations
and terminology

ADF	Automatic Direction Finder or Radio Compass.
ADS	Air Delivery Service.
ALG	Advanced Landing Ground.
AOC	Air Officer Commanding.
AOP	Air Observation Post.
ASI	Airspeed Indicator (instrument).
ATC	Air Traffic Control.
Casevac	Casualty Evacuation.
CATO	Concealed Approach and Takeoff.
CSM	Company Sergeant Major.
DI	Direction Indicator (instrument).
DZ	Dropping Zone.
ETA	Estimated Time of Arrival.
FL	Flight Level.
FRA	Federal Regular Army.
GCA	Ground Controlled Approach.
GPO	Gun Position Officer.
G2	G (Operations) Staff Officer Grade 2. Usually holds rank of major.
HF/VHF/UHF	High Frequency/Very High Frequency and Ultra High Frequency radios.
IFR/VFR	Instrument Flight Rules/Visual Flight Rules.
ILS	Instrument Letdown System.
IMC/VMC	Instrument Meteorological Conditions

	or Visual Met Conditions. (Often abbreviated and expressed on the radio by using the first two letters of the phonetic alphabet: 'India Mike' or 'Victor Mike').
OT/BT	Observer to Target/Battery to target. The lines in the gunnery triangle with points for the Observer, Target and gun Battery.
Pitôt	A tube usually protruding forward of the wing in clean air, to obtain the atmospheric pressure. The tube has a heating element inside it to prevent freezing.
REME	Corps of Royal Electrical and Mechanical Engineers.
RPM	Revolutions per Minute.
RSM	Regimental Sergeant Major.
RTU	Returned to Unit.
SMG	Sub Machine-Gun.
SLR	Self-Loading Rifle.
QFE 'Q code'.	Pressure given to set the altimeter to read zero feet at airfield elevation.
QFI/CFI	Qualified Flying Instructor. Chief Flying Instructor.
QGH	'Q code'. Type of Instrument Letdown procedure.
QNH 'Q code'.	Pressure given to set the altimeter to read zero at sea level, in a given region.
QSY	'Q code'. Changing radio frequency to...
VSI	Vertical Speed Indicator (instrument).
Zulu time.	Greenwich Meantime.

Printed in the United Kingdom
by Lightning Source UK Ltd.
116011UKS00003B/202-207